African Musicians in the Atlantic World

New World Studies
Marlene L. Daut, Editor

African Musicians in the Atlantic World

LEGACIES OF SOUND AND SLAVERY

Mary Caton Lingold

University of Virginia Press

Charlottesville and London

University of Virginia Press
© 2023 by the Rector and Visitors of the University of Virginia
All rights reserved
Printed in the United States of America on acid-free paper

First published 2023

9 8 7 6 5 4 3 2 1

Library of Congress Cataloging-in-Publication Data
Names: Lingold, Mary Caton, author.
Title: African musicians in the Atlantic world : legacies of sound and slavery /
  Mary Caton Lingold.
Description: Charlottesville : University of Virginia Press, 2023. | Series: New World
  studies | Includes bibliographical references and index.
Identifiers: LCCN 2023024500 (print) | LCCN 2023024501 (ebook) |
  ISBN 9780813949772 (hardcover) | ISBN 9780813949789 (paperback) |
  ISBN 9780813949796 (ebook)
Subjects: LCSH: Black people—Caribbean Area—Music—History and
  criticism. | Music—Caribbean Area—History and criticism. | Slaves—Western
  Hemisphere—Social life and customs.
Classification: LCC HD52.9 .S682 2023 (print) | LCC HD52.9 (ebook) |
  DDC 780.89/960729—dc23/eng/20230612
LC record available at https://lccn.loc.gov/2023024500
LC ebook record available at https://lccn.loc.gov/2023024501

Cover art: A Negroes Dance in the Island of Dominica, Agostino Brunias, 1779.
(Yale Center for British Art, Paul Mellon Collection, B1981.25.1958)

In remembrance of enslaved African Atlantic musicians

Contents

List of Illustrations   ix

Acknowledgments   xi

Introduction   1

1. Musical Encounters in Early Modern Atlantic Africa   19

2. Circulating African Musical Knowledge to the Americas: Macow's Xylophone   50

3. Plantation Gatherings and the Foundation of Black American Music   67

4. Race and Professional Musicianship in the Early Caribbean: In Search of Mr. Baptiste   94

5. African Traditions and the Evolution of Caribbean Festival Culture in the Eighteenth Century   108

6. Songs from the 1770s: A Musical Moment   123

Epilogue: Listening for Tena   153

Notes   165

Bibliography   203

Index   225

Illustrations

Captain Mahu and musical entourage stop in Cape Verde, 1602   25

Kongo military clothing and instruments, 1591   27

African ivory horns, 1600s and 1700s   31

Gambian bala and bala player, 1698   37

Kongo instruments, 1692   55

Baptiste's notation from Sloane's *A Voyage to the Islands*, 1707   76

Instruments from Sloane's *A Voyage to the Islands*, 1707   77

Festival in St. Vincent, 1794   116

African musical instruments of Suriname, 1770s   121

Barbados work song, 1770s   126

Musical notation from Stedman's *Narrative*, 1796   136

Musical notation from the manuscript version of
Stedman's *Narrative*, 1790   137

Musical notation from the "Jamaican Airs," 1770s   140

"Queen or 'Maam' of the Set-Girls," 1837   150

Tena's song in *The American Songbag*, 1927   154

Acknowledgments

Many people and many institutions supported me as I wrote this book. At VCU, I wish to thank the Department of English, the College of Humanities and Sciences, the Humanities Research Center, the James Branch Cabell Library, members of the Pre-Modern Study Group, and the many colleagues and mentors who have engaged with my work and offered encouragement and intellectual community, including Kimberly N. Brown, Kelsey Cappiello, Gretchen Comba, Michael Dickinson, Carolyn Eastman, Joshua Eckhardt, Adam Ewing, Shelli Fowler, Grace Gipson, John Glover, Richard Godbeer, Michael Hall, Les Harrison, Chioke I'Anson, Catherine Ingrassia, Shermaine Jones, Joshua Langberg, Adin Lears, Sarah Meacham, Bernard Moitt, Kathryn Murphy-Judy, Brooke Newman, Matteo Pangallo, Greg Patterson, Kate Roach, Jenny Rhee, Sachi Shimomura, Ryan Smith, Cristina Stanciu, Rivka Swenson, and Mimi Winick. To my VCU students, thank you for your kindness, your curiosity, and your creativity. Your energy and words of encouragement have fueled me.

The earliest rumblings of this research began at a 2013 NEH Summer Institute at the Newberry Library in Chicago on the subject of "Music and Travel in the Early Modern World." Helmed and conceived by Carla Zecher, this was an incredible experience, and I am thankful to Carla, the NEH, the Newberry Library, and all my co-participants, especially Heather Koppelman, Jason Farr, Jennifer Linhart-Wood, and the late Bill McCarthy, who were wonderful to be in conversation with.

I also want to acknowledge the extraordinary staff at the James Ford Bell Library at the University of Minnesota, where I was in residence for a William H. Reese Company fellowship. Marguerite Ragnow, Anne Good, Margaret Borg, and student staff members all answered countless questions and offered generous support over the years as I continue to engage your collections. The time I spent at the Bell Library transformed this project, in part because that was when I began to read African travelogues intensively. I am grateful to the Research Center for Material Culture in Leiden, the Netherlands for a fellowship that made it possible for me to examine instruments of Suriname collected by John Stedman. It was mind-expanding to connect with your research community and collections, and I am grateful to Wayne Modest, Alessandra Benedicty, and Ilaria Obata for your generosity and warm welcome. Several other research institutions and archives also made my research possible, and I thank particularly the staff members of the Jamaica National Archives, the National Library of Jamaica, the Registrar General's Department in Jamaica, the British Library, the Augusta Genealogical Society, the International Library of African Music, and the Rubenstein Rare Book & Manuscript Library at Duke University. I wish to thank the Museu Nacional de Arte Antiga, Portugal, the Virginia Museum of History and Culture, the Gloucester Archives, the Newberry Library, the John Carter Brown Library, and the Yale Center for British Art for permission and assistance in using images of materials in their collections.

It is hard to imagine this book coming into existence without many collaborators. Creating *Musical Passage: A Voyage to 1688 Jamaica* with Laurent Dubois and David K. Garner was a pivotal experience and I thank them both. Thank you also to Matthew J. Smith for supporting my research and *Musical Passage* in many ways, and for helping to bring the project to life in performance with Herbie Miller, the Institute of Jamaica, the UWI-Mona Department of History and Archaeology, Chinna Smith and Inna da Yard, Shawn Wright, and the UWI-Mona Chorale. I am grateful to 4VA grant collaborators, Emily Green, Bonnie Gordon, and Michael "Doc" Nickens for valued exchange around early Black music in Virginia. I also thank attendants of the Performing Early Black Music Symposium at George Mason University in Summer 2022. I was honored to participate in the Living Histories of Sugar project, funded by an AHRC grant in the UK led by Marisa Wilson at the University of Edinburgh. Thank you to Marisa, and team members Phillip "Black Sage" Murray, Marva Newton, Jodie Lyn-Kee-Chow, Nathalie Bertaud, Michael Nicholson, Yvonne Lyon, Diana Paton, and Lynette Goddard. I remain inspired by our time together.

Many people from near and far generously answered my research questions, offered inspiration or encouragement, and discussed this project with me in various stages. I wish to thank Nicole Aljoe, Elizabeth Ault, Desirée Baptiste, Catey Boyle, Sarah Balakrishnan, Will Clark, Ashon

Crawley, Marlene Daut, James Delbourgo, Jeroen Dewulf, Elizabeth Maddock Dillon, Ainehi Edoro, Patrick Erben, Sarah Eyerly, Cécile Fromont, Rebecca Geoffroy-Schwinden, Mary Ann Girvan, Alan Howard, Susana Ferlito, Sarah Finley, Kristina Gaddy, Katharine Gerbner, Roger Gibbs, Glenda Goodman, Cynthia Greenlee, Miles Grier, Trey Hall, Jerry Handler, Tunde Jegede, Gracie Joyce, Javier Marín, Eric Martinel, Otosirieze Obi-Young, Brooke Newman, Diana Paton, Grégory Pierrot, John Rickford, James Robertson, Pete Ross, Danielle Skeehan, Cassander Smith, Matt Smith, Matt Somoroff, Linda Sturtz, John J. Sullivan, Ann Waltner, Roxann Wheeler, and Kelly Wisecup. I'd like to offer special thanks to Rich Rath, a generous interlocutor whose research inspired me to pursue this topic. I never had the opportunity to meet Dena Epstein or Eileen Southern but I return to their writing continually and with gratitude. I also wish to thank the anonymous reviewers of both my book proposal and the full manuscript for their time and effort in making this a much stronger project. I extend particular gratitude to Lisa Voigt, who identified herself as one of the reviewers and whose generosity, insights, and example I greatly appreciate. I also want to thank the NCFDD Faculty Success Program, my group members and our mentor, Susanna Ferlito, for the practical tools I needed to complete this project.

I am deeply grateful for the community of scholars who have joined me in forming a working group on Early Caribbean Music. Our regular meetings have given me a sense of community, and through each of you I have learned a great deal. Before we came together, I felt somewhat isolated working on the topic, and now I feel very much a part of something bigger than myself. Thank you to founding members Maria Ryan, Wayne Weaver, David Hunter, Rebecca Geoffroy-Schwinden, Henry Stoll, and Devin Leigh, and thanks to all those who continue to join the group. Special thanks are due to Maria Ryan and Wayne Weaver, who have shared many sources and insights about early British Caribbean music with me over the years. I am so grateful to be in conversation with you. I also wish to acknowledge the generations of historians of early Caribbean music who came before us, some of whose work I am still discovering.

Several symposia and events nurtured the development of this research. In particular, I thank participants of an event at Boston University's Center for Early Music Studies, "Atlantic Crossings: Music from 1492 through the Long Eighteenth Century," organized by Victor Coelho, and also participants of a workshop on eighteenth-century Africa organized by Bronwen Everill at Cambridge. Joanna Marschner organized two symposia on Black music in eighteenth-century Britain hosted conjunctively by the

Paul Mellon Centre for Studies in British Art, Yale Center for British Art, Hendrix and Handel in London, and the Historic Royal Palaces, with support from James and Laura Duncan. These events were instrumental in fomenting my ideas. I am also grateful to Sarah Finley, Miguel Valerio, and Sarah Eyerly for co-organizing with me a symposium, "Intersections: Black and Indigenous Sound in the Early Atlantic World," in Fall 2022. Thanks to the participants, attendants, funders, and performing ensemble, Lua, for a memorable and inspiring exchange.

This book evolved from my dissertation research at Duke University, where I was fortunate to learn from many professors who shaped my thinking, especially Pricilla Wald, Laurent Dubois, Cathy Davidson, Louise Meintjes, Tsitsi Jaji, Fred Moten, the late Srinivas Aravamudan, Deborah Jenson, Guo-Juin Hong, and Jaqcueline Waeber. I am especially grateful to my dissertation director, Priscilla Wald, who gave me the freedom and the guardrails necessary to pursue a deeply interdisciplinary project. Cathy Davidson inspired me in many ways, and I learned invaluable lessons from my time as her research assistant. Laurent Dubois taught me an enormous amount about Caribbean and Atlantic world history and culture, and I am grateful for his ongoing mentorship. At Duke, I also wish to thank the Franklin Humanities Institute staff, and especially Chris Chia, as well as librarians Carson Holloway, Laura Williams, Elizabeth Dunn, the late Sara Seten-Berghausen, and Liz Milewicz. Many of my graduate school colleagues remain valuable interlocutors and dear friends, and I wish to thank especially Whitney Trettien, Darren Mueller, Rebecca Geoffroy-Scwhinden, David K. Garner, Allison Curseen, Cheryl Spinner, and Meghan O'Neil. From my time at CU-Boulder, I gained a lifelong friend and trusted sounding board in Michele Speitz, for whom I am also very grateful.

Many academic mentors and music educators have touched my life and had a hand in making me the thinker I am today. I wish to thank Claudia Stokes for her mentorship at Trinity University, and also Jordan Stein for seeing me through my MA years at the University of Colorado. It is hard to imagine that I would have made it into this career without inspiration and continued guidance from both of you. I wish to thank the public schools in Marshall, Texas for the education and strong music foundation I received. Scott Macpherson brought me to new heights musically under his choral direction at Trinity University. To the Lyons Jam and bluegrass community surrounding Boulder, Colorado: you taught me how to learn with my ears, a transition that made this book possible. Special thanks to K.C. Groves, Rob Clark (and his red van), and Planet Bluegrass. I am also very grateful to the Walltown Children's Theatre in Durham, NC for welcoming me in and teaching me what can be accomplished in artistic communities that center Black and brown experiences. Thanks especially to all my singing students, and to Cynthia Penn-Halal. Recently, Hope Armstrong Erb has spurred me into a new season of study in her piano studio in Richmond, just as I was finishing this book and needing to rediscover a joy in music.

To the entire staff at the University of Virginia Press, I am very thankful for your expertise and labor in bringing this book to publication. Nadine Zimmerli is a stalwart editor who has championed and challenged this project in the most productive ways, from day one. I also thank Marlene Daut for making a home for the book in the New World Studies series, which is an honor. I also wish to acknowledge the journal *Early Music* for allowing me to reprint in chapter 4 a revised version of an article, "In Search of Mr. Baptiste: Early Caribbean Music, Race, and a Colonial Composer," which first appeared in volume 49 of the journal in 2021. Parts of "Peculiar Animations: Listening to Afro-Atlantic Music in Caribbean Travel Narratives," published in *Early American Literature* 52.3 (2017), appears in much revised form in chapter 3. I thank these journals, their editors, staff, and reviewers for contributing to the development of this book.

I have a wonderful circle of friends who keep me grounded and bring me great joy. To my running, swimming, and walking buddies in Richmond, Molly, Sarah, Mary, Sara, Lynn, and Jenna, thank you for the early morning camaraderie and for keeping me sane while writing this book. To my best college girls, Kira, Nora, and Sarah, you remain my dear sisters in all life's seasons. Shermaine, I would walk through fire with you and probably manage to laugh the whole time. Kimberly, thank you for Zooming and writing with me throughout endless pandemic days, which brought joy and got this book written. Thank you also to many other friends, neighbors, and loved ones, too numerous to name here, for being part of this journey, and a cherished part of my life.

To my family: above all, I thank my Mom for her unfaltering love and support, which is a constant blessing to me. I am also deeply grateful for the love and support of my brother, Bradley, and his family, as well as Aunt Emily, Uncle Chase, and many beloved Untermeyer cousins. I also wish to thank all my Olsten in-laws, and especially Jann and Renee for supporting and loving my family to great ends. To my son, Henrik, I love you dearly and I hope you get to pursue hard questions and big dreams, as I have in researching and writing this book. And, Eric, thank you for walking alongside me with love, kindness, and patience. You are my beloved partner in music and in life.

And finally, I wish to thank and honor the memories of those whose lives and musical performances inspired this book. It has been a humbling and daunting task to try to tell their stories in a way that even begins to do justice to what they endured and to what they accomplished. I offer this book in a spirit of gratitude and respect.

My greatest hope is that my work here will be of some use to researchers and performers of the future. If that is you, then I thank you for picking up where I left off.

African Musicians in the Atlantic World

Introduction

SOMETIME IN the late 1640s, a man named Macow sat at the foot of a plantain grove in Barbados, carving the keys of a musical instrument. Little information about his background survives, but we do know that he was an accomplished musician. On the plantation where he was enslaved, he was also responsible for tending the plantain crop and dispensing bundles of fruits to his fellow captives. Details about Macow's life come to us in the words of an Englishman named Richard Ligon. An avid musician in his own right, Ligon eventually wrote about Macow after returning home to the British Isles in poverty, having failed to find profit in the Caribbean. There, he penned an influential travelogue, *A True and Exact History of the Island of Barbados* (1657), from debtor's prison, hoping to earn enough from the sale of the book to regain financial footing.[1]

When Macow had crossed the Atlantic Ocean in bondage years earlier, he did not have the luxury of ensuring safe passage of an instrument, but Ligon had traveled to the West Indies with his Italian theorbo in tow. The lavish object—double-necked and resplendent with strings—was all the rage in Europe at the time. Macow played a stately instrument, too, one that was prominent in courts across numerous early modern African nations. Ligon described the xylophone Macow built, but he did not record whether or not it was a West African bala, a Central African marimba, or another instrument. We do not know where Macow came from, or when he made landfall in the West Indies. Seafaring under the best of circumstances was trying at the time. For enslaved captives, it was a lesson in suffering and endurance that foretold what was to come. Like other Africans pressed into American slavery, when Macow wanted to enjoy music, he had to build a new instrument, making use of what materials he could come by.

The musical encounters these two men had had on a Barbadian plantation exemplify the circumstances that gave rise to the circulation of African music around the Atlantic world in the era of slavery. Every Sunday,
Macow gathered with other Africans to make music and socialize. When
he did so, he participated in a growing trend that extended across the
plantation Americas. When Richard Ligon witnessed Macow's performances and wrote about it for European audiences, he became part of a
growing outsider discourse about the music of African-descended people.
Writers like Ligon forged conceptual ties between race and music that
have remained influential for centuries. Musicians like Macow transmitted sounds across space, creating worlds of musical expression that came
to define the diaspora. Both helped to write the story of early African
Atlantic music. Ligon crafted a narrative with the pen and the printing
press; Macow did so when he picked up an ax to fell timber and carved
the wood into an instrument. By creating the conditions for producing the
music that he wanted to hear and to feel, and perhaps pray to—Macow
etched musical knowledge into the body of his newly built instrument and
into the soundscape of the region, just as Ligon wrought ideas in a book.
By tuning into Macow's musicianship, like a story within a story, or a
sound within a song, we can begin to understand how Macow and his
contemporaries transformed global music under the conditions of slavery.

Atlantic African sound systems followed in the footsteps of captives,
kings, and free people, wherever they sailed and trod and wherever tales
of their experiences were told. When Africans like Macow came to the
West Indies under captivity, they brought their ways of life with them.
And though they were displaced from kin and country, enslaved people
took great care, at great cost, to revive their most precious and pleasurable traditions in a new land. Their efforts ultimately transformed musical practice on a global scale. Enslaved performers planted musical seeds
that grew into countless genres, many of which have become part of the
soundtrack to modern life. Whether listening to rock, reggae, kompa, jazz,
merengue, Afro-pop, R&B, gospel, hip-hop, or country, our ears have all
heard the legacy of enslaved performers. In fact, it is through listening,
and by thinking about sound, that the broader history of music and slavery can best be understood.[2] Sound, after all, was the primary means of
circulating musical knowledge across the Atlantic World. Likewise, sonic
experience—that of musicians, listeners, dancers, and observers—drives
the narrative of this book. But sound does not exist in isolation, not at
all. The musical festivities of Africans and their descendants in the plantation Americas involved a tremendous range of modalities.

African Musicians in the Atlantic World explains how captive Africans established thriving musical traditions while facing the immense difficulties of enslavement. In order to address this history, the book's scope—both in terms of geography and temporality—parallels the rise of plantation agriculture and transatlantic trade, spanning roughly from the early 1600s through the end of the eighteenth century. During this time period, increasing maritime travel facilitated economic exchange between Africans, Americans, and Europeans. Goods, people, and their cultural practices—like music—followed this triangular route, bringing distant lands into intimate relation. Toward the end of the seventeenth century, the sugar industry intensified and human trafficking grew apace, dramatically shifting demographics in many plantation colonies. This trajectory continued throughout the eighteenth century as European settlers purchased more and more African captives to develop and sustain their land. Enslaved Africans were subjected to the will of their enslavers, their daily lives constrained by the profit-driven demands of those who called themselves masters. Yet captives found ways to establish their own expressive domain within the plantation sphere.

Enslaved Africans and their descendants thus founded a massive arts movement: African Atlantic music. By African, I mean music created by people who came from Africa. By Atlantic, I refer to the interconnected world between parts of Africa, Europe, and the Americas created by oceanic travel during the era of expanding global trade, slavery, and colonization. And by music, I mean a vast realm of expression—the music itself, the dancing and worship that so often accompanied it, and the records of those who heard and wrote about it. At times, I also use the term "Black music" to refer broadly to the performance traditions created by enslaved people and their descendants. As a concept, "Black music" can be applied capaciously to describe music from long ago and music from our own time. But in this book, when I use the term "African Atlantic," I mean specifically to refer to the historical moment when captives were trafficked from African ports to American plantations. It was in this "African Atlantic" context, that enslaved communities gave birth to "Black music."[3]

African knowledge and culture did not alight on American shores in a single era, rather a process unfolded across generations as captives were continually trafficked across the ocean over the course of three centuries. This book examines an era when plantation slavery became the dominant economic engine of the British, French, and Dutch colonies in the Western Hemisphere. In the world of plantation agriculture, enslavers treated African people as disposable commodities, and when disease and dangerous labor conditions took the lives of captives, planters purchased more people to replace them, investing in a cycle of violence that ensured suffering and also ensured that African people and their traditions continued to flow westward across the Atlantic Ocean. This process became a time-bending collective experience for enslaved Africans and their descendants—what we now understand as the common roots of the diaspora.

It was in the Caribbean, and along its outer rim, in places like Louisiana, South Carolina, and Suriname, that plantation slavery grew most conspicuously. In the West Indian basin, large numbers of captive peoples from disparate African societies forged new cultural processes on American plantations. The particularities of the region help to explain broad realities about enslaved peoples' lived experiences and artistic legacies. Because of the centrality of the Caribbean to circum-Atlantic maritime travel, the archipelago was uniquely influential throughout the era of European exploration and colonization. When the sugar economy boomed, the region also became the financial engine fueling imperial interests on both sides of the Atlantic. Multiple empires, languages, and cultures shaped life in the West Indies, forming a microcosm of vast colonial-era histories. Individual islands and territories often changed hands from one empire to another and a culture of enslavement and plantation colonialism transcended borders, especially when planters began to exploit enslaved laborers in an effort to manage single-crop agricultural production. This book focuses primarily on the Caribbean, and particularly the British Caribbean, but it also draws from sources and events connected to West and West Central Africa, as well as slave societies in mainland North and South America. While recognizing the distinctiveness and diversity of plantation colonies, I hope the material in *African Musicians in the Atlantic World* will be of interest to scholars of African Atlantic life across broad geographies.

African Musicians in the Atlantic World tracks musical expressions as cultural phenomena tied to American slavery, but the story must begin on the Atlantic coasts of Africa, where enslaved people were from, and where musical encounters between Africans and Europeans set the stage for what was to come. Europe and Africa did not meet in America; rather they had long-standing exchanges along the migratory routes of the Eastern Hemisphere. Music was central to many aspects of life across diverse African nations, and the opening chapter examines records of performances from Atlantic Africa, focusing on the long seventeenth century, when Atlantic slavery became a prominent fixture of Euro-African trade.

The book then shifts its focus to American plantations, unfolding in a rough chronology that tracks the development of musical life during the rise of plantation slavery across the seventeenth and eighteenth centuries.

Throughout, *African Musicians in the Atlantic World* spins on an Afro-centric axis, privileging the stories of African-born musicians and their communities. In fact, one of the book's revelations is that diverse African musical genres continued to be practiced in the plantation Americas for quite a long time and to a remarkably influential degree. These traditions also were practiced alongside Afro-American traditions that were unique to the cultures of enslaved and free people of the Americas. Many enslaved and free people also practiced musical traditions rooted in European ways of life, as professionals, amateurs, religious subjects, and in the context of forced labor. I have chosen in this book to focus primarily on musical practices that took place within enslaved communities and for their own enjoyment. There were many African-descended musicians who performed for white audiences in the plantation sphere, and the space of enslaved musical gatherings often swelled to include white colonial inhabitants and free people of color. Especially during feast days and in urban settings, African music and dance formed the heartbeat of events involving much wider publics. As Macow and Ligon's interactions suggest, there was no fixed wall separating the musical worlds of planters and captives, and yet I strive in *African Musicians in the Atlantic World* to foreground the experiences and tastes of enslaved audiences to better understand how they shaped the musical world of the Americas through their listenership, participation, and performances. By focusing on survivors of the Middle Passage, I aim to illuminate important early moments in the rise of Black music in the Americas.

Music and Slavery

Unfortunately, the story of music and slavery has been crudely mischaracterized in the popular imagination in a number of ways, across several eras, and these mischaracterizations have obscured important aspects of the history of early Black music. The late-eighteenth century was one key moment when white audiences began to twist the story of music and slavery into outright fantasy. At that time, when abolitionism grew in Britain, the subject of music became part of public debates about the morality of slavery. Abolitionists argued that the institution caused great suffering, while pro-slavery advocates retorted that on the contrary, enslaved people were well-cared for and even "happy." Pro-slavery voices pointed specifically to musical practices in plantation colonies as evidence of captives' contentment and even betterment, a subject I discuss at length in chapter 5. Thus, the trope of the "happy slave" was born and it lived on and on, continuing to shape debates about slavery years later in the United States.

In the 1830s, the explosive popularity of blackface minstrelsy in the United States and later abroad gave further currency to the trope as white performers portrayed enslaved people in jocular caricatures. The minstrelsy-era also flooded the historical record with portrayals of Black musical experience throughout the nineteenth century, making it difficult for scholars to discern which records reflect actual Black performances and which are merely the product of white fantasy. Minstrelsy's false and degrading representation of slavery became fixed in the public imaginary, leaving a deep scar on popular culture in the U.S. and beyond.[4]

Many nations have traditions of caricaturing Black music on stage and in popular culture. In early modern Spain and its colonies, for instance, writers and performers mimicked African dialects in theatrical and literary works, a practice known as *habla de negros*.[5] In late eighteenth-century colonial Haiti, then French Saint-Domingue, white artists performed the dances of enslaved Africans on the popular stage.[6] The widespread practices of racializing and mocking Black people's musical lives have made it difficult to uncover a truer history of enslaved people's experiences.[7]

For different audiences, and to different ends, the *idea* of music and slavery has become an emblematic cultural touchstone, often invoked in an effort to grapple with the vexed legacies of slavery's past. Although outsiders cheapened the history of early Black music by portraying performances as comical and degraded, some working within Black intellectual traditions developed alternative narratives celebrating the accomplishments of enslaved musicians. For many of these writers and performers, enslaved people's musical practices exemplify the central paradox of African diasporic culture—the twin realities of tremendous suffering and vibrant creativity.[8] This conceptualization of music and slavery emphasizes a story of resistance and redemption, one in which Black artists transformed difficult circumstances into fertile ground for creative expression. There are considerable stakes to how we interpret the symbolic significance of music and slavery. Both minstrelsy tropes and narratives of cultural survival run the risk of perpetuating the assumption that it was solely the historical conditions of slavery that engendered the rise of Black music.

This book aims to emphasize that Black music was not caused by slavery, it was created by the people who endured slavery. The second half of that sentence is no happy story, and attention to it must never white-wash or romanticize a devastating history of violence and loss. So, too, must the creative lives of enslaved people be acknowledged and properly memorialized. That this needs to be explained is because of centuries-old narratives that cast African captives as pure subjects to white power. People of European descent authored cultural fictions that robbed people of African descent of their knowledge and history, but these racist nar-ratives were never totalizing realities. Scholars debating questions of historical "agency" have established that enslaved people led full and complicated lives and that they influenced their own experiences of cap-tivity and indeed global history.[9] The flourishing arts of the diaspora are proof enough of that.

Music flourished despite the fact that colonial regimes tried to suppress it, and despite the fact that enslaved people had so little time, and so few resources, on the whole, to undertake it. People found ways to make music while working, and with objects that were not originally designed to be musical instruments, but that nonetheless made great sounds. The insistence and persistence with which Africans in the Americas partici-pated in musical activities cannot be denied. Musical arts proliferated under slavery because enslaved people chose to make that happen. *African Musicians in the Atlantic World* seeks to offer a deeper understanding of how they did so.

But to imagine ourselves outside of Western paradigms that project white reason and history against Black ignorance and lostness remains difficult because these ideas are baked into the methodologies we use to study the past, as many scholars have poignantly addressed.[10] Disciplin-ary conventions largely privilege evidence and sources emanating from the powerful, casting undue suspicion on traditions of knowledge that emerge "from below."[11] Studying the early history of Black music requires a careful confrontation with these obstacles. And unfortunately, while the *symbolic power* of music and slavery has been much invoked, the historical specificities have not been as extensively attended to.

Obstacles in the Study of Early Black Music

Some of the challenges of studying early Black music have to do with the nature of available sources, and others have to do with the nature of academic disciplines and institutions. The discipline of musicology would seem to be a welcome home for the topic, but research on ver-nacular Black music from before 1800 has been rare in the field. This is because historical musicologists generally focus on notated traditions, and thus white European genres, whereas ethnomusicologists and folklorists explore musical practices from broader geographies and ethnicities, but typically in the context of living practice. There are, and have always been important exceptions, including, in particular, a handful of groundbreaking studies of Black music history written in the 1970s.[12] Also, scholars from the Caribbean publishing throughout the twentieth century produced research on music histories of the region, but unfortunately not all of this body of work has been fully appreciated, nor is it fully accessible due to exclusionary practices and institutional barriers in Western academia that continue to marginalize scholarship emanating from the global South.[13] For similar reasons, research addressing musical practices in early modern Africa is even more rare.[14]

Much of the existing publications relevant to the study of music and slavery remain scattershot across generations, disciplines, geographies, and time periods, making it difficult for scholars to engage with one another and learn from prior research. Yet, the study of early Black music history is alive and well and beginning to expand, thanks to scholars bridging the gap between historical musicology and ethnomusicology, as well as academics, writers, and performers bringing attention to the subject from a variety of fields and perspectives. Scholarship on Black music histories from the era of slavery has tended to focus on the nineteenth century, which has to do with the fact that there are more available records from the period.[15] A growing body of literature addresses the eighteenth century and earlier eras, and many of these studies emphasize specific traditions and locations within the colonial British and French Caribbean.[16] Work focusing on Iberian empires is illuminating the circulation of African performance traditions across Africa, Europe, and colonial Latin America in far earlier periods.[17] Several books and projects on broader cultural histories of the Atlantic world include material relevant to the study of music and performance.[18] Recently, writing on the history of the banjo has brought welcome attention to the circulations of musical knowledge from Africa to the Americas, and there are many writers and thinkers working outside academia to bring historical sources on early Black music to light for broad audiences.[19] There are also many scholars highlighting the widespread influence of African-descended performers who participated in European genres, both in Europe and the Americas.[20]

To this growing conversation, *African Musicians in the Atlantic World* brings an understanding of the musical practices of African-born survivors of the Middle Passage who arrived in the Americas during the rise of plantation slavery, between roughly 1600–1800. In so doing, I track the growth of Black music precisely during the crucial period when enslaved people firmly established the practices that we now understand as the basis of African diasporic music. This was also a time when few Atlantic Africans had the opportunity to generate records that would become preserved in archives and other historical repositories. Insight into enslaved people's cultural experiences at the time generally comes from sources created by Europeans–often the very same people who were actively trafficking, enslaving, and oppressing them.

In spite of these obstacles, researchers in slavery studies have shown that examining available records with a careful and critical eye can reveal a surprising amount about the cultural history of the African diaspora. In the last several decades, a swell of restorative work has opened up possibilities for exploring the lives of enslaved people in far greater depth. The methodological innovations guiding the turn toward an Afro-centric understanding of the era largely have entailed a shift in perspective, as scholars bring new questions to old documents, training their attention to the experiences of people whose lives they track painstakingly across records that at first glance often seem to portray only the perspectives of elites and oppressors.[21]

I take inspiration from these efforts as I, too, bring fresh questions to sources that are familiar to many scholars of slavery and early American and Atlantic studies. *African Musicians in the Atlantic World* draws extensively from written accounts authored by European travelers. Within these types of narratives, it became formulaic to describe musical practices, and a wealth of first-hand descriptions of performances in Africa as well as America survive. Many travelogues even contained illustrations of instruments and excerpts of musical notation.[22] Some of the accounts were published and widely read in their own day, but others languished in manuscripts. In this book, I draw from a sprawling array of such sources to amass a significant trove of records documenting early African Atlantic musical expression.

These European memoirs on which I draw to recover African musical expressions became an immensely influential literary genre during the long era of expanding global trade. Some authors were missionaries, others settlers, traders, sailors, and colonial officials, and they were all educated elites, typically male. In books that often read like how-to manuals for prospective travelers, narrators described what they saw, heard, and ate on their journeys. Other written accounts focused on documenting island ecologies and weather. Readers turned to the genre for information about what to pack in their trunks, how to approach a rocky coastline, and how to manage enslaved laborers. Travelogues were read by monarchs and merchants who were invested in global trade and imperial power. They were also read by landlocked adventurers who were curious about the wider world.

Travel memoirs preserve compelling details about the past but they are also fraught with bitter legacies. Works in the genre drew deeply upon discourses of savagery and otherness, helping to spread countless cultural stereotypes and to foment modern conceptions of race. It is impossible to overstate the degree to which published travelogues influenced and encouraged European practices of colonialism, slavery, and genocide around the globe by helping to normalize and to advertise methods of conquest and exploitative trade of many kinds.[23] Global travel writing also had a hand in creating what we now would call ethnography and cultural anthropology, shaping the way that Western academics would seek to understand the non-white and non-Western world for centuries.

Given these realities, it may seem surprising that many scholars turn to these types of records for information about subaltern perspectives and experiences from the past. But these works preserve eyewitness accounts of the Atlantic world as it developed and of colonial American history. Books written by tradespeople, settlers, missionaries, and other travelers recorded remarkable detail about peoples, practices, and languages, that would otherwise remain undocumented. Scholars across numerous fields have turned cautiously and critically toward these sources to address African and Indigenous American perspectives.[24] Similarly, I consider the musicians and musical audiences documented in these kinds of works to be historical actors and creatives that shaped the cultural discourses of their time; even in the context of pronounced power imbalances, the narratives and material objects born of cross-cultural encounter were co-constitutive.

One of the enduring challenges that comes with trying to bring the story of African Atlantic music into the study of history, literature, and the performing arts is the difficulty of recuperating personal histories. Throughout the book, I illuminate individual lives and experiences whenever possible, joining other scholars of the early African Atlantic world working to personalize the story of slavery.[25] In addition to examining Macow's musicianship in this introduction and again more thoroughly in chapter 2, I also tell the story of a musician named Mr. Baptiste in chapter 4, while addressing the difficulties that come with trying to secure biographical details even of performers who were free people of color.

Mr. Baptiste's name appeared in Hans Sloane's travelogue and natural history of Jamaica, alongside the notated excerpts of African music he transcribed in 1680s Jamaica. Sloane explained nothing about the man except that he was considered to be "the best musician" at a festival gathering of Africans. My research reveals that he was probably a free person of color, with possible roots in the Afro-Iberian world.

The book closes with the story of a song sung by an enslaved woman named Tena, who lived in Georgia in the 1820s. Her biography represents, in many ways, the end of a long line of African-born performers who made their mark on American music during the era of enslavement. I learned about Tena's music in a book of folk songs published by the poet and orator Carl Sandburg in 1927. In searching for more information about her past, I uncovered fascinating details about the circulation of her song to South Africa and what is now Zambia, in the mid-twentieth century. Many enslaved and free musicians left enormously influential legacies that span continents and centuries, yet their stories surface in written records in mere glimmers and glints.

To put further pressure on the weight of white authorship in the available sources, and to bring attention to the experience of individual Africans, I also draw extensively on writings by African Atlantic memoirists like Gustavus Vassa (also known as Olaudah Equiano), Ukawsaw Gronniosaw (also known as James Albert), and others. The slave narrative genre owes its heritage in part to the genre of travelogue, and in the second half of the eighteenth century, these memoirs brought an important corrective to the one-sided portrayals of Africa and the Americas documented in earlier works by Europeans, although they, too, were mediated by the perspectives of white gatekeepers and audiences.

In addition to analyzing published writing, *African Musicians in the Atlantic World* also draws from manuscript sources, material objects, visual art, and other records that together build a multifaceted body of evidence. In chapters 3 and 6, for example, I examine surviving examples of musical notation documenting vernacular African Atlantic music from the period. Some of these sources were published in works of travel writing, while others survive in manuscripts that were never published. These excerpts, which are also complicated and heavily mediated by the system of notation, open a window into the subtleties of African Atlantic performance practice.

Throughout *African Musicians in the Atlantic World* I blend an approach grounded in literary analysis, sonically informed musical interpretation, and historical inquiry. By bringing together the methodologies of disparate disciplines, I seek to carve out a space for early Black music in the interstices. In doing so, this book joins a broader effort to uproot and to overthrow the white knowledge order in the study of slavery and the colonial past by further amplifying the expressive arts of Atlantic captives.

Music history is the primary subject of this book, and written records comprise a significant portion of the relevant archive, while sound provides a key analytical intervention. I also draw from my training and experience as a musician to inform my understanding of performance—both vernacular and textual—as a process of knowledge production. When musicians gathered to create and share music together, they transferred information and ideas across time and space. Through their musical practice, enslaved musicians ensured the transmission of sounds and sound systems that they held dear, building a legacy at once coherent and multiplicitous.

Sound Methods

Western travelers, missionaries, and settlers often did not like nor understand the music that they heard. They interpreted performances to be odd or exceptional that may have been experienced as mundane and unremarkable by participants. Indeed, hearing and observing without fully understanding became a hallmark of white listening practices in spaces of cross-cultural contact.

I deploy interpretative strategies emanating from the field of sound studies as a key methodology for navigating the perceptual gaps between European listeners and African performers. Examining narrative accounts for sound and sonic experience productively decenters the perspective of outsiders who strove to document experiences beyond their comprehension. Sounds do not exist in and of themselves, they make their meaning when interpreted by listening subjects. In order to understand what sounds "mean" we must consider who is making the sound and why, and how it may have been experienced by a variety of people. Listeners interpret sound subjectively, according to cultural training and individual experience. With this in mind, I approach sound as a prismatic system that must be interrogated for multiple possible meanings.[26]

What is the difference between *sound* and *music*? In the context of this project, I consider sound to be a capacious realm of which musical performance is merely a part. Music is a highly aestheticized and formalized type of sound production. It is also deeply experiential and communal, especially in the early African Atlantic performance settings examined here. Neither sound nor music excludes other senses or practices; on the contrary, the particularities of African Atlantic musical practice demand that sight and sensation be considered integral to musical life. For me, one of the theoretical interventions of sound studies on the field of music has been to emphasize that music is an embodied process experienced subjectively by different listeners and performers.[27] Much of the music explored in this book took place during communal gatherings that involved an array of expressive practice—dance, costuming, spiritual communication, and much more. Intricate cultural boundaries shaped musical practice in the African Atlantic world, but they did not always map onto European norms.[28]

In this book I aim to further destabilize what we think we know about sound and music from a Western perspective by illuminating the way Africans constructed and preserved musical knowledge across space and time. I argue for the historical coherence of their efforts, insisting that cultural processes that unfold in the realm of sound have as secure and demonstrable a legacy as other historical phenomena.[29] Indeed, one of the biggest impediments to recovering the earliest history of Black music has been the presumption that early performances by enslaved people were irrevocably lost because they were not sufficiently written down or recorded through mechanical sound reproduction technology (which had not yet been invented). I contend that the musical production of Atlantic Africans established a remarkably *sound legacy,* one as preservable and coherent as any other historical phenomena. This book thus reconsiders the historical weight of written texts and documentary archives, imagining them in relationship to comparably weighty sounds and sound systems that may not survive in physical form, but that survive abundantly in expressive tradition and in audible traces recorded in written description, illustration, and notation.

We must take sound as seriously as print and material records if we want to understand the lives of Africans in the plantation Americas in the seventeenth and eighteenth centuries. The sounds of the performances that enslaved musicians created did not evaporate into an unrecorded past. Rather, they were heard and documented by many, as the numerous accounts I uncover in this book attest. Musicians and those who gathered with them also reproduced sound every time they sat down to play, as did their descendants who carried forth across spaces and through centuries. Both the problem and the solution, then, is a matter of the historical imagination, and what we consider to be possible to know about the past.

Turning to sound and performance as a sphere of knowledge production helps to disrupt the preeminence of white narration in records of cross-cultural encounter. European writing dominates historical records from the period but Africans were prolific authors of other media, including, especially, sound. By drawing attention to the sounds that Africans created, and which European authors heard and described, I aim to illuminate a vast alternative archive of early modern Atlantic experience. Until Africans and their descendants are brought to the center of the story of slavery's past, we will never begin to understand the foundations of Atlantic modernity. The sounds and sound systems that enslaved people brought with them to the Americas were diverse and abundant. They were local and global, reflecting cultural exchange in the Eastern Hemisphere that proceeded European conquest. So, to understand what sound means to people is to understand in some sense, who they were and what mattered to them.

A Revolution in Knowledge

Global travelers from Europe took pains to portray customs that were unfamiliar to them, and this ultimately helped to establish cultural criticism as something indelibly rooted within an imperialist, racial frame. And as a result, white European tastes and aesthetic predilections became the terms through which diverse cultures were written into history. The problem of cultural imperialism has not faded away, in fact it remains a cornerstone of Western academic humanistic inquiry. The very carving of disciplines into colonial languages like English, and divorcing subjects from one another as history, music, and literature, speaks to imperialist Enlightenment efforts to sort out, explain, categorize, and conquer. Most of what we actually want to know or to understand about the past or the present could never be neatly packaged in a single discipline's purview. That this study is interdisciplinary, therefore, is not so much by design as by necessity. The story of early Black music transcends borders, sensory modalities, language traditions, and academic fields.

The musical observations of colonial travelers record the fact that enslaved artistic performances operated as a fundamental challenge to colonialism, white supremacy, and imperialism. I do not mean to romanticize enslaved performances as though their sole purpose was to resist oppression, but I do mean to point out that they were interpreted by outside observers as communal acts that threatened the protocols of the slavocracy. Just as racism is best defined by those who are subjected to it, it may also be that resistance to oppression can be well-observed by those bent on practicing it. White listeners reacted to, feared, explained, coveted, and attempted to interpret African musical performances. The music interrupted them, it made them listen, it made them want to stop it, to get closer to hear it, to copy it down, to explain it, to write about it, to prevent it, to allow it, to control it. But they never, ever, could.

Black music has always meant something to Black people that is quite different from what it means to non-Black people. And indeed, Black theorists across generations have interpreted the birth of Black music as a politicized response to the condition of enslavement.[30] We must take it as given that white colonial elites' recordings of enslaved performances were not accurate, and yet the recordings are nonetheless a product of those performances. The one came first, then the other. This book, then, also necessitates a careful examination of white listening practices.[31] At the same time, while *African Musicians in the Atlantic World* interrogates works authored by white listeners, the book aims to foreground the soundworlds of enslaved Africans and their descendants. Other scholars have suggested that the earliest records of Black music are so drenched in European perspectives that they are primarily a record of white racism rather than a record of Black music.[32] While there is some truth to the observations that the records can tell us more about white perception than about Black performances, I also believe that the extant records are nonetheless useful for exploring the sounds and the significance of early Black music. Historians of all stripes construct stories about the past without perfectly reliable information all the time. Why should the music of enslaved people be deemed unknowable?

Black music is one of the most revolutionary knowledge traditions to emerge from the Western hemisphere.[33] Indeed, it would be impossible to name any other American art form that has done more to influence the way people spend their time, how they listen, sing, worship, and protest. And yet Black creatives, like the musicians documented in this book, have often faced intense scrutiny around the question of "authenticity," scrutiny that is rarely, if ever, trained toward white knowledge production, then or now. Early Black Atlantic authors also faced endless scrutiny from white editors and readers about their identity and the veracity of their narratives depicting enslavement.[34] The scrutinizing that African-descended creatives have had to endure about their identity, origins, and the substance of their cultural production is now subsumed under the cover of scholarly convention. *African Musicians in the Atlantic World* dispenses with this narrative of lostness and inauthenticity to reveal abundant traces of early Black musical life across diverse sources.

Border Crossing

The chapters and epilogue of this book unfurl in an approximate chronology, beginning in the late sixteenth century and closing with a musical episode from the early nineteenth century. The organization is meant to provide readers a sense of change over time, beginning from the founding of plantation slavery in the Caribbean through its rise, as Africans were trafficked to the region in ever-increasing numbers, ultimately forming a majority of the population and a prominent cultural force. To center African knowledge and experience, the narrative of this book opens and closes in Africa. After an opening chapter focusing on early modern Atlantic Africa, the following chapters shift to the West Indies and North America, looking specifically to the rise of plantation slavery in the British Caribbean and other nearby territories, including Suriname. These chapters track the establishment of African musical tradition in the Americas, considering how, why, and under what circumstances captives circulated musical knowledge around the Atlantic world, establishing cultural institutions in the midst of slavery. While some chapters focus on stories of individuals and their historical moments to provide an intimate portrait of musical life under slavery, other chapters broaden in scope to offer larger insights about the development of African Atlantic music under slavery over time.

Chapter 1 shows that African performances that took place *in Africa* were central to the emergence of Atlantic trade and Atlantic world cultures, both. The chapter also demonstrates the subjective nature of sonic experience and shows how cultural listening practices shaped European authors' portrayals of African performances, and ultimately the racialization of Black music. European perceptions of African music shifted according to location and context. Travelers heard performances differently when they encountered them in Africa, compared to slave societies, and they also interpreted sounds differently based on the context of the performance. Monarchic and military performances were largely revered whereas music tied to indigenous African religion was disdained. The subjective nature of sonic experience is key for understanding not only the emergence of African Atlantic music but also the discursive writing about it created by Europeans who traveled to Africa and the Americas.

The second chapter bridges African and American contexts by following the story of a survivor of the Middle Passage and his instrument. I revisit the anecdote that opened this introduction, taking a deeper look into the life of Macow, who lived in Barbados in the 1640s, a time that was crucial for the founding of plantation culture in the Americas. Ultimately, I interpret Macow's xylophone as a material artifact of African Atlantic sound. Studying this artifact illuminates a broader story about the processes by which captives like Macow circulated musical knowledge to the Americas.

While chapter 2 focuses on an intimate story, chapter 3 considers the role of collectives in creating space for musical life under slavery. This chapter argues that enslaved people founded the bedrock of African diasporic culture by choosing to gather regularly during evenings, on Sundays, and during feast days. These types of performances became a prominent cultural institution in the Americas over the course of the seventeenth century. Participants created space for social life and performance remarkably early in the history of plantation slavery's rise, and this chapter surveys these types of performances, what they meant for enslaved participants, and how they were portrayed by outsider witnesses.

Chapter 4 zooms in again to tell the story of one individual and his historic moment. Mr. Baptiste composed an important record of the types of festivals analyzed in the previous chapter. He transcribed music performed by enslaved Africans in 1680s Jamaica that was later published by Sir Hans Sloane in his 1707 account of the island. Baptiste lived at a time when slavery began to boom in the Caribbean and life for Atlantic Africans became increasingly conscribed by racial hierarchy. Through archival research, I show that Baptiste was likely a free person of color and that his life and story are emblematic of a class of professional musicians living amidst diverse traditions in the late seventeenth century. Baptiste's story also draws attention to the connections between British Jamaica and nearby French and Spanish colonies, revealing a complex and intimately networked circum-Caribbean.

Chapter 5 grapples with how musical life in enslaved communities did and did not change over the course of the eighteenth century. Ultimately, I argue that distinct African traditions continued to be performed extensively in plantation societies even as uniquely Afro-American traditions also began to emerge and circulate widely. Focusing on extensive records of musical life in Suriname assembled by Anglo-Dutch author John Stedman, I document the persistence of African traditions in the plantation Caribbean at a time when discourses about slavery and enslaved people's cultural practices were changing.

Chapter 6 continues the focus on the late-eighteenth century, and a particular decade—the 1770s—which produced a remarkable number of notated musical pieces portraying enslaved performances in the British Caribbean. I assemble several of these musical texts as a compilation album that reflects a diversity of genres and practices that were also deeply in conversation with one another. The 1770s were a time of great change and flourishing in the performance sphere of the Caribbean, and musical records that survive provide a vivid portrait of enslaved life at labor, at pleasure, and in political thought.

The epilogue centers on a woman named Tena, who was enslaved in Augusta, Georgia, in the 1820s. She sang a song that traveled across centuries and voices, an example of the power of sound to preserve histories and narratives of slavery's past. Tena's music, and the way it was remembered and studied by U.S. Americans and Africans in the twentieth century helps to reveal the ties between distant eras and our own. The epilogue addresses how in our own historical moment, an engagement with the music of the early eras of slavery can be a productive way to memorialize the legacy of some of the world's most influential artists.

The impact of African Atlantic music and slavery is all around us, and the legacy of enslaved musicians and dancers and listeners lives on whether or not we tune in. But engaging the history of early Black music helps to bring clarity and consciousness to the stories of people who created the worlds we inhabit and did so in the midst of grave challenges. This book is for them and for their legacy, may it continue to live long, proud, and loud.

1 Musical Encounters in Early Modern Atlantic Africa

UKAWSAW GRONNIOSAW was a young teenager when he made a long journey westward from what is now Eastern Nigeria toward the Gold Coast in the 1720s. A traveling merchant had approached the boy's family and offered to take him under his wing. They agreed to the plan, seemingly unaware of the fact that nothing could be more perilous than for a young Black African to travel toward the Atlantic Ocean in the care of a tradesman. His trek delivered him right into the hands of a Dutch slaver who trafficked him to the West Indies. After living in captivity for several years, he eventually claimed freedom in New York and later emigrated to England. It was there that he published a religious autobiography under the name James Albert.[1] But before embarking on the Middle Passage, and the epic journey that followed, he made an inland crossing of more than a thousand miles on foot.

Gronniosaw's intra-African migration resembles journeys that many captives bound for American slavery were forced to make. He endured cultural confusion, disillusionment, and loss before undergoing further traumas at sea.[2] And like everyone crisscrossing the ocean at the time, both free and unfree, African, European, and American, his migratory experience was shaped by what he heard—the things he understood, and those he did not. During the overland journey toward the Atlantic Ocean, Gronniosaw and the traders shepherding him spent evenings hard at work cutting wood to build bonfires, hoping that the flames would deter predators from attacking the campsite. In daylight, they crossed through rugged terrain and villages that were increasingly foreign to Gronniosaw. The journey terrified the young man who was "in continual fear that the people I was with would murder me."[3] Moving through these spaces, he would have experienced familiar sounds that helped him to make sense of his changing surroundings, perhaps crackling fire and the fall of his own feet. But he also would have encountered things that were strange and new to him, including unfamiliar languages and eventually, the sound of ocean breezes rippling across Atlantic waters.[4]

Upon arriving in the unnamed kingdom on the ocean's shore, Gronniosaw heard something astonishing: a loud blast of trumpets and drums. Startled by the unusual noise, he asked about the meaning of the music, and was told that the sounds came from the king's musicians, who intended to honor him with a royal welcome. The narrative explains that, "I heard the drums beat remarkably loud, and the trumpets blow—the persons accustom'd to this employ, are obliged to go upon a very high structure appointed for that purpose, that the sound might be heard at a great distance: They are higher than the steeples are in England. I was mightily pleas'd with sounds so entirely new to me, and was very inquisitive to know the cause of this rejoicing and ask'd many questions concerning it: I was answer'd that it was meant as a compliment to me, because I was Grandson to the King of BOURNOU."[5] Later, the traveling merchant's sons—boys about his own age—told Gronniosaw a very different story. They warned him that their king considered Gronniosaw to be an enemy of the state—a spy. The boys told Gronniosaw that he was to be executed the following day. In an instant, the imperial greeting transformed into the sound of impending doom. The narrative never clarifies whether or not the boys or the other townspeople were simply ribbing young Gronniosaw with their shifting explanations for the musical pronouncement, but terror eventually did come when the King sold the young traveler to a Dutch slaver. Gronniosaw's story shows how the very same sounds—those of a proud horn and a thunderous drum—can be experienced differently across space and time, and for different people: one moment regal but inviting, the next powerful and terrifying. Importantly, this episode also illustrates the role of musical production in statecraft during the precolonial era in Africa.

During my research into representations of music in Africa during the rise of Atlantic slavery, I noticed that European travelers often described African performances witnessed in African settings very differently compared to the way they portrayed similar music in the context of American slavery. Largely speaking, European documentarians wrote favorably about the monarchic and military music they witnessed in Atlantic Africa, but in the Americas, these very same traditions induced fear and scrutiny. Drums and horns in particular became emblems of enslaved resistance in the Americas, and many colonial powers instituted laws to ban their use. But in Africa, during the era when European travelers were establishing the trade networks along coastal regions that became crucial to the rise of slavery, Europeans revered these same horns, drums, and other instruments of state, as I chronicle in the first part of this chapter.

Europeans also wrote admiringly about some African religious music, particularly when it intersected with Islamic and Catholic faith practices. However, they were critical of indigenous African spirituality and the types of performances that often attended it. The second part of the chapter will parse some of the hierarchies of sound quality that European authors applied to diverse African musical traditions. These descriptions help to illuminate some of the aesthetic trends animating performance traditions along the Eastern Atlantic, and they also illuminate the origins of enduring racial stereotypes about Black musicality.

To understand the world of slavery that Gronniosaw entered in 1720, we must look further back, to the history of African-European contact and trade on the Atlantic coasts of Sub-Saharan Africa. This chapter examines records of musical production along the Atlantic coasts of Africa. Like I do in much of this book, in this chapter I examine records of musical production along the Atlantic coasts of Africa by analyzing both Europeans' perception of African performances as well as the musical experiences of Africans themselves. Just like Gronniosaw heard the trumpets and horns differently based on what he thought they meant, Europeans interpreted African musical sounds depending on the contexts in which they heard them, and according to their prejudices. Sounds can facilitate diplomatic alliances and sounds can drive fear and prejudice into the hearts of travelers. As I show, sonic experience was crucial to the way people encountered one another in the Atlantic World and crucial to the ways in which they manipulated and resisted power in the context of commerce, diplomacy, and slavery.

Atlantic Africa as Point of Origin

From the end of the fifteenth through the early seventeenth century, Africans and Europeans established trade networks that laid the groundwork for the rise of slavery. At this time, cultural exchange between Africans and Europeans expanded rapidly, and not only through maritime traffic. Trade routes connecting parts of Africa, the Mediterranean, Iberia, and the Middle East also facilitated migration and contact that included musical exchange.[6] Musical performances in Atlantic Africa were essential to shaping imperial strategy and intercultural relations during the era of exploration.

The Atlantic economy took a sharp turn toward chattel slavery over the course of the seventeenth century, but maritime commerce between Africans and Europeans and had been on the rise for some time. Trade expanded when European ships began to travel more broadly during the "age of exploration," roughly between 1400 and 1600. Africa was among the first distant regions that Europeans explored extensively, in part because of the geographic proximity and oceanic currents that connect the two continents. Even when Europeans were traveling to territories in the Pacific Ocean, they commonly stopped along the Western African coastline to trade and replenish resources. As settlements in the Americas expanded, African outposts also became frequent ports of call for travelers to the Caribbean and North America. In this way, Africans influenced Europeans *in Africa* during the period as much as they did through the presence of enslaved Africans in America and in Europe. As many other scholars have pointed out, studies of the Atlantic World and the triangular trade tend to center on European and American metropoles, all too often eliding the role of Africans in shaping international trade and cultural developments during the era.[7]

By focusing on African settings, I, too, wish to underscore the significance of the region to the development of global trade and the cultural transformations that came with it, especially in the realm of music. African shores are not simply where enslaved performers came from—the artists whose stories comprise the primary subject of this book—but Sub-Saharan African coastal regions also served as an original point of perspective for European maritime travelers, traders, and enslavers who wrote the travelogues that inform much of this book. Musical exchange was absolutely vital to the way European travelers and African sovereigns and subjects interacted.

This chapter spans a broad geography, examining musical practice from places as distinct as Cape Verde, Senegambia, the Gold Coast, and parts of Central Africa. These spaces contained a great diversity of peoples and cultures and yet they were also bound together through Atlantic trade networks. I make no claims for sameness across these regions, far from it, but there are notable continuities shared between Africans and also between Africans and Europeans, and these similarities became fruitful for commentary by travelers. My examination of travelogues reveals that music provided far more than mere accompaniment to the story of Atlantic African trade. Africans and Europeans alike used music to signal power, wealth, and military prowess to adversaries and allies. These kinds of performances in turn helped to shape the encounters and exchanges that came to define the African Atlantic world for several centuries.

Music and Scenes of Diplomacy, Monarchy, and Militarism

Europeans traveling in West and West Central Africa in the sixteenth and seventeenth centuries sought key trading partners and strategic alliances with local leaders. Because of this, many written portrayals of performances in the region focused on militaristic and state functions of music. Motivated by imperial imperatives to trade and conquer, migrants—whether Catholic missionaries or naval explorers funded by European monarchs—needed to assess social hierarchies and local distributions of power. They saw themselves as influential representatives of their Crown or their Church, and so they pursued counterparts of equal stature with whom they could negotiate commerce and protection.[8] Prospective travelers were keen to anticipate the threats and alliances they might find among different states and peoples around the world, so they turned to published narratives for information about military practice and political hierarchies. Judging from the commonality of such descriptions in travel writing across the early modern era, explanations of combat strategy, terrain, and potential vulnerabilities were important to the genre's success and influence.

Many publications included costly maps and detailed illustrations designed to aid in navigation, and to ensure that newcomers knew how to protect themselves in unfamiliar territories. Images in publications connected to global travel and trade were typically created in Europe by artists who had little to no firsthand knowledge of the encounters they reimagined for publication, so they borrowed from what they knew in order to visually enhance written narratives. The resulting images often include some measure of tropified representation, but they do, at times, also depict useful details garnered from eyewitnesses. Most importantly, these visual records reveal the political and ideological perspectives shaping how Europeans saw the world.[9]

Two illustrations exemplify the role of music in diplomatic encounters between Africans and Europeans during the rise of Afro-European trade. Both were published around the turn of the sixteenth century, when commercial ties between Eastern Atlantic nations were deepening. The first image, from 1591, offers insight into European uses of music in diplomatic pageantry. The second, from 1602, portrays a military musical production from the Kingdom of Kongo. Together, these images illustrate that musical performances played multiple important roles in the development of trade and cultural exchange between Africans and Europeans in the early modern era.

The first illustration portrays a 1598 meeting between Dutch captain Jacob Mahu and an unnamed Cape Verdean leader. It was composed by Theodor de Bry, an influential publisher and illustrator whose representations of voyages had an enormous influence on European perceptions of the wider world for centuries.[10] In the image, five trumpeters flank Captain Mahu during a ceremonious conversation between the two figureheads. Mahu's ship docked at St. Iago, in the Portuguese-held Cape Verde islands while en route to Asia via the Strait of Magellan.[11] The scene portraying the voyage emphasizes the importance of trumpeters and horn players in diplomatic exchanges on African coasts.

The engraving also introduces falsehoods meant to stylize the encounter for European audiences. In his voluminous catalog of exploration-era illustrations, De Bry drew from stock descriptors to signal otherness and savagery. The iconography he helped to popularize taught Europeans how to "see" people who differed from them, especially Africans and Indigenous Americans. The portrayal of Mahu's voyage includes several of these sorts of exoticizing details, like the animal rug placed beneath the Cape Verdean's feet. By contrast, the Dutch captain sits upon a square, woven tapestry symbolizing his modernity and wealth. In reality, of course, many African commodities were highly sought after in Europe at the time, and especially exquisite textiles.[12]

And while the illustration stylizes the diplomatic parties in such a way that viewers might mistake the scene to be portraying a "first contact" of sorts between Europeans and Africans, Cape Verde was hardly a remote outpost in 1598. The islands were a common port-of-call for voyages traveling Atlantic waters, and locals were probably far more globally savvy than many of the Europeans who visited. Having been colonized by the Portuguese, the islands were home to multilingual people, some of whom had both African and European ancestry. The Cape Verdean leader himself presumably was Portuguese, yet the image stylizes him as vaguely non-European. Ironically, the Dutch and other Northern European explorer-traders were following in the footsteps of the Portuguese, learning from their tactics and protocols.

Building on Portuguese imperial custom, when European vessels like Mahu's approached African coastlines, their trumpeters would declare arrival from the bow of their ships. These same musicians would often

Jacob Mahu's voyage stops in Cape Verde. Theodor de Bry, et al., *Americae nona & postrema pars* [. . .], plate 18, "QVOMODO HOLLANDI REGVLVM QVENDAM LITTORALIS tractus Guinaea inuiserint" (Francofurt, 1602). (Virginia Museum of History and Culture, G159. C697 v.4)

join their captains in smaller diplomatic parties that rowed to shore to greet African leaders. The Portuguese developed this method of what scholar Ian Woodfield terms "musical diplomacy" because they believed that Africans were more friendly to outsiders when music was present. This assumption grew from the fact that African leaders often greeted the Portuguese with their own court musicians in tow. Later, other European empires adopted the Portuguese methods of musical contact, establishing common rituals of international trade that transcended empires and geographies.[13] Musical diplomacy was very much a two-way street for Africans and Europeans.

Horns and horn players were especially significant to African-European musical exchange, both on African coasts and in Europe. They served to communicate across distances at sea, to warn of impending danger, natural or human, and they were key to formal shows of state and the rituals of colonial possession and trade.[14] The practice was so widely known that it features as a minor plot point in Aphra Behn's *Oroonoko; or, the Royal Slave* (1688). In the narrative, an English ship captain lures the titular character onto his ship by greeting him in a long boat with "all his Musick and Trumpets, with which *Oroonoko* was extreamly delighted." Once lured aboard the boat with music and a feast, the captain entraps Oroonoko and his entourage, shipping them across the Atlantic into slavery in Suriname.[15]

Africans also traveled northward in the sixteenth century, both as captives and as free people, and some of these migrants were musicians of notoriety.[16] In Germany, lords were keen to have Black African trumpeters as part of their court. The musicians signaled prestige in a tradition that began in the Middle Ages and grew throughout the early modern period. The practice extended to England, where African-descended trumpeter John Blanke performed in the royal entourage of King Henry VIII.[17] African sovereigns also adopted foreign performers into their courtly ensembles. For example, a king from Sierra Leone recruited a German horn player into his band of court performers in the early 1600s.[18] Horn players held significant roles in musical exchanges between Europeans and Africans in this era, in part because their instruments were prominent implements of state pageantry and warfare in both regions. The horn players in the De Bry image stand alongside armed soldiers. One man hoists a gun over his shoulder, another wears a sword, and a battle ax stands tall behind Mahu's entourage.

Illustrations depicting African music also emphasized the relationship between martial arts and musical instruments, including horns. While there are no horns in the engraved image of military music from the Kingdom of Kongo, the accompanying narrative describes the role of ivory horns in battle extensively, a point to which I will return. First, I will examine the sights and sounds conveyed in the image itself, which comes from a narrative detailing the travels of a man named Duarte Lopes. Lopes was a Portuguese Jew who journeyed to through several Central African kingdoms, and his narrative was written down by Italian cosmographer Filippo Pigafetta. Lopes's memoir remains an important source for the study of the Kingdom of Kongo in the sixteenth century. Originally published in Italian in 1591, the book was translated into multiple languages, with an English edition appearing in 1597.[19] Like Cape Verde, the Kingdom of Kongo had a long-standing engagement with Portugal by this time, and many locals were practicing Catholics. As Cécile Fromont put it, "Since the first landing of Portuguese explorers and clerics on Kongo shores in 1483, a sustained flow of people, objects, and ideas circulated and wove ties between the Kongo and Portugal." Kongo monarchs were

Kongo military clothing and instruments from Duarte Lopes's narrative. Lopes and Pigafetta, *Relatione del reame di Congo,* plate 4. (James Ford Bell Library, University of Minnesota, 1591 Lo)

extremely influential on the Atlantic stage and many elites in the kingdom traveled to Europe for their educations.[20]

At first glance, viewers of the engraving might mistake the light-skinned warriors as ancient Greco-Romans.[21] The soldiers march above a fortressed village that is difficult to locate in space and time. On its own, the image is difficult to interpret, but when examined in conjunction with the narrative descriptions, the engraving comes to life as a multi-layered illustration of Kongo martial performance. The words "suono militare" (military sound) and "habito del soldato" (soldier's dress) index the information conveyed visually. As explained by Lopes in the narrative, elite Kongo lords wore hats festooned with "sundry plumes" that the narrator believed were designed to increase their stature and fearsomeness. Lopes speculated that the feathers made soldiers appear tall and intimidating, and that the chains of iron reflected "pompe and bravery."[22] Naked from the waist up, the lords wore large iron chains "with rings upon them as bigge as a mans little finger." In her scholarship on the visual culture of the Kingdom of Kongo, Fromont explains that ironwork was closely linked to wealth and kingship, so these decorative chains likely did signal prestige. The striking feathers and substantial iron chains are both depicted with dramatic ornamental flair.[23]

Kongo soldiers employed multiple kinds of musical instruments in battle. Some were carried by musicians, and others were worn on the body, like jingling bells that soldiers attached to their belts.[24] The image portrays two instruments, a drum and a *lunga,* a conically shaped iron bell struck with a mallet. Strangely, the *lunga* depicted has only one side, whereas other records of the instrument from the period portray them as double-sided.[25] Another puzzling absence has to do with the fact that although horn playing features prominently in Lopes' commentary, the instrument does not appear in the engraved representation.

Lopes was struck by the similarities between the ivory horns used in Kongo and the cornets Europeans used on the battlefield. He claimed that the Kongo horns "yeelde as warlicke and harmonious musicke as the *cornet* doth, and so pleasant and jocund a noyse, athat it moveth and stirreth up their courages, & maketh them not to care for any daunger whatsoever." In both military traditions, instruments were used to direct armies in combat. Lopes explained that, "The removes of their armie are guided and directed by . . . soundes and noyses, that proceede from the *Captayne Generall,* who goeth into the middest of the *Armie,* and there signifieth what is to bee put in execution." The "Captayne Generall" would direct the army to march left, right, or to fall back, by orchestrating instrumental signals, just as "we here among us doo understande the pleasure of our *Generall* by the soundes of the *Trompet.*" Each band of Kongo troops were armed with a set of musical instruments, but the "Captayne General's" were larger than the others, so that his would make the loudest, most distinctive sounds. When the captain issued sonic commands, each troops' musicians would respond, affirming that the message was received.[26] Sounds from horns, drums, and other loud instruments were crucial for being able to communicate efficiently across great distances in chaotic situations like battle and seafaring during the era.[27]

Kongo military strategy involved complex, highly orchestrated sound production and body movement. Not only did soldiers use music, dance, and costume to advance their goals on the battlefield, they also performed military scenes at court in ceremonious displays of state power and patronage. Lopes's narrative presents information about the sounds and sights of Kongo warfare as though he witnessed them in battle, but it is possible that he also observed these activities at court, in the form of performances known as *sangamentos.* Explaining *sangamentos* of the eighteenth century, Fromont notes that they "served dual purposes. On the one hand, they acted as preparatory martial exercises for soldiers and as demonstrations of might and determination in formal declarations of war. On the other hand, they accompanied joyful celebrations of investiture, complemented courtly and diplomatic pageants, and lent their pomp to pious celebrations on the feast days of the Christian calendar."[28] Whether performed at court, or on the battlefield, military arts produced state power.

Surviving African ivory horns from the period underscore the close ties between militarism, material culture, and performance. The Portugal National Museum of Ancient Art collection boasts four ivory horns from sixteenth and early seventeenth-century Africa in its collection. One of these objects has a very distinctive decorative pattern that clearly resembles the knot-like imagery common on Kongo designs from the era.[29] The horn may be an example of the types of instruments that Duarte Lopes described in his memoir. Like other aspects of early modern African music, the use of ivory horns transcended expansive geographies. Museum records indicate that the other horns in the collection are from Sierra Leone. The Sierra Leone carvings combine African and European images, including crosses, deer, and monarchic seals. These artifacts document the cultural exchanges that took place in the context of military music performed in African courts and they emblematize the centrality of musical exchange to African statecraft and Atlantic trade.[30] The horns had utility on the battlefield, and they were also prestigious emblems of wealth and power. Ivory was a highly sought-after commodity, and the use of these instruments reflected the combined military and commercial power of African kingdoms.

While the material resonance of African horns speaks volumes today about the production of power in early modern African kingdoms, the sounds of the instruments would have been impactful in their own time. If you can hear a sovereign's trumpeter, then are you not in their dominion? King's trumpeters and other court musicians helped reinforce their leaders' sovereignty through public performance. As has been much explored by historians of sound, church bells in European villages would not only mark the time and orient the day but also create a sonic periphery drawing together communities as much as any wall or gate.[31] In Islamic societies the call to prayer had similar effects.

European travel authors often made particular note of the great distances that some sounds traveled. For instance, a Capuchin priest visiting the Kingdom of Kongo in the 1660s commented that "they fell a playing upon several Instruments, a dancing, and shouting so loud, that they might be heard half a League off." An Englishman noted that along the Gambia river the sound of a bala traveled "a good English mile."[32] Indeed, sound in this era traveled effectively for a number of reasons. Common building materials often did little to dampen acoustics and a general lack of what we now call noise pollution meant that in many cases, distant sounds could be heard more readily. Europeans were disempowered when they heard sounds that they could not interpret. Over time, their curiosity and confusion about sounds that were unique to African societies became drenched with anxieties. These anxieties increased in the context of slavery and colonial occupation, when Europeans maintained tenuous control over large populations of Africans.[33] The drumming-in-the-distance trope germane to many scenes of white fear lives on to this day and has its roots in portrayals of early modern exploration and conquest.[34]

However, Lopes's descriptions did not simply tropify Kongo performers as "wild natives." Instead, he emphasized the similarities between African and European sound-making. This serves as a reminder that while Europeans came to see Africans and African culture as dramatically different from their own, during this era, they were also interested in identifying commonalities and building strategic partnerships. Eventually, ideas about the distinctions between Africans and Europeans hardened into racial stereotypes that fueled the rise of slavery and colonialism. Records like De Bry's engraving, Lopes's account, and the ivory horns remind us that these outcomes were not inevitable, and that Africans and Europeans were mutually engaged in the performance of power in the theater of the early modern Atlantic world. Yet, in these narratives and objects we are also reminded that the tide of history was bending quickly towards disaster.

West African Court Music

European travelers' investment in diplomatic relationships with African monarchs and other leaders drew their attention to many different kinds of court performances. So far, I have discussed ceremonies of state involving horns and drums in the Gold Coast (Gronniosaw's narrative), European trumpeters in Cape Verde, and military music from the Kingdom of Kongo. Records of trade in the Senegambia region of West Africa highlight another unique tradition of court music. The music of *jeliya* or *griot* attracted a great deal of commentary from European travelers, and their early records document musical traditions that are also well-preserved in the realm of oral history.

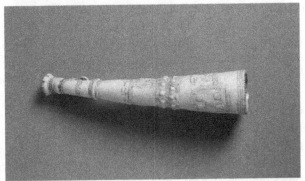

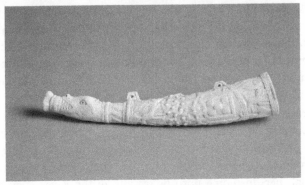

Early sixteenth century African ivory horns held in the
Museu Nacional de Arte Antiga, Lisbon, Portugal. *Top:*
from Congo, Zaire, or Angola (inv 21, photographed
by Luis Pavão); *center:* from Sierra Leone (inv 932,
photographed by Luis Pavão); *bottom:* origins
unknown, possibly Sierra Leone (inv 989, photographed
by José Pessoa). (Direção-Geral do Património Cultural
and Arquivo e Documentação Fotográfica, Portugal)

Portrayals from the era have had a long impact on the way the tradition is perceived by outsiders. In fact, the most widely recognized word for the musicians, "griot," is an artifact of European travel writers' misapprehension; practitioners do not use the word to describe themselves. French travelers coined the term "guiriot" beginning as early as 1636, but the scholar of West African music Eric Charry explains that "there is no term in any of the local languages that can refer to hereditary professional musical-verbal artisans generically without specifying the ethnic group they belong to."[35] Still today, the term "griot" is generally used by non-Africans to describe musical artisanship while tradition-bearers identify themselves in clan-specific terms. When Englishman Richard Jobson described the practice in 1621, he used the term "Juddie," an anglicization of "jeli" or "jali," the terms used by Mandinka and Maninka people.[36] Griot music is tied so strongly to family, community, and clan, that a singular word does not reflect the way myriad practices are understood by the communities who created the tradition. However, the terminology *does* reflect the influence of travel writing on discourses of African music, and it has become widely recognized as a genre within music scholarship and popular discourse.

Griot musicians inherit their status as a birthright, and the tradition is passed down to male heirs across generations. Griot performers are strongly tied to individual clans and leaders, with one of their roles being to preserve community history and lineage through musical storytelling. The musicians provide far more than entertainment; they are also aural archivists. Their ancient practices stretch back centuries, with some modern musicians performing songs that are more than 600 years old. The tradition spans several ethnic groups, including the Mande, Fulbe, Hausa, and Wolof peoples, among others.

In the early modern era, griot musicians' courtly responsibility to praise and trumpet their leaders resonated with European travelers whose own monarchs practiced similar forms of musical patronage.[37] An English traveler in Gambia, Richard Jobson, observed that "at any time the Kings or principall persons come unto us trading in the River, they will have their musicke playing before them, and will follow in order after their manner, presenting a shew of State."[38] He also described the way griot extolled their sovereign by "exalting his antientry" and recalling local histories.[39] There were other similarities between African and European court music at the time. Both traditions emphasize virtuosity and use intricately constructed chamber instruments, and in both regions, concerts were often intimate affairs involving an elite group of performers.[40]

While there were many interesting overlaps and continuities between European and West African court music, there were of course important distinctions as well. Griot were set apart, in some ways, from the mainstream of their societies, which confused outsiders and led some to assume that the musicians were classed as outcasts.[41] Some travelers wrote derisively about griot music, including Jean Barbot, an influential late-seventeenth century French traveler, who described the musicians as "buffoons" and "sycophants" in his widely circulated narrative.[42]

Europeans were not the only ones to express distaste for outsider musical practice. Jobson noted that when Gambians heard his companions "play upon any Lute or Instrument which some of us for our private exercise did carry with us . . . they would in a manner of scorn say, he that played was a Juddy (jeli/griot)." Jobson seemed to believe that the Gambians dismissed his companions' music-making because of perceived prejudice against *jeli,* but he may have been misinterpreting what was simply a disregard for European music. This is but a small glimpse into the perspective of Africans who are typically the ones listened to in these accounts of early modern encounter. Such episodes offer an important reminder to consider the variety of listening experiences present in a recorded scenario, especially when the written portrayal is so one-sided. I chose to open this chapter with Gronniosaw's story, in part because I wanted to begin a discussion of music and power in Africa with the perspective of an African, who nonetheless was a foreigner in the Gold Coast kingdom where he became enslaved. His story reminds us of the diversity of African experiences, and it also demonstrates the power and influence of African elites. For these elites, musical performance was an important tool, both on the battlefield, at court, and in diplomatic trade.

For European travelers in African settings, music that was neither militaristic nor monarchic eventually became classed and raced. Duarte Lopes's narrative linked class status to sound quality explicitly: "the common people use little rattles and pipes, and similar instruments, which are harsher and ruder in sound than those used by the nobles."[43] European traders, travelers, and diplomats had far more respect for African sovereigns during the early modern period than they would come to have in later eras. By the nineteenth century, as the continent became extensively colonized, its peoples became subject to horrendous stereotypes and false assumptions about African history and culture. But before there was primitive Africa for Europeans, there was ancient, civilized Africa, and as Hermann Bennett argues, Europeans shifted from imagining "African kings" to "Black slaves" in part because of the slave trade and the racist ideologies that grew alongside it.[44]

Ukawsaw Gronniosaw's passage from African kingdom into the hands of a Dutch slave ship captain illuminates the forces shaping the tragic story of Atlantic slavery. When he heard the king's trumpets and drums, he initially felt startled, then welcomed, and ultimately terrified. European listeners also heard early modern African performances differently depending on many factors. Generally, in African territories the sound of military trumpets might have meant that a European was traveling under the protection of a powerful trade partner, but on slave ships, the same instruments signified the threat enslaved people posed, especially given that many were highly trained in combat. Duarte Lopes praised the virtues of military sonic orchestration in the Kingdom of Kongo in 1590, but a century later, European colonists in the Caribbean tensed in fear when they heard drums rumbling from the hills adjoining their plantations. In what follows, I continue to listen carefully to the ways in which Europeans heard African musical performances during the era. Tuning in to sound qualities recorded by travelers reveals important details about African musical aesthetics as well as the origins of Western tropes of "Black musicality."

Searching for Early Modern African Aesthetics

In the 1620s, when Richard Jobson traveled up the Gambia River in search of precious metals and trade partners, he passed through lands marked by centuries of transcultural change and migration. He met Mande and Fulbe people along his journey, as well as Portuguese merchants and people of Afro-Portuguese descent. Before the Portuguese came to the region, Islam had come, influencing local culture and politics. So, too, had the rise and fall of the great Malian empire shaped alliances and divisions in greater Senegambia. The region contained remarkable diversity, and also deeply rooted ways of life. Jobson sought to make sense of the political and cultural divisions he encountered as he traveled inland against the flow of the river. His observations loom large in Western histories of the region and they have also influenced the way scholars understand African-European musical encounters during the period.[45] The memoir he wrote about his journeys, *The Golden Trade: Or, A Discovery of the River Gambra, and the Golden Trade of the Aethiopians* (1623), marked the dawn of an English fascination with and economic investment in the Gambia river region that lasted well into the next century.[46]

Ever keen to identify metalwork and riches, Jobson took particular note when he spotted a musician wearing elaborate bracelets during a performance. The man was playing the bala, a xylophone of great prominence and significance in the region, especially for the Mande *griot,* also known as *jeli,* whose traditions I discussed previously.[47] (The next chapter will discuss African xylophones in greater detail.) When the musician worked his hands over the keys of his instrument, the large metal bracelets shook, creating intricate noises that complemented the sound of the bala. Often called balafons in the West, balas have wooden keys, and hanging below each of these keys is a gourd.[48] The gourds function as resonators that amplify and modify the sounds created when a musician strikes the keys with a mallet. These designs produce a highly distinctive sound that has a buzzing, almost effervescent quality. The Gambian musician's bracelets further embellished the performance by contributing a finely textured sound of shaking metal while also decorating the musician's virtuosic movements, drawing visual *and* aural attention to the embodied act of performing. This is all to say that the designs of the instrument worked in concert with the musicians' technique and attire to achieve a musical ideal that was at once seen, felt, and heard.

But when Jobson described the musicians' performance, he was less than laudatory about the sophisticated musicianship and craftsmanship he observed. He wrote that the bala player wore "upon either arme . . . great rings of Iron: out of which are wrought pretty hansomly smaller Irons to stand out, who hold upon them smaller rings and juggling toyes, which as hee stirreth his armes, makes a kind of musicall sound agreeing to their barbarous content."[49] By writing that the musical sound was "agreeing to their *barbarous* content" he characterized Gambian musical aesthetics as uncivilized and debased. He also emphasized the performers' experience—"their content"—as that which he deemed "barbarous." Outsiders' perceptions about musicians' *experience* were key to the construction of stereotypes about Black musicality, as we shall see.

Atlantic commerce brought new listeners to African genres, and these listeners created a discourse of their own that responded to and analyzed African music. Many travel writers described scenes of musical life in Atlantic Africa, and in so doing they helped to introduce prejudicial narratives that eventually hardened into racial stereotypes of Black musicality. These records also lend insight into the musical knowledge and aesthetics shaping diverse performance traditions, from African to American Atlantic shores.

Jangle, Buzz, and Rattle

Gambian bala performers were not the only musicians to deploy metal adornments and other jangling musical devices as part of their musical practice. Similar objects and instrument designs were documented across expansive geographies, from Senegambia, to the Gold Coast, and the Central African Kingdoms. Rattling objects, shells, and metal rings were put to different purposes in many different genres. They could be attached to the strings of instruments, or near gourd resonators like those hanging below bala keys. Kongo court musicians attached small metal rings to instrument strings according to Duarte Lopes, the Portuguese traveler who also described military instruments of the region. The English translation explains that these objects were "very thinne . . . These ringes doo make a sounde of sundrie tunes, according to the striking of the stringes. For the stringes when they are striken, doo cause the rings to shake, and then doo the plates that hang at them, helpe them to utter a certayne mingled and confused noyse."[50] The original passage in Italian offers a clearer indication of the "mingled and confused noyse," describing a subtle metallic sound that best translates to "tinkling" in English.[51] The slippage in the translation, though, speaks to the fact that Europeans interpreted these sounds as aberrant rather than ideal.

An English traveler to the Sierra Leone River region identified similar sounds in the late eighteenth century that were created by an entirely different instrument: "a kind of cymbal . . . they are held between the fingers, and played upon by striking them with a small iron ring worn upon the little finger, and give a shrill tinkling sound."[52] This author, John Matthews, also mentioned enormous drums ornamented with "shark's teeth or bits of copper. . . . Which make a jingling noise." In a rare acknowledgment of African influences on European music, he surmised that the "trombone and tambourine, appear to have been borrowed from the Africans" because of their similarities to the instruments he saw.[53] The rattling metal discs of a modern tambourine clearly recall this legacy. The tambourine's construction gestures broadly to the global circulation of musical designs in the period since the instrument is associated with Turkey, Persia, Iberia, Greece, and elsewhere.[54] Trends in sound design spanned disparate regions, which speaks to the significance of diverse cross-cultural exchanges and multidirectional trade routes both during and prior to the era of Atlantic trade.

The aural aesthetic echoed decorative arts across broad regions, blending aspects of material culture with sound design. Blacksmithing and mining

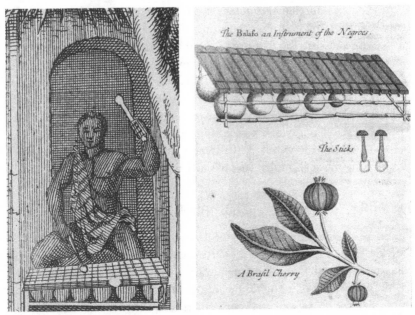

Gambian bala and bala player from Froger, *Relation of a Voyage*. (James Ford Bell Library, University of Minnesota, 1698 Fr)

were economically central across many parts of West Africa and records reveal the ties between industry, artistic production, and state power.[55] The audio-visual implements I identify here also played a role in the types of militaristic and monarchic musical performances discussed previously. For instance, when the Gold Coast monarch Kwamena Ansa of Elmina greeted Portuguese emissaries in 1482 he was "covered with bracelets, necklaces and jewels made of gold on his arms, legs and neck, and had many small golden charms hanging from his hair, his beard and his head." The monarch's courtly procession also included "musicians playing horns and rattles made of shells." In his work contextualizing early interactions between Europeans and Akan states (Ghana, Togo, and parts of Côte d'Ivoire), Toby Green highlights Ansa's impressive display of wealth and power during the stately greeting in contrast to the "poor, feverish, and desperate" Portuguese men who arrived with hopes of trade in the 1480s.[56] King Ansa's decorative items signaled his wealth and the sophistication of his artisans. These designs echoed, quite literally, the musicians who paraded as part of the courtly entourage.

Intricate adornments played a role in fashion and in music in varied traditions, but the execution and meanings behind these types of designs varied widely. It is not my intention to argue for homogeneity in the use of these musical implements across diverse early modern African musical genres. Rather, my goal is to pull on a single thread of information—a musical idea, an attribute, a practice—that musicians and performers of many kinds wove into diverse modes of expression. These "jingling" and "tinkling" designs emphasized and embellished the relationship between movement and musical sound. When the Atlantic trade in precious metals and later captive peoples expanded, African musical aesthetics of this sort would begin to have even broader influence across the globe. For now, let us look further to how different listeners interpreted the sounds created by vibrating musical implements in early modern Atlantic Africa.

Theorizing Sonic Misperception: "Black Musicality" Is Born

Jingling, tinkling, and rattling sound designs foreground and embellish the kinesthetic aspects of musical performance. The buzzing gourds of the bala and mbira, the quivering membrane of vocal masks, and the bright, tremulous bowing of a goji fiddle are sounds from diverse traditions that emphasize the sensations that performers and listeners experience when making and appreciating music. Some theorists of sound argue that all sound, and therefore also music, is essentially vibration.[57] Vocal sounds are created by the vibration of vocal chords, string music is created by the vibration of strings, and listeners perceive sound through the vibration of their ear drums, and to a lesser extent through the vibrating sensations of other body mass. If you have ever stood too close to a speaker at a loud concert, then you probably understand what it means to feel sound through bodily vibration. I interpret the jangling, tinkling, and buzzing implements that were a part of many early modern African traditions as a design aesthetic rooted in an appreciation for the multisensory properties of vibration.

All music involves the manipulation of vibration, and Europeans also held deep beliefs about the connection between what they understood as musical harmony and the vibration "of the spheres," a metaphysical theory that combined mathematics and astronomy.[58] European instruments also were designed to emphasize vibrational qualities, such as the harpsichord, which was very popular during the early modern period. When played vigorously, the instrument has a remarkably buzzy and rattling quality reminiscent of the sound qualities I am identifying in African contexts. This is to say that the relationship between musical aesthetics and vibration was not uniquely "African." Neither was musical vibration manipulated, theorized, or embellished in a universal manner across the continent.

The sounds Jobson and his peers heard went a touch beyond their listening preferences, leading to their confusion about and distaste for the role of vibrational implements in African performance. In the centuries that have passed since these moments of encounter, classical music originating in Europe has only grown more attached to an aesthetic privileging of tones that practitioners of Western art traditions are taught to interpret as "clear" or "well-articulated" as opposed to "muddled" or "rough" sounds. Indeed, these adjectives are so thoroughly freighted with aesthetic judgment from a Western cultural perspective, it is difficult to compose sonic descriptions that do not implicitly otherize aspects of African musical aesthetics.

Cultural listening practices shape more than aesthetic taste; the science of human hearing has shown that aural perception actually adapts on a neurological level to what we hear regularly in our environments. Our ears are not objective when it comes to perceiving sounds. What we have been taught—both informally and formally—to appreciate affects our ability to consciously recognize and distinguish sounds.[59] Scientific theories of auditory perception help explain what is already self-evident to many musicians and language learners. As one learns a new instrument, genre, or idiom, degrees of awareness build, making what was once "foreign" far more comprehensible and in many cases more pleasurable. This is all to say that early modern European travelers may not have been able to hear much less make sense of the subtleties of performances they witnessed. Just as languages may sound like mere "noise" to unfamiliar listeners, musical styles might sound "barbarous," as Jobson put it, to those unacquainted with the genre.

The inability of Westerners to appreciate the refined characteristics of classical music originating in Africa continues to bear negative consequences today. Modern recording technologies developed in Western labs are ill-suited for the reproduction of many centuries-old African genres because they are not designed to capture articulations like the buzzing and jangling that puzzled early modern travel writers.[60] This has frustrated modern tradition-bearers, like the eminent Malian kora player Toumani Diabaté, who explained that the characteristic buzzing of the bala and other instruments is becoming less prominent within the tradition because of the constraints of audio technology. In an interview with the anthropologist Merlyn Driver, Diabaté said that "he viewed buzzing as the 'sound of Africa,' but that 'sound engineers don't like the way it interferes with other inputs.'"[61] Driver argues that for Mande *griot* musicians, this "buzz aesthetic" is tied to "technologies of enchantment" that work as a vector to ancestral spiritual connection. The buzzing is not simply a stylistic preference; it also conveys deep metaphysical meaning and spiritual power. Driver's understanding, brought about by conducting fieldwork with musicians maintaining historic traditions, underscores the ongoing significance of sound-making that emphasizes vibration and texture within African musical aesthetics and theory.[62] Over time, Western observers began to reductively code African practices of embodied expression principled on vibrational sound as "rhythm." Outsiders had only a superficial sense of what it meant to anchor musical thought around what it means *to feel* rather than simply *to hear* or *to do*.[63]

The misperceptions of European travelers had long-standing effects on the cultural landscape in which African Atlantic musical traditions evolved over the next centuries. Jobson's use of the term "barbarous" to describe African performance exemplifies tropes portraying African and other non-European traditions as uncivilized, sometimes denoted by the term "antique" during this period.[64] He also gave currency to a stereotype that was already appearing at the time but grew bolder by the centuries: the idea that African-descended people are naturally gifted in music. Jobson generalized what he observed of Gambian music in this way: "There is, without doubt, no people on the earth more naturally affected to the sound of musicke then these people; which the principall persons do hold as an ornament of their state."[65] Importantly, the substance of his comment, that the people he observed are "naturally affected to the *sound* of musicke" (emphasis mine) differs from the idea that Africans have a particularly natural ability to *make* music (the stereotype that would come). It is possible that Jobson was attempting to explain something of significance about the character of the musical performances he observed. He noted that the musicians seemed to be "affected" by "the sound of music," which says more about his impressions of their listening *experiences* rather than their performance *abilities*. This is an important distinction because musical performance would eventually become linked to physical ability in racial fictions of biological difference, helping to establish what Jennifer Stoever has termed the "sonic color line," or the "process of racializing sound."[66] Jobson's observation may have been a poor attempt to document defining characteristics of Gambian performance. That is, like most stereotypes, this one was created by outsiders who witnessed something of significance, but failed to understand it, and as a result, twisted the truth for ever more and to great and damaging consequence.

"Black musicality" is now a racial stereotype of global proportions. Behind the history of the trope lies a story about the vast circulation of African music and musical ideas in the age of European exploration and conquest. Traditions of African sonic knowledge could be said to have conquered a cultural terrain as vast as any empire, and yet in the making of this triumph, African performers faced scrutiny, prejudice, and outright violence by many outsider listeners. The misperceptions of outsiders ring loud in the historical record, but so do the musical performances of Atlantic Africans. I insist that it is possible to tune in to both. Through cross-cultural encounters along the Atlantic coasts of Africa, and the publications that documented them, Europeans learned to hear through the filters of cultural prejudice and fear, which worked to racialize Africans according to sound characteristics and embodied practice. As Europeans began to associate specific sounds and musical styles with perceived wickedness and metaphysical threat, religious prejudice hardened.

Religion and Ritual

For many early modern Africans, music and other forms of sonic expression were deeply intertwined with religious practice. But it can be challenging to interpret the spiritual significance entailed in musical episodes documented in surviving records. If Western observers strained to convey what they heard with accuracy, they struggled mightily to make sense of religious beliefs that they found foreign and frightening. It is beyond the scope of this book to fully survey music and religion across the expanse of early modern Atlantic Africa, but in what follows I highlight important themes and indicative episodes that illuminate some of the ritual aspects inflecting Atlantic African music.

If Europeans tended to write favorably about regal performances in African settings, they were far more wary of ritualistic gatherings. They reserved their harshest criticism for practices connected to indigenous African faiths, and especially music and body movement associated with spirit possession and material implements of the divine, or what outsiders often referred to as "fetishes."[67] By contrast, Europeans were largely accepting of Islamic and Christian musical practice, even when the musical styles and instruments had local origins. As historian Peter Mark puts it regarding the Senegambia region in particular, "French and English observers gradually established a sliding scale with Christians at the top, Muslims somewhere in the middle, and followers of local African religions

at the bottom."[68] Richard Jobson wrote extensively about Islamic practice in the region, referring repeatedly to his interactions with marabout,
or holy men, whom he referred to as "Marybucke." Jobson's grasp of
indigenous Gambian religion was so weak that his descriptions of ritual
practice are difficult to interpret. For instance, the narrative refers repeatedly to a spiritual being or leader he termed "their devil ho-re," but Jobson gave little meaningful explanation about what he meant by the term.
And, in a cruel critique of the spiritually inflected performance of one
vocalist, he wrote that "with his mouth gaping open, [he] makes a rude
noyse, resembling much the manner and countenance of those kinde of
distressed people which amongst us are called Changelings."[69] In Jobson's
era, the word "changeling" was used to describe people with intellectual
impairments, and the term also connoted beliefs that mental disabilities
and illnesses were caused by being possessed by evil spirits or otherwise
spiritually harmed.[70]

While the English and French focused on establishing trade in the
Senegambian region in the seventeenth century, further South along
the Atlantic coasts, missionaries from Portugal, Spain, and Italy already
had established outposts in the Kingdoms of Angola and Kongo, where
many Africans, including influential monarchs embraced Catholicism,
beginning in the fifteenth century. As Cécile Fromont and others demonstrate, African Catholicism emanating from West Central Africa, and
especially the Kingdom of Kongo, was enormously influential to the
emergence of African Atlantic performance traditions on both sides of
the Atlantic.[71] Some African Catholic rituals entailed a blending of local
and European traditions.[72] For example, in the 1680s, Italian Capuchin
traveler Girolamo Merolla da Sorrento visited a market-place "where the
people, almost innumerable, and divided into two choirs, were singing of
the *Rosary* in the *Gonghese* [Kongo] tongue."[73] A manuscript painting in
Capuchin records documenting 1740s Kongo portrays a liturgical scene
in which African clerics kneel and sing from what is likely a hymnal, supported by a band of musicians playing traditional Kongo instruments,
including xylophones, ivory horns, and a drum.[74]

The cross-cultural musical encounters documented in European travelogues were not simply important because they were the performances
that happened to be written down. These interactions, which took place
within a uniquely Atlantic-oriented performance sphere, became the fertile ground upon which Black music would erupt into prominence during the rise of slavery. As I address further in subsequent chapters, in
the context of plantation slavery in the Americas, rituals of healing and

bereavement became some of the most visible and widely documented expressions of African faith traditions. There was such an extremely high rate of death for enslaved people that funerals became all too common. Here, I look to related scenes of ritual healing and bereavement documented in African settings. One early eighteenth-century portrayal lends insight into women's healing arts in the Kingdom of Loango. The kingdom was situated to the North of the Kingdom of Kongo, and it spanned a territory that includes the modern-day Republic of Congo and parts of Gabon. An English sailor, Nathaniel Uring, described overhearing drumming in the streets of an urban center in the kingdom, which prompted him to inquire about the source of the sound. After being told that the music was coming from a house where a gravely ill woman was being tended, Uring intruded upon an intimate scene, where a women laid on her deathbed. She was surrounded by loved ones who ministered to her with medicines and music.

Through his eyes and ears, readers catch a glimpse of highly ritualized performances that took place in private homes, where outsider observers generally had little access. The healer deployed herbal medicines and divine implements over the woman's body during the solemn performance. Six or eight other women used rattles full of beans and stones to fill the room with sound. They also sang from time to time. To the side of the room, a drummer carried a complementary rhythm. Uring reports that the infirmed woman later died, a fact he relays to deride the communal efforts. But the healing arts of the participants may well have been successful in other ways. For all he knew, the herbs were there to ease the woman's suffering rather than to cure her outright. The women gave their ailing loved one ceremonious attention and care in her final moments. They attended sickness with ritual sound, just as they would voice their mourning, together, after the woman's passing. Perhaps the communal ministrations were intended to guide her safely on her journey through the door of death.[75]

Vocalization was an important part of ritualized mourning within many African traditions of bereavement. These expressions of grief drew cruel critique from outsiders who found the sounds unpleasant. Uring wrote at length about the mortuary rites that observed in Loango.[76] Late one night, he overheard community members' lamentations after the death of a newborn infant. The vocal expressions blanketed the night with unsettling sound, and for Uring, who coldly recounted the scene, the occurrence was notable because of his poor night's sleep. For the family and loved ones of the infant, it was an evening of wakeful attention to the child's loss. Uring explained that "A Child died soon after it was born. . . . all the Neighbours round came to cry over it, which made such an intolerable Howling, that we could not sleep; they began about One or Two a Clock in the Morning, and continued till about Nine. This being the Mode of the Country, they try to excel each other in making most odd and loud Bawling: As we value a good Singer, they esteem those which excel in Howling."

The next day, Uring ventured to observe the bereaved family and their infant laid in repose. When he arrived, he noticed a man that he recognized participating in the ceremony. He asked this man, a linguistic interpreter whose name he spelled as Masucca Malimbo, "how he could be so stupid" to express pain at the loss of an infant who "was but just born, which was neither capable of Pleasure or Pain, nor no relation to him." Malimbo replied that it was "in Complyance to the Custom of his Country, and that it was in Respect to the family. . . ." Uring scoffed at the community's tradition, but for modern readers Malimbo's explanations appear far more reasonable and admirable than Uring's cold assessment of infant loss. Child mortality rates were of course high at the time, both in Africa and Europe, which may have shaped Uring's calloused attitude. It is not clear whether or not the Loango custom related to expressions of grief, or perhaps a communal practice meant to expel any spiritual forces that may have contributed to the child's death.[77]

Uring's point of view as a listener frames the story in his printed text, but it is also true that his words document the cries themselves, and what they meant to the community members that created them together. He criticized the rituals extensively. In my discussion of the episodes I have chosen to paraphrase much of his language, not in an effort to sanitize, but rather to honor the intimate scenes of grief that he portrayed, and so suggest an alternative way of making sense of the past that he documented. Many scenes of cross-cultural witnessing unfold in similar terms: the observer portrays what they hear with a lack of dignity, respect, and understanding. And yet they seem obsessively concerned with what they heard—as if the outsiders cannot get the sound to stop ringing in their ears. They were forced to listen, and listen they did. This fact speaks to the enduring political power of African Atlantic sound-making, even as it came to be violently suppressed in slave societies and under colonial regimes—maybe especially so. To create sounds, loudly, and together is to claim space and communal territory, a practice that took on special significance under slavery, as the following chapters address.

Uring's irritation at the sound of public mourning brings to mind modern cases in which white residents in gentrifying neighborhoods call police on their Black and Brown neighbors for playing music "too loud" while gathering. Uring's irreverent point of view as narrator is far from benign—it is part of a long history of racialized sonic oppression.[78] By shifting attention from Uring's mishearing to the mourner's communal practice of grief, it is possible to reconstruct a sonic imagining of the past that is more attuned to the experiences of Atlantic Africans. Uring's cruel interpretation will never be fully silenced, but neither will the mournful sounds that spurred him to write. Those cries, recorded obliquely in the printed narrative, live on as a monument to the child's brief life, and as an artifact of early modern sound.

The African-born Atlantic traveler and abolitionist author Olaudah Equiano also wrote about ritual mourning practices among the Igbo people of modern-day Nigeria. Nigeria and Loango are not especially similar, nor are they close in distance, but vocal mourning rituals were common across many parts of Africa and indeed around the world. This became a shared context in the Americas that drew the attention and disregard of those for whom such practices were foreign. Because death rates were so high in slave societies, the sounds of ritual mourning became prominent within the local soundscape. Reflecting on his early life, Equiano described the way his mother would visit his grandmother's gravesite, perform lamentations, and make offerings. The funereal practices among the Ibo people did not conceal the terrible nature of grief and loss with silence and solemnity. He wrote that when he accompanied his mother to his grandmother's tomb, she "made her libations, and spent most of the night in cries and lamentations. I have been often extremely terrified on these occasions. The loneliness of the place, the darkness of the night, and the ceremony of libation, naturally awful and gloomy, were heightened by my mother's lamentations; and these, concurring with the cries of doleful birds, by which these places were frequented gave an inexpressible terror to the scene."[79] Through the ears of a child who later became forcibly exiled from his natal community, his mother's mourning proved deeply unsettling for Equiano. For both Equiano and Uring, the sounds of lamentations were unforgettable and disturbing. Perhaps the vocalizations were intended to be disturbing, terrible, and unforgettable. Through the two writers' recollections, we may be able to hear echoes of historic sounds while also understanding that the meanings assigned to those sounds, both then and now, are profoundly subjective.

A Celebratory Performance and Communal Resistance

Music accompanied life's most mournful and sacred moments, and performance was also important for celebratory public events combining
ritual and revelry. Cool evening temperatures made nighttime a preferred
setting for musical gatherings in many hot climates. In the Gambia River
region Richard Jobson described nightly music-making as a consistent
part of daily life, as routine as mealtime and sleeping. During celebratory gatherings bonfires were used to dissuade predatory wildlife from
attack.[80] The fires surely also provided light and ambience. He wrote that
"every night after it seemes they have filled their bellies, they repair to
this Court of Guard, making fires both in the middle of the house, and
in the open yard, about which they doe continue drumming, hooping,
singing and makeing a hethenish noyse, most commonly untill the day
beginnes to breake, when as we consceive dead-sleepes take them, by
which meanes sleeping one part of the day, it makes the other part seeme
shorter, untill the time of feeding come againe."[81] Jobson emphasized the
routine nature of nightly music-making, an aspect of Atlantic African
music culture that extended to plantation settings. In chapter 3, I expand
upon this point to argue that nightly performances and festival celebrations tied to calendrical rythms enabled enslaved Africans to claim space
for musical life in the Americas.

Jobson documented a multi-day celebratory festival tied to yearly rites
of ritual circumcision. He witnessed the events because a young man,
Samgully, who had accompanied his ship up the river as translator and
guide, was set to undergo the rite. Music and dance were important components of the multifaceted celebration. Of the young man, Samgully,
Jobson wrote that he "had learned to speak pretty English; and withal
had taken such an affection toward us; that he did seem even heartily to
neglect father and mother, and his own home, in his desires to follow us."
Samgully previously had been part of a different Englishman's Gambia
River crew and now he was commissioned in Jobson's. The boy's mother
was very anxious to bring him home. She found the traveling party along
the river, approaching from the riverbank to scold her son into coming with her. As Jobson described it, she "made grievous moan to have
him sent back" in order that he might undergo the ritual.[82] Apparently
Samgully's circumcision was overdue by a year and his mother was adamant that he take part in the coming events. Jobson wrote as though the
boy did not want to go ashore, but his mother took matters into her own

hands, and soon enough he went home to participate in the multi-day affair, which Jobson then invited himself to observe.

Samgully was subject to competing social hierarchies while trying to pursue a modicum of personal and economic freedom under significant constraints. He may have felt torn between two authority figures—his mother and Jobson—both of whom placed him under obligation. He may have wished to placate Jobson (possibly his enslaver, although Jobson wrote as though Samgully had been hired to assist in the trek) as well has his mother, who wanted him to fulfill societal expectations within the family and community. Samgully's experiences shed light on some of the circumstances faced by non-elite free individuals participating in international trade on the Atlantic African coasts.

Jobson described the exuberant gathering as being like "our fairs here in England" where "under every shady and convenient tree, there was great fires, . . . their pots a seething, and their victuals addressing, and also their mats laid, to take up their lodging, sorting themselves together in great companies, and in most places, having music, drumming, and dancing; akin such a noise and din, as might well proceed from such kind of Actors."[83] While the crowds were trading goods at the encampment, the young men who were to be circumcised set off from the group, where they were accompanied by other young men, including those who had recently undergone the ceremony. At this second location, there was "a greater noise of voices; as also drumming, and thumping, more clamourously . . ." Jobson distinguished between the noise levels of particular groups in the community as well as the type of music and merrymaking that they undertook, of which there was a broad range. One evening, Jobson attended what was apparently an elite gathering, hosted by the "maister of the towns house" who extended an invitation to dine on a "brace of partridges." At this dinner he found "the Ballards [bala], or best music, and the younger sort of women gathered together."[84] Jobson watched the women dancing and eventually joined them, along with his men. He reported this as if it was welcomed by the ladies, but his intrusions may well have been merely tolerated by them.

In the narrative, Jobson projects confidence in his abilities as an observer, but he comes across as a fish-out-of-water, one who was not particularly welcomed by the celebrants. Some community members evidently embraced trade and interaction with outsiders like Jobson to a degree, but others were vocal about protecting local custom and authority from interference. Upon first arriving at the festive encampment

Jobson found "many people, and much musick; but after a while that we had been there, they all quitted the place."[85] Jobson interpreted this as a "kind of modesty, not to disturb us," but it is easier to imagine that the celebrants preferred to continue their activities in private, away from the outsiders' curious intrusion. Jobson tried to prevent Samgully from undergoing the circumcision, but his mother's active intervention put a stop to the Englishman's influence. It was her vocal performance from the riverbank that set the terms for the lengthy encounter that followed. Jobson's party attempted to cross from the river into the community's sacred spaces. While they witnessed some of the celebrations, they were prevented from impeding the ceremonies. After the circumcision took place, Jobson attempted to follow the young men as they left the ceremony, but a group of elders adamantly prevented him from doing so. The men "in haste overtook us . . . made a shew of much displeasure to such as were going with us, and would by no means suffer we should come amongst them."[86] There may or may not have been a general willingness to accept the presence of Jobson's crew during the festivities, but the elders clearly did not wish the Europeans to interrupt or participate in important aspects of the ritual.

The episode is illustrative because it documents the wide-ranging roles of music and dance within a multi-day gathering. Through Jobson's records we learn about the food revelers ate and gain insight into how social hierarchies and gender roles influenced who danced when, and with whom. These kinds of details underscore that African Atlantic festivals entailed a variety of entertainment that was experienced differently by different people. Elder men met generational obligations when overseeing circumcision rites and Samgully's mother fulfilled familial duties by ensuring her son's participation. Jobson's account sheds light on individual experiences, as well as the larger social worlds of early modern Africans that shaped performance practices. And yet, there are limits to what Jobson can teach us, and that is made clear when members of the Gambian community explicitly resist his intrusion and observation.

Indeed, many of the practices Jobson attempted to portray remain shielded from view. The blurred images and muffled sounds Jobson described record a variety of culturally significant music, ritual, and embodied performance, but the author's fear, ignorance, and confusion—and that of other travel writers—became sown into Western cultural discourse. At the very same time, multifaceted festival performances became a prominent cultural stronghold of Atlantic Africans. This chapter has emphasized that in order learn about early modern African performances, one must also learn about the way Europeans heard, interpreted, and mediated these events in their written accounts.

Sound is and has always been key to white perceptions of racial difference. Early modern travel writers helped to birth the "sonic color line" into being through copious portrayals of musical encounters on both sides of the Atlantic.[87] But the process was not straightforward; European perceptions of African music changed according to specificities of space and time. On Eastern Atlantic shores, the sonic color line functioned more like movable fencing that Europeans shifted according to their interests, embracing practices in one setting, especially when present at African courts, and condemning them in others, often in ritual contexts. The power to do so, and the presumptions about cultural dominance that were implicit in the ways travelers heard and analyzed African performances contributed to the development of racial taxonomies and racialized listening, which are of a piece with the long arc of white supremacy in the Americas and the history of European trade and eventually colonialism across Africa.

Europeans may have born witness to some performances, but they were not full participants in nor authors of African Atlantic sonic experience. The following chapters will show how Africans forced into slavery created opportunities for musical expression, eventually founding one of the most prominent cultural institutions in the colonial Caribbean and across the plantation Americas. Despite and perhaps also because of the triangular slave trade, enslaved and free Africans circulated musical forms across and beyond the Atlantic world under the cover of European cultural confusion. If as Jobson put it, Africans were "naturally affected to the sound music," it was the sound of *their own* music which affected them.

2 Circulating African Musical Knowledge to the Americas
Macow's Xylophone

I OPENED this book with the story of a musician named Macow because his experience represents a crucial moment in the history of African Atlantic music. Macow, who lived in Barbados in the 1640s, was likely a survivor of the Middle Passage, and he was among the earliest generations to perform in plantation settings. While Indigenous and African slavery had been practiced in the Americas prior to Macow's era, plantation agriculture did not become prominent until the seventeenth century. And as plantation agriculture grew, so did slavery, resulting in dramatic demographic changes. As captive Africans came to the Americas in ever-increasing numbers, African music began to circulate ever more widely around the Atlantic world. Macow and his contemporaries did not know it at the time, but when they gathered to perform with each other, they were helping to found a diverse constellation of traditions, including musical ones, rooted in the collective experience of New World slavery.

This chapter is about Macow and his instrument—two characters in the broader epic of African Atlantic music that help us to understand the connections between western coasts of Africa and the plantation Americas, and how life under slavery built upon and also transformed African musical practices. The following chapter will consider the role of collectives in establishing musical traditions in plantation colonies, whereas here I look to the story of one man and his instrument to tell a more intimate tale. Doing so allows me to illuminate enslaved performers' techniques of musical transmission as well as the musical aesthetics motivating instrument design.

Instrument construction amounts to a foundational act: without instruments, musicians could not practice much of their music. I argue in this chapter that surviving documentation of instruments and their sounds constitute significant artifacts that record the processes by which enslaved musicians circulated musical knowledge to the Americas.[1] Macow played a xylophone, which was a very prominent type of instrument across many early modern African traditions. African xylophones were not especially prominent in the Americas, but they were no less influential to emergent African diasporic soundways than the banjo, which other scholars have examined. Musical objects represent precious sources within the archives of African Atlantic sound, in part, because looking at the construction and use of instruments shifts our attention from white-authored narration of African performance and toward sounds and ideas created by Africans themselves.[2] My analysis of African xylophones in the early modern period and Macow's musicianship teach us that enslaved people transmitted musical knowledge to the Americas using aural techniques of sound reproduction. These techniques inflected musical instrument design, as well as the use of found objects for musical purposes, a practice that became central to African diasporic musical aesthetics.

Information about Macow and his instrument comes to us from the words of Richard Ligon, whose travelogue has long fascinated those seeking to understand life on the ground as the English turned full bore toward plantation agriculture and Atlantic slavery in the 1640s. The timing of Ligon's memoir adds to its value as a record of musical life among enslaved communities because Ligon and Macow lived in Barbados at the precise moment when settlers in the young colony began to invest heavily in sugar production and therefore also, the vast importation of African captives. As captives like Macow poured into the island, they charted pathways for those who came after them. The island surged to the vanguard of the English empire, paving the way for the rise of large-scale plantation agriculture across the Americas.[3] As Karen Kupperman explains in her indispensable modern edition of the text, Ligon hailed from a well-to-do family, but he struggled financially. A royalist who fled the English Civil War, he hoped to achieve profit in Barbados. There, he rubbed shoulders with the island's elite but he also labored for a living, probably as an overseer, plantation manager, and possibly in food service. He was in his sixties by the time he made landfall in the West Indies.[4]

Ligon's descriptions of Macow's musicianship document an individual performer living under slavery. Typically, Europeans writing about African music among the enslaved described groups of revelers without differentiating performers, a fact that reflects a broader practice of dehumanizing and universalizing the experiences of the enslaved. This means that although we know a great deal about some aspects of early African Atlantic music, the stories of individual lives and their intimate complexities are far more rare. Thus, Ligon's records of Macow's musicianship and instrument-building preserve a sliver of insight into what it was like for captives as they adapted performance practices to life in a new and challenging environment. So, who was Macow, and what did Ligon record about his music?

Italian Lute and African Xylophone

Ligon's travelogue documents two significant musical encounters between the author and Macow. First, the narrative reports that Macow approached Ligon while he sang and played his Italian lute, called a theorbo. Some days later, an inverse exchange occured, when Ligon happened upon Macow at the plantain grove, where he sat, building the xylophone. During the initial interaction, after Ligon finished playing the theorbo, Macow took the instrument from him and began exploring its tuning, plucking "one string, stopping it by degrees upon every fret, and finding the notes to varie, till it came to the body of the instrument; and that the neerer the body of the instrument he stopt, the smaller or higher the sound was, which he found was by the shortning of the string."[5] Ligon chose to characterize Macow's actions as wide-eyed curiosity, but the text also documents Macow's experience as an instrumentalist. Throughout the twin incidents, Ligon's narration drips with condescension. Imagining himself to be the bearer of all musical knowledge, he was incapable of perceiving Macow's abundant expertise.

Ligon presumed that Macow had never before encountered a device like the theorbo, but it would be far more surprising if Macow *had not* been familiar with the instrument's basic characteristics.[6] Stringed instruments were numerous across African traditions, and as a prominent musician, Macow would have been very familiar with some of them. To be sure, Ligon's theorbo was rather unique because of its size and numerous strings, but the basic playing techniques of all chordophones (whether lutes, guitars, banjos, or ngoni) is the same: moving the placement of fingers along the headstock changes the pitch. Macow knew this, which is why he worked his fingers up and down the fretboard to figure out how to play the instrument. Ligon imagined Macow to be an unschooled instrumentalist even as he documented his studious explorations of the theorbo's capacity for sound-making.

When Ligon then encountered Macow building his own instrument along a plantain grove, his prejudice did not allow him to see a master musician at work either. Macow had "before him a piece of large timber, upon which he had laid crosse, sixe Billets, and having a handsaw and a hatchet by him, would cut the billets by little and little, till he had brought them to the tunes, he would fit them to; for the shorter they were, the higher the Notes which he tryed by knocking upon the ends of them with a sticke, which he had in his hand." Ligon mirrored Macow's curiosity, taking the stick from him to try out the instrument's keys. He observed "the six billets to have sixe distinct notes, one above another, which put me in a wonder, how he of himselfe, should without teaching doe so much." Ligon tried to persuade Macow to conform the scale of his instrument to his own tastes, writing that "I then shewed him the difference between flats and sharpes, which he presently apprehended, as between *Fa* and *Mi:* and he would have cut two more billets to those tnnes[sic], but I had then no time to see it done, and so left him to his own enquiries. I say this much to let you see that some of these people are capable of learning Arts."[7] Ligon recorded Macow's musical expertise in detail and yet he could not fathom the display of knowledge before his very eyes. His portrayal of the exchange with Macow exemplifies narrative patterns that Europeans deployed during and well after the colonial era as they observed and evaluated knowledge traditions that were unfamiliar to them.

Europeans silenced African history and erudition precisely because of their failure to imagine and understand what they witnessed. This was the intellectual terrorism of colonial-era encounters, because as ignorance led to silencing amid a backdrop of dramatic power imbalances, entire knowledge systems were rendered obscure and ahistorical. The evidence of Macow's knowledge, learning, and mastery was abundantly clear, but nonetheless Ligon wrote a story that imagined European culture as the center from which all knowledge flows.[8] My objective is to reverse that script by drawing out from within erroneous narratives like Ligon's the plain evidence of African cultural knowledge recorded quietly—but audibly—in the folds of textual blind spots. Doing so reveals that Africans transmitted and preserved sonic knowledge through instrument design.

Xylophones in Early Modern Africa

Because there are so many different types of African xylophones, it is impossible to know what instrument Macow may have been creating. Most balas, a West African Mande name for the instrument, were larger than the object Ligon described, and they would have had gourd resonators attached beneath the keys. Yet not all African xylophones have gourd resonators, and they vary widely in size and construction. Some are free standing, whereas others are played on the ground, and yet more are worn at the waist, held by a strap that encircles the musician's shoulders.[9] Macow was in the process of constructing the instrument's keys, so we do not know the eventual design characteristics.

We do know that xylophones were important within numerous traditions, and that they held particular significance among West African Mande people, for whom the bala was central to the rise of the great Malian empire under the leadership of King Sundiata. The epic of King Sundiata, sung by Mande *griot* or *jeli,* recalls the origins of the bala. The legendary *griot* who played the instrument, Bala Faseke Kouyate, was pivotal to Sundiata's rise to power. Kouyate's descendants today still preserve his historical memory as well as his ancient thirteenth-century bala.[10] As the empire of Mali expanded and eventually fell, migration, and domestic slavery took place in its wake, which led to cultural transformations and the dissemination of instruments and musical styles. The conquests of the Malian empire, coupled with the spread of Islam across parts of West Africa, brought cultural and political transformation across the region in the eras just prior to the European age of empire. This historical context may help to explain why balas and similar xylophones are so common and so similar across broad parts of West Africa.[11]

The word many Westerners use to describe African xylophones, "balafon," is an artifact of European trade in the region. In Mandinka, *bala* means "wood" and *fo* means "speak." French traders morphed these words into "balafon," just as they also morphed local terms into the word "griot" to describe the region's music-bearers (see chapter 1).[12] Today in the United States and in Latin America, the word "marimba," is more commonly used to refer to xylophones. The term "marimba" comes from the Kikongo language of West Central Africa, where the instruments were also common. The strong ties between Iberian empires and the central African kingdoms of Kongo, Angola, and Loango, may explain why the term "marimba" has had such a lasting presence in Latin American settings. (I return to the subject of Afro-Catholic influence on Atlantic African tradition in the Americas in chapter 4.)[13] An illustration from Girolamo Merolla da Sorrento's 1692 narrative of the Kingdom of Kongo catalogued musical instruments and their musicians, including a marimba displayed prominently. Merolla was one of many European writers who described xylophone performances on the African continent in the seventeenth century. Indeed, the prevalence of European accounts documenting

Kongo instruments from Merolla, *Breue, e succinta relatione*. (James Ford Bell Library, University of Minnesota, 1692 Me)

balas, marimbas, and similar instruments speaks to how important xylophones were within many different Atlantic African musical genres.

When travelers described African xylophones in their memoirs, they often compared them to European organs or harpsichords, placing the instrument into their own lexicons. Englishman Richard Jobson, whose writing I discussed at length in the previous chapter, and French sailor François Froger, both noted the importance of *balas* along the Gambia River region. The river was a trading outpost of intense interest to both the English and the French during the period, and as Ligon mentions, many enslaved people in Barbados hailed from "The River of Gambia." Jobson called the bala, which he spelled "ballards," their "principal instrument," noting that it had "some seventeene wooden keyes standing like the Organ," and that it could be heard at a great distance, or what he called "a good English mile."[14] Writing in 1698, Froger noted that Gambians incorporated the instrument in Islamic scriptural study, entertaining themselves by "discoursing about the *Alcoran,* or with play-ing on a certain Musical Instrument, which they call *Balafo.*" He, too, observed that the gourds "perform the same effect as our organ-pipes." Froger's narrative included a woodcut diagram as well as an image of a performer playing the instrument (see p. 37 in this book).[15] The Italian cleric Michael Angelo of Gattina, who traveled to the Kingdom of Kongo in the 1660s, also praised the sophisticated design of xylophones while comparing them explicitly to organs.[16]

Both organ pipes and gourd resonators amplify sound while bring-ing a softening and breathy effect to an instrument's tone. But, as dis-cussed in the previous chapter, the gourds of African xylophones create a unique buzzing sound, which is created by vibrating membranes that cap the gourds under the instrument keys.[17] Organ pipes are constructed of wood or metal, and they are long cylinders, open on both ends, whereas gourd resonators are enclosed, round, and bulbous. That is to say, the sound effects of the implements are not the same, although it is under-standable that European authors leaned on the comparison to illustrate the instrument for European audiences. Their observations also help to explain why the modern orchestral marimba resembles traditional African xylophones, but with organ pipes attached beneath the keys rather than gourd resonators. Indeed, the design of the modern instrument recalls, in its material form, the way European eyes and ears interpreted African performances during the era of Atlantic encounter. At the same time, the eventual replacement of the gourd resonator with the Western construc-tion visually erases an explicitly African influence. The modern Western "marimba" hides its African ancestry in plain sight. Nonetheless, the ubiquitous object tells a story about the circulation and transformation of musical knowledge across the African Atlantic world. Clearly, xylo-phones were of such great importance that one enslaved man, Macow, went to great lengths to create one in Barbados, as did other enslaved performers elsewhere. Together, they gave the instrument new life in the western hemisphere.

"Chief Musitian" of a Barbados Plantation

What do we know about Macow and the instrument he built in Barbados? Ligon did not describe Macow's background at all, but he did explain a bit about the broader demographics of Africans in the colony, writing that "some of them are fetch'd from *Guinny* and *Buinny,* some from

Cutchew, some from *Angola,* and some from the River of *Gambra.*"[18] These regions refer broadly to the slave-trading territories of West and West Central Africa, and offer little in the way of precision, except for an understanding of the heterogeneity of the enslaved population in Barbados at the time.

One other curious detail survives that may provide insight into Macow's natal heritage. He seems to have been from a part of Africa wherein twin births were taboo. Ligon reported that after Macow's wife delivered twins, Macow "provided a cord to hang her," adamant that she be killed. In Ligon's dubious interpretation of Macow's actions, he speculated that Africans believed that twin births signaled infidelity.[19] More likely, Macow's fury had to do with a spiritual doctrine that connected twin births to the presence of evil forces. A similar taboo seems to have some lasting historical presence among Igbo (Nigerian) and Yamba (Cameroonian) West Africans.[20] (For some Africans, such as the Yoruba, twins were especially prized and considered high blessings.) The evidence is slim at best, but it is worth noting that the name "Emeka" is a common Igbo name. Ligon's spelling "Macow," could be a transliteration. There are also log xylophones among Igbo in Nigeria and peoples of Cameroon that are traditionally constructed of banana stem, which may be a similar, if not the same plant as the trees Macow tended.[21]

The issue of gender violence against enslaved women shades Macow's story. He was prevented from killing his wife, but he abandoned her after the incident. The birth of Macow's twins also speaks to the fact that for enslaved women, their reproductive capacities placed them in the crosshairs between the competing demands of patriarchy and race-slavery.[22] Macow saw himself as lord over his wife, and his enslaver saw her and her offspring as his property. The chilling episode serves as an important reminder that musical arts were never insulated from the mundane and horrific realities of plantation slavery. Gender divisions and cultural norms, both among Africans and Europeans, shaped women's musical lives tremendously. As I discuss in subsequent chapters, women's musical roles often were restricted and their performances were far more sparsely documented in the historical record, especially during the early eras of slavery.

Macow's conflict with his wife also reminds us that he was part of a community of enslaved people, and his roles within that community shaped his life in many ways, including in terms of his musicianship and labor. Describing Macow, Ligon wrote that "we had an excellent Negre in the Plantation, whose name was *Macow,* and was our chief Musitian; a very valiant man, and was keeper of our Plantain-groave."[23] Every Saturday afternoon, those enslaved alongside Macow would assemble in a line to receive bundles of plantains, their weekly allowance of food. In Ligon's eyes, it was "a lovely sight to see a hundred handsome *Negroes,* men and women, with everyone a grasse-green bunch of these fruits on their heads, all coming in a train one after another, the black and green so well becoming one another." The anecdote reveals that Macow was enslaved on a relatively large plantation, surrounded by at least one hundred other captives, and it also reveals Ligon's paternalistic and romanticizing attitude toward enslaved people and their experiences. He coldly noted that Barbados captives were given nothing else at all to eat or drink by their enslavers, nor any bedding on which to rest at night. And yet, he chose to portray their circumstances as contented, remarking also that they were "very good servants, if they be not spoyled by the English."[24] Ligon's belittling attitude toward Africans extended to his perceptions of their music, as well. To his peers, Macow may have been a figure of influence and power, given his ties to planters and because he was responsible for administering the chief source of food. Perhaps he also had expertise in several languages, acquired in a trading context in Africa, or in the Americas, that recommended him for a managerial role to his enslavers.

Those enslaved on the plantation gathered weekly on Sundays to play music, dance, and recreate. (The following chapter examines these types of gatherings.) Ligon did not explicitly describe Macow's participation in the events, but we can assume that he was among those participating. He wrote that all men played the "kettle drums," but "upon the smallest the best Musitian plays, and the others come in as Chorusses." Perhaps Macow, the "chief musician," played the smaller drum, which because of its size, would have been higher in pitch, and therefore more audible above the rest. Ligon wrote at some length about the drumming styles he heard in Barbados, marveling at the complexity and novelty of the rhythms, but ultimately he criticized African music for lacking a "varietie of tune." In Ligon's opinion, "time without tune, is not an eighth part of the Science of Musick."[25] Ever confident in the superiority of his abilities and taste, he believed that if he had stayed in better health during his visit to the island he would have taught enslaved performers techniques that would have improved their musicianship. As other scholars have observed, the memoir transparently preserved Ligon's pompous musical prejudices, while it obscured the beliefs and aesthetics motivating Macow.[26] Yet some of them can be recovered still.

Listening for Macow's Music

Attempting to gain some insight into Macow's instrumental practice, I looked to modern research on African xylophone tuning and design. There are, of course, limits to what we can learn about the past by examining living practice, and yet musicians possess immense knowledge about the history of their own traditions. I am grateful to scholars of ethnomusicology and anthropology who have worked to make some of this knowledge legible across cultures and languages.[27] Heather Maxwell's work on West African xylophones proved especially useful for understanding the intercultural aspects of Macow and Ligon's encounter.

Maxwell reveals some of the fissures between European and West African theorizations of tuning that likely shaped Ligon and Macow's encounter. Emphasizing the degree to which "musical sound can be culturally constructed," she recalls her own struggles as a Western-trained musician trying to grasp the fundamentals of xylophone tuning when studying the instrument. She writes that while her prior training caused her to think about tuning in terms of higher and lower pitches, and intervals in-between those notes, when she observed a master xylophonist building an instrument, she learned that he conceptualized tuning in terms of the distance between the wooden keys and the ground. Duga Koro Diarra, a Bambara musician of the Minyanka area of Mali, described the relationships between keys in terms of familial metaphors, so that one key might be the "little brother" of another. Diarra's primary concern was not "pitch" (highness or lowness) but rather with what Maxwell describes as the "spatial relationship between the keys and the ground."[28]

Maxwell's description of the way Diarra constructed xylophones bears an uncanny resemblance to Ligon's portrayal of Macow's instrument design. She wrote that "in Mali, Diarra's system of tuning a new xylophone involved a long and concentrated series of alternate tapping and striking, from one key on the model xylophone[. . . .] He adjusted the pitches (and intervals) by scraping either the top end of the keys, the underside, or the top middle of the key." Ligon described a similar process when he observed Macow: "having a handsaw and a hatchet by him, would cut the billets by little and little, till he had brought them to the tunes, he would fit them to."[29] Maxwell's and Diarra's musical exchange suggests that Macow and Ligon didn't just use different scales for their music, their conceptualization of tuning and the relationship between the sounds that instruments make was wrought in musical-cultural specificity.[30]

Maxwell explained further that initially she was unable to perceive some of the sounds that xylophones make, even when she had been studying the instrument seriously for some time. Her frustration and confusion mirrors Ligon's; he insisted that Macow's instrument was missing *"Fa and Mi,"* and that he ought to "cut two more billets to those tunes."[31] Both musicians searched for notes on the keys that they felt to be missing. Maxwell's observations are worth quoting at length for what they can teach us about xylophone tuning and aspects of West African music theory.

> One day in particular, when I could not locate a minor third near the bass notes, I remarked to my instructor, Brehman Mallè, that the xylophone was "missing" the minor third from the lowest A-sharp (there is no C-sharp key on the instrument). I played the third pitch, then the fourth, and then sang the interval in between that I wanted to play. I said, "You see, you don't have this note!" Mallè quickly looked at me, smiled, and said, "Oh yes we do, it's here!" He played notes 3 (C) and 4 (D) together and what resulted was a clear C-sharp. He asked me if I could hear it then, and after a few repetitions (and several other influencing voices), I finally did. Once having heard it, I noticed that it was quite clear.[32]

Like the "hidden" xylophone pitches that Maxwell was not initially able to hear, Ligon's portrayal ultimately hides Macow's musical knowledge within the text. And yet, it rings out, just the same, if you know how to listen for it. As with all of the sounds discussed in this book, the sounds of the balafon, the pipe-organ, and the modern marimba are made legible through culturally specific listening practices. Froger and Jobson heard the sound of an organ when they heard a balafon, and Ligon heard an incomplete scale. Heather Maxwell, too, heard what she thought were absent notes when she initially learned to play. What Macow heard, we do not know precisely, but we do know that he chose to reproduce what he heard by constructing an instrument that would preserve and amplify the sounds from his African homeland within the social worlds of the American plantation.

African Xylophones in the Americas

A few accounts of xylophone music in the plantation Americas offer a
window into the way the instrument functioned in enslaved communities. In the 1770s the instrument, called a "barrafou," was documented
in Virginia, and as late as 1791, the planter William Young, observed
the instrument on the island of St. Vincent. During Christmas festivities
he witnessed a group of musicians who arrived on scene "with an African
Balafo" and "played two or three African tunes." Hearing the sound of
the instrument "about a dozen girls . . . came from the huts to the great
court, and began a curious and most lascivious dance, with much grace
as well as action."[33] This moment signals the relationship between instrumental performance and dancing, and also shows the appeal and importance of this particular instrument. Upon hearing the familiar sound, the
women rushed out to join the musicians. The presence of the dancers was
not simply incidental or marginal to the music, it was of course the whole
point of it. The gathering and togetherness, and the encouragement that
came from the women's performance, made possible the playing. Even
in 1791, about 150 years after Macow's performances in Barbados, the
African xylophone was still ringing out in Caribbean communities. It is
interesting to speculate about what the *bala* may have meant to second
and third generation enslaved people who may have been living alongside
African-born survivors of the Middle Passage. Chapter 5 revisits this issue
in a discussion of how African Atlantic music changed for generations of
enslaved people born in plantation societies.

Unlike the small stringed instrument that came to be called the banjo,
the balafon tradition did not flourish in the Americas. It never died out,
either, and the instrument's sounds and playing technique became an
important part of the tapestry of the soundworlds of the African diaspora, especially in parts of Latin America. But the xylophone became
less prominent among enslaved people of North America and the Caribbean, especially compared to drums and stringed instruments like the
banjo. Laurent Dubois argues that one of the reasons the banjo became
the quintessential African diasporic instrument during this period is
because it adapted well to the available construction materials in the
Americas, and to the condition of slavery. The instruments were relatively
small and made of just a few simple materials that were readily available in the Americas. As Dubois shows, banjos—sometimes called *banza,
bania,* or *banjar*—were abundant across disparate plantation societies
by the end of the seventeenth century. By the dawn of the nineteenth

century, the instrument had an iconic status associating it with the music of enslaved people that led to it being the premier instrument of blackface minstrelsy.[34] Why did banjos explode, and African xylophones wane from prominence in enslaved communities, when they had been so important to Atlantic African tradition?

We can only speculate about the constellation of reasons that eventually marginalized xylophone performance among enslaved communities. Xylophones were so intricately designed and sophisticated in their construction that it would have been logistically difficult to build them in plantation contexts. The instruments were often large and quite fragile, not the sort of thing anyone would build if they didn't know how long they might be in a place. Making these large, specialized instruments would also have been less of a priority for captives whose energy was consumed simply by surviving the brutal regimen of plantation labor while being exposed to life-threatening ailments and malnutrition. Macow's position tending the plantain grove probably gave him the time and opportunity to build the instrument that most other enslaved people would not have had. Xylophone construction requires an enormous amount of both wood and time. In order to cure the wood before constructing the instrument, it would need to be exposed to wood-burning fire for several days. Ligon neglected to describe this process, which would have taken place long before Macow sat tuning the keys.[35] Yet while the balafon fell out of prominent use in most parts of the Americas, the quality of its sound, and the techniques used to play the instrument continued to shape performances across the diaspora.

Found Instruments and African Diasporic Aesthetics

Many enslaved people came to the Americas with a tremendous amount of musical knowledge and training, but many of them never again had access to the instruments that they had played at home. Some musicians like Macow built new instruments from the materials that they could come by, while others creatively repurposed available objects and European instruments to reproduce the sounds they longed to hear, imbuing new materials with old sound.[36] The result, of course, was the creation of many new sounds, sound systems, performance genres, and instruments.

One thing that binds together many musical traditions of the African diaspora is performers' highly developed method for transferring sounds across instruments and objects. This technique was shaped by the conditions of slavery, as people were forced to make use of the objects and materials at their disposal, but the practice probably also has roots in African performance techniques.[37] When enslaved people were prevented from using drums in their performances (a subject I return to in later chapters) musicians innovated means to recreate the percussive patterns they longed to hear. This practice survives in living traditions, such as "patting juba," in which North American musicians create complex rhythms by clapping hands against their shoulders, knees, legs, and sides. Similarly, when buck-dancing, stepping, or tap dancing, performers create percussive patterns with their feet. Transferring sounds across instruments became an aesthetic principle and a carefully honed technique among performers across diverse African diasporic genres.[38] In an interview with Paul Gilroy about Black aesthetics and music, Toni Morrison commented on the centrality of appropriating found objects, saying, "The major things black art has to have are these: it must have the ability to use found objects, the appearance of using found things, and it must look effortless. It must look cool and easy. If it makes you sweat, you haven't done the work."[39]

Consider the buzzing sound of the many African xylophones in relation to the soft and yet wonderfully piercing and metallic tones of the steelpan drums, an instrument invented using repurposed oil drums in Trinidad and Tobago in the 1930s and 1940s.[40] Practitioners and scholars believe that steelpan performance developed from Afro-Caribbean drumming traditions, and yet the playing techniques and sonic attributes of the instrument also share elements with other instrumental traditions, including xylophones. In the previous chapter, I discussed the sonic qualities created by gourd resonators as well as the jangling bits of metal, shells, and other materials that were attached to African instruments. I argued that these musical implements were emblematic of some of the vibrational aesthetics of early modern trans-African sound. Many modern genres rooted in the Black experience, such as blues, zydeco, hip-hop, rock, and others feature characteristics that accentuate vibration with twangy, thumping, buzzing, and scratchy sounds. The instruments deployed and the sounds themselves have changed over time, but an audible legacy remains perceptible.

Throughout the twentieth century, African diasporic musicians maintained the practice of using found materials innovatively for the purpose of crafting musical instruments. Indeed, many mid-twentieth century blues artists explained that their earliest instruments were repurposed household items. Some blues greats recalled that as children, they played guitars made of cigar boxes as well as diddley bows, which are a type of single-string zither adapted from similar African instruments that can be constructed with little more than a wire and a nail.[41] The innovative use of found objects translates to creative deployments of recording technologies as well. Genres like dub reggae, Jamaican dancehall, and hip-hop all emerged because musicians creatively manipulated recording and amplification technology to produce novel sounds.[42] Indeed, the ties between the creative uses of instruments and the creative use of recording technology are not incidental.

Musical Instruments as Recording Devices

In order to follow the path of particular sounds and styles across instruments over time, we might do well to consider musical instruments—whether designed or found—as recording devices.[43] Musical instruments facilitate recording because "recording" is a practice of learning. Let me explain. The term's Latin roots (*re* as in repeat and *cordare* as in heart) signify memorization, or "learning by heart." Before the rise of written communication, education centered around memorization and oral performance. Many knowledge traditions continue to emphasize memorization. For instance in religious traditions like Islam, students memorize and recite lengthy holy texts. Memorization plays an important in many musical traditions, even those that rely heavily on notation like Western classical music. These practices are fundamentally a way of recording information in the human body and mind so that they can be reproduced on command. People enter all kinds of vital records—births, deaths, and marriages—into public registers. These records are not mechanical reproductions of the events themselves, but a manner of documenting their existence.

In today's colloquial use, we use "recording" synonymously with mechanical forms of audio reproduction, but these practices are principled on much older ways of preserving and circulating information, much of which did orient around sound. Historians of technology have insisted that when we study the formation of new technologies—like phonographs and telephones—that we consider the way that the devices grew out of existing beliefs and practices. For instance, Jonathan Sterne shows that while we consider audio technologies to have transformed cultures of sound, they actually might be better understood to be reflective of beliefs about hearing and practices of listening that came before.[44]

Put simply, audio recording existed before inventors like Thomas Edison and his peers developed a process for playing audio records mechanically. And performers practicing before the invention of mechanical recording technologies were also exposed to music from near and far. Especially in the early modern era, musical styles and instruments were in wide circulation, largely because of the vast movement of people and goods throughout Europe and Africa, and around the Atlantic rim. Ligon played an Italian theorbo, Macow played a xylophone reflective of trans-African soundways, and both brought instrumental traditions to the Caribbean.

Before there were automated playback machines like phonographs and record players, musicians recorded tremendous amounts of sonic knowledge in their minds and through their practice. They, too, used technologies to do so. Musical notation is one way of recording and circulating sonic information and I argue that building and adapting musical instruments is another. Instrument builders like Macow inscribed musical knowledge into the surface of objects by designing and constructing a set of possibilities for making sound. The number and length of strings on an instrument determine the pitches that may be produced from it; the shape and size of a drum will affect the object's tone and loudness. Of course, instrument design is only part of what creates possibilities for making instrumental music. Performers routinely stretch instruments to their limits, adapting new styles, as enslaved musicians did when they brought traditional African sounds, techniques, and rhythms to traditional European instruments like the violin.[45] African Atlantic musicians not only created possibilities for musical performance through instrument construction, they also surmounted the limitations of musical objects, bending them to their musical will. This interplay between object and performer is an important site of experimentation and innovation.

By emphasizing the role of instruments in performance, I do not intend to de-privilege musicians' agency, but rather to reveal the way that instrument designers and musicians manipulated sonic technologies for the purposes of sustaining existing traditions and inventing novel sound systems, especially under the horrific and constraining conditions of American slavery. Encoded in these practices, I argue, is a form of "recording" that animated musical life long before the dawn of modern audio reproduction. When a musician learns a song by heart they record it in their body and mind for the purposes of reproduction. Musical objects instrumentalize this process by bringing structural possibilities and limitations to bear.

Understanding the way aural knowledge was transmitted before the dawn of modern recording helps to reveal the sounds of the supposedly unrecorded past. Within the vernacular traditions of the early African diaspora, sonic information traveled great distances and expanded widely.

As this chapter has shown, musical instruments facilitated these processes, and their physical trace is a form of evidence that can be studied to reveal the deep grooves of an audible story.

Macow's story as an individual performer and the larger story of the instrument he built in Barbados reveal how Atlantic Africans circulated sounds and sonic knowledge across space and time. The following chapter zooms out to focuses on what groups of people accomplished through collective action. Communities of enslaved people continually created opportunities for musical performance, and their efforts ultimately established norms and practices that ensured a space for African Atlantic cultural expression in the colonial Americas.

3 Plantation Gatherings and the Foundation of Black American Music

THE PLANTATION system robbed people of most of their time and much of their strength, yet, whenever they could, enslaved Africans gathered together to partake in music. These events became the most recognizable cultural institution in American slave societies. This is unsurprising given that performance was a central part of life in many African nations, but it is remarkable given what we know about the living conditions of those held in bondage. After enduring the Middle Passage, survivors found themselves in a dramatically different social order in which the grueling demands of plantation agriculture were compounded by racial violence. Transforming rugged landscapes into productive farms was backbreaking work, and many Africans on seventeenth and eighteenth-century plantations struggled simply to stay alive. Vast numbers of people perished under the weight of disease, overwork, malnourishment, and physical and mental abuse.[1]

In light of these realities, how did people have the energy and time to participate in communal festivities, much less establish lasting cultural traditions under duress? In this chapter, I explain how musical gatherings became prominent and widespread in plantation societies, focusing primarily on the British Caribbean during the rise of plantation agriculture, while also noting commonalities and divergences across geographies and empires. I show that a confluence of factors contributed to the rise of musical life among enslaved communities, yet most importantly, enslaved laborers took advantage of calendrical norms in the colonial system to carve out time and space for musical gatherings. Their actions helped to normalize musical performances very early in the history of American slavery, essentially institutionalizing practices that led to the growth and development of numerous African diasporic traditions in the Americas.

Musical gatherings were held consistently and they were audible across broad spaces, so much so that they became a staple of colonial American experience much commented upon by observers. Indeed, the wide circulation of portrayals of the gatherings may have contributed to the acceptability and predictability of the practices. The substance of the events—instruments, genres, costumes, and dances—varied widely according to the expertise and tastes of specific populations. Despite this diversity and variability, throughout the Americas, at the edges of plantations and in urban centers both, enslaved Africans gathered with regularity to make music and dance. Often, the performances could be heard from a distance, which helped to broadcast events and draw people into participation. Outsiders often described these activities simply as "music" or "dances," but the performances entailed a great variety of creative expressions and traditions. Participants engaged in martial arts, costuming and fashion, ritual healing, ancestral communication, religious worship, political organizing, amorous courtship, and commerce.

Enslavers and colonial authorities eventually grew fearful of musical gatherings because of their association with uprisings. They enacted prohibitions to control the size and nature of the events, but efforts to subdue performances were inconsistently enacted, and ultimately futile. Enslaved communities were strategic about adapting to shifting rules and regulations, especially in the Caribbean, where people of African descent comprised the vast majority of the population. There was only so much authorities could do to interfere when people were determined to engage in musical activity. By choosing to gather, to revel, and to worship with regularity, African captives established a social space of their own. They created rich sensory worlds outside of, but also within oppressive colonial structures, and they institutionalized customs that became key to the development of diasporic cultures and identities, laying the foundations for Black American music.

African Customs and the Plantation Calendar

In the 1680s, an Englishman named John Taylor expressed surprise at the fact that enslaved Africans in Jamaica would stay up late into the night making music and dancing together, even while exhausted from a long day's work in the fields. Their daily routine began at four-thirty in the morning when they were awakened by the sound of a horn or a conch shell. With the exception of a roughly two-hour rest during the hottest part of the afternoon, they labored until "light permit." He wrote that "those poor slaves leave off work and repair to their houses, where they get their suppers, make a great fire, and with a kitt (made of a gourd or calabash with one twine string) play, sing and dance according to their own country fashion."[2] He was aghast that after "making themselves all mirth" the men and women "lay themselves naked on the ground all round their fire, the whole family together in a confused manner to sleep; for tho' the country is so hot, yet they can't sleep without a fire, and thus these ignorant pore souls spend away their time."[3] Taylor pitied the celebrants and wrote with disdain about the displaced Africans' practices, but for the enslaved, nightly gatherings were well worth the sacrifice of rest. By participating in performances out of doors and around a fire, they strove to organize evening hours according to their own customs. Nighttime was preferred for musical production in many parts of Africa, and firelight often accompanied routine celebrations.[4] Taylor regarded the late-night revelry as an aberration, but the performances represented a return to something resembling known routines for many captives. Nightly celebration brought a measure of normalcy and pleasure to people's uprooted lives, helping to make life under difficult conditions more bearable.

One of the reasons that African musical gatherings flourished in the Americas had to do with the fact they could be adapted, in some sense, to the rhythms of colonial and plantation practice. Musical gatherings often occurred in three specific settings: on plantations in the evenings after a day's work, on Sundays when enslaved people were relieved from agricultural and other duties, and on feast days in the Christian calendar. Each of these types of gatherings became a prominent and somewhat regularized performance context within the emergent culture of plantation societies. These practices were interrelated, and yet they were also distinctive.

Because European colonists observed the sabbath as a day of rest for all, Sundays became renowned as a day during which enslaved Africans participated in musical gatherings. High holy days in the Christian calendar enabled even more elaborate celebrations, especially in Catholic colonies, where public procession and festivities were integral to religious observance.[5] Enslaved people made use of opportunities to gather in the evenings, on Sundays, and on holidays, bending the colonial calendar to their own wishes. Through their efforts, Africans established social norms around communal performances by the seventeenth century, remarkably early in the history of American slave societies. The gatherings became fertile ground for the emergence of yet more traditions, many of which seeded diasporic art forms that continue to this day.

Because of the earliness and extensiveness of Spanish settlement in the Americas, coupled with Portuguese and Italian engagement in Atlantic

Africa, performance traditions oriented around Catholicism proved influential to the establishment of many African Atlantic musical practices.[6] African Catholics shaped Atlantic traditions far and wide, from the Kingdom of Kongo, to Iberia, New Spain, Brazil, and beyond.[7] Africans who practiced or were simply exposed to Catholicism from places like the Kingdoms of Kongo and Angola also represented a significant and influential demographic on some American plantations. There were other Africans and Indigenous people who embraced the religion under colonial rule, whether by necessity or expressions of faith. Even in British North America where the Spanish and Portuguese held few strongholds, many enslaved people were trafficked from and through societies touched by Catholic celebration. The African captives famously taken to the Virginia colony in 1619, for instance, were stolen from a Spanish slaving vessel. They had been captured in Angola and trafficked through the Caribbean.[8]

In the Catholic tradition, public processions and elaborate performance traditions associated with feast days were not only allowed, they were encouraged. The calendrical rhythm of Christian festivities probably also resonated with enslaved people who practiced indigenous African religions that entailed seasonal celebrations and festival traditions. The Christian calendar also reflected seasonal rhythms that helped make it possible for enslaved people to gather at natural pauses in the agricultural schedule, when demand for enslaved labor was lower.[9]

Perhaps because Catholic empires set the stage for colonial practice in the Americas, enslaved gatherings tied to the religious calendar became conventional across all American slave societies. It was on Sundays and holidays that enslaved people were released from plantation obligations and allowed to congregate across distances. Records documenting such performances—from narrative accounts to pictorial illustrations—proliferate in the historical record. Sunday and festival gatherings differed in size and character depending on their location. In demographically diverse urban centers, for instance, festivals were more likely to draw European colonists and other onlookers into the events. On rural plantations, evening performances, Sundays, and feast days were more likely to be spaces where enslaved people gathered exclusively amongst themselves, especially in the seventeenth and early eighteenth century.[10]

While there were differences across American geographies and empires as to the experiences of the enslaved and the general structuring of plantation life, there were important overlaps and multidirectional influences as well. Protestant British colonists largely discouraged the religious conversion of enslaved people until the late eighteenth century, which may be part of the reason why Sunday gatherings were so regularly documented in accounts of the British West Indies and North America.[11] If enslaved people were not expected or even in some cases allowed to attend religious services, then they would have been free to conduct their own weekly ceremonious gatherings.

Sunday Gatherings, Domestic Labor, and Women's Roles

Sunday musical celebrations took place against the backdrop of domestic labor. Planters generally did not demand agricultural work from the Africans they enslaved during the Sabbath "rest," but they did force them to grow much of their own food. This meant that enslaved people spent much of their spare time tending to small farms of their own. They also needed to maintain other necessities, like clothing and cookware. Sundays provided an opportunity to tend to such pressing matters. Writing about the weekend respite in 1640s Barbados, Richard Ligon praised those who chose to toil at making ropes and other commodities during free hours, comparing them favorably to those who spent their time making music.[12] A prominent chronicler of Jamaica, Hans Sloane, also commented on the household tasks that took place on Sundays and holidays in the 1680s, writing that "they have Saturdays in the Afternoon, and Sundays, with Christmas Holidays, Easter call'd little or Pigganinny, Christmas, and some other great Feasts allow'd them for the culture of their own Plantations to feed themselves from Potatos, Yams, and Plantanes, etc. which they plant in ground allow'd them by their Masters, besides a small Plantain-Walk they have by themselves."[13] Sloane offered these observations about food cultivation as a preamble to his lengthy description of enslaved people's musical practices on Sundays and feast days.

Also describing weekend domestic labor and music-making in 1680s Jamaica, John Taylor noted that "On Saturday at noon they leave off work (unless at sugar-boyling time) and their master gives to each Negro man and his famally a quart of rum and mollosas to make merry withall; this part of the day they spend in their own plantations, and on the Sundays these slaves gather together in great companys, goeing to visit their countrymen in other plantations, where according to their own country fashon they feast, dance, and sing [sic]."[14] Because Hans Sloane and John Taylor lived in Jamaica at the same time, their portrayals are useful for corroborating details about life on the island. The two authors do not appear to have met one another, and John Taylor's manuscript was written long before the first volume of Sloane's narrative appeared publicly in 1707. Richard Ligon represented an earlier generation of West Indian travel authors, yet the world he described in Barbados decades earlier shared important similarities with 1680s Jamaica, especially for enslaved inhabitants.

Barbados was the first productive colony in the British empire and Jamaica soon followed, ultimately surpassing Barbados to become the wealthiest British holding in the West Indies because of the success of sugar planting on the much larger and more fertile island. For the very same reasons, Jamaica was home to a deadly and vicious slaving system. When Ligon, Taylor, and Sloane lived in the West Indies, the islands they inhabited were at comparable stages of colonial development, a period when planters aspired to transform undeveloped landscapes into productive farms, relying on a steady increase in enslaved laborers, the majority of whom were African-born.

These three authors described Sunday and festival music amid lengthy characterizations of plantation customs—from farming techniques to culinary tradition. Questions of culture are always tightly bound to questions of labor and economy in these types of West Indian narratives. But enslaved gatherings did not increase profits nor were they meant to delight the ears of enslavers. In the seventeenth and early to mid-eighteenth century, music on plantations largely took place in collective spaces created by the enslaved for themselves. That we learn about them through the voices of men like Ligon, Sloane, and Taylor, is merely a byproduct of history. Their written reflections provide a point of departure from which to imagine and interpret more expansive histories, histories that center the experience of the enslaved and the legacies they wrought.

I noticed in the course of my research into written portrayals of Sunday gatherings and other musical festivities that women were rarely documented as musicians, especially in the seventeenth and early eighteenth centuries. Observers commented on women's roles as dancers, but rarely, if ever, as singers or primary instrumentalists in these settings. (Men also danced, sometimes alongside the women, and sometimes separately.) The lack of documentation of women's musicianship probably reflects the fact that in many African musical traditions, gender norms restricted women from prominent roles. Still today, among West African *jeli* or *griot*, instrumentalists are male, while women are largely restricted to vocal performances.[15]

To grasp the meaning and significance of the musical gatherings described in colonial sources, it is important to consider who was there but also who may not have been there, and why.[16] Pondering the relative absence of women's contributions to Sunday music caused me to reflect further on how gender roles would have shaped women's and men's experiences of performances differently. Women's gender roles in Africa and on American plantations involved overlap but also important differences. When competing norms collided in plantation settings, enslaved women bore the burden on all sides. Historian Jennifer Morgan has shown that enslaved labor was always gendered, even though surviving records often fail to differentiate between men and women's experiences of slavery. She observes that "African women on both continents produced the agricultural goods that were the base of the respective economies. As they cleared fields and cultivated and harvested crops, enslaved West African women found themselves performing familiar tasks whose cultural meaning had radically changed."[17] The same was probably true for enslaved women's musical lives. Women were responsible for a majority of fieldwork, and they likely did a disproportionate amount of domestic work in enslaved households, meaning that they were probably less at liberty to participate prominently in Sunday gatherings.

Enslaved women faced especially grueling demands—from the domestic and reproductive labor that they performed to the sexual violence they endured. Despite these hardships, they carved out innovative and entrepreneurial roles, particularly in the Caribbean, where they became key to the region's emerging subsistence economies. "Market women," as they came to be known, took advantage of the small garden plots they were allotted to sell excess produce as well as handcrafted goods, a practice reflective of economic practice in many African nations.[18] These markets were also held on Sundays, and by the late eighteenth century, customers at Sunday markets included enslaved people, poor whites, and also planters who purchased food from free and enslaved African growers.[19]

Written portrayals of music in enslaved communities often marginalized women's participation by focusing on the musical production of instrumentalists, especially drummers and stringed instrument performers, but pictorial representations help to fill in the gaps in narrative accounts. Extant illustrations, including the one on this book's cover, portray women clapping, or playing handheld percussion instruments that we would now call rattles, castanets, or tambourines, especially in the late eighteenth century. As later chapters will address further, women's roles as instrumentalists and public performers increased in the latter part of the eighteenth century. Yet, even in scenes of plantation performances from the earlier eras of slavery, women are front-and-center. Two paintings in particular highlight the role of women in early festive gatherings: one by Dirk Valkenberg from 1707 Suriname and the other by Zacharias Wagenaer from 1641 Dutch Brazil.[20] The images portray male and female congregants, as well as young children, and in both, some women are nude or topless, while others are elaborately styled in fashionable clothing, which has the effect of drawing attention to enslaved women's sartorial creativity while also undressing and sexualizing them for European viewers. Both female and male celebrants are sexualized in the scene, which has an orgiastic character. I have elected not to reproduce the Valkenberg or Wagenaer images in this book because of their sexualizing and objectifying nature.

Europeans often judged African festivation and dance practices in terms of sexual morality. For instance, Hans Sloane wrote that "The Negros are much given to Venery, and although hard wrought, will at nights, or on Feast days Dance and Sing; their Songs are all bawdy, and leading that way."[21] The paintings created an exoticizing spectacle of female nudity and body movement, but they remain useful because they document enslaved women's diverse roles within musical gatherings, helping to complement narrative accounts that narrowly focus on male musicianship. Yet, the pictorial record introduces new problems, serving as a stark reminder of the way that enslaved women were made especially vulnerable to both sexual and racial degradation—in works of art portraying slavery, and in life itself.

When we look at and listen to records of African women's performances from the era of Atlantic slavery, we must hold simultaneously in mind that outsiders generated degrading and sexualizing representations of their bodies, but also that enslaved women were people with wide-ranging motivations and interests, including sexual appetites. Indeed, some may have sung "bawdy" songs. Historian Jessica Marie Johnson argues that African Atlantic women, enslaved and free, "took embodiment and aesthetics seriously," as they negotiated measures of freedom in a world conscribed by class, race, gender, and slavery. She writes that "embodiment (the intersection of the material and the metaphorical) and aesthetics (an expressive culture of selfhood) informed African women and women of African descent's practices of freedom." Johnson's scholarship offers instructive ways to ponder how enslaved women may have negotiated the space of the musical festival on Sundays and feast days. Women were edged out of some roles, but also their labor and artisanship proved absolutely central to other aspects of the celebrations.[22]

Women's fashion, ululation and praise, dancing, caretaking, social-izing, and culinary and entrepreneurial arts made gatherings possible and pleasurable.

Outsider observers who documented musical life in plantation societies tended to focus on larger gatherings held in public view. When women made music of their own as principal performers much of it would have taken place in more intimate settings as they worked over fires, in gardens, with children, and in fields, in spaces somewhat shielded from enslav-ers' views. Descriptions of women's musicianship in Sunday and feast day gatherings in the seventeenth and early eighteenth-century Caribbean settings may have been somewhat rare, but women began to enter the historical record as prominent performers more frequently as part of sec-ond and third generation enslaved people who blended European arts, fashion, and theater with traditional African genres.

A Festival in 1688 Jamaica

Sometime in 1687 or 1688, a large musical gathering took place in Jamaica. This particular festival inspired one of the most unusual and elaborate accounts of early African Atlantic music. While there are many surviving written descriptions and illustrations connected to Sunday and feast day gatherings in the Caribbean and broader plantation Americas, just one source attempted to fully capture the sounds of performance in notated form. Hans Sloane, natural historian and traveler to Jamaica, asked a man named Mr. Baptiste to transcribe the music performed by ensembles of enslaved musicians from several different parts of Africa. Sloane's book also included illustrations of African instruments and explanations of enslaved Jamaicans' musical practice. Together, the mate-rial preserves a multi-layered portrait of musical festivals in the early era of plantation slavery.[23]

The musical festival that inspired Mr. Baptiste's notations was notable because of the amount of musicians present. Explaining the event and the transcriptions, Sloane wrote that "Upon one of their Festivals when a great many of the Negro Musicians were gathered together, I desired Mr. Baptiste, the best Musician there to take the Words they sung and set them to Musick, which follows." He also indicated to readers that "You must clap Hands when the Base is plaid, and cry, Alla, Alla."[24] His words suggest that he expected his audience in Europe to attempt to perform the music on their own. Mr. Baptiste's transcriptions offer a glimmer of insight into the musical character of performances, and

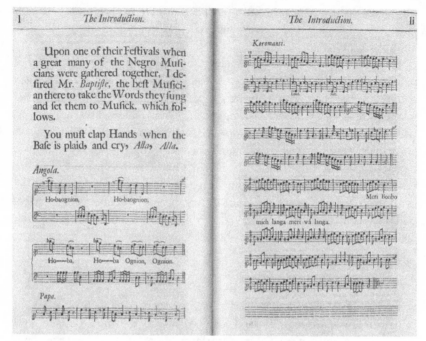

Musical notation from Hans Sloane, *A Voyage to the Islands Madera, Barbados, Nieves, St. Christophers and Jamaica, with the Natural History* [. . .] *of the last of those Islands* (London, 1707), vol. 1, l–li. (David M. Rubenstein Rare Book and Manuscript Library at Duke University, QH109.J5 S6 1707 v.1 c.1)

they raise fascinating questions about the world of the enslaved musical festival. The pieces are some of the earliest notated records of not only African diasporic performances but also early modern African music in existence, and, I would argue, the first notated record to usefully portray African genres themselves (as opposed to African influences on European traditions).[25]

Baptiste appears to have been someone with considerable insight into the musical practices of enslaved Africans, but like all of the material examined in this book, his transcriptions offer a story about Black music that was assembled for primarily European audiences. The disjuncture between recorder and recorded feels acute in the case of the notation published by Sloane. Musical notation is designed for the reproduction of Western musical genres; the system was not designed to accurately replicate music from other traditions. The notations represent a remediation of the music for European audiences, and this foretells practices of white

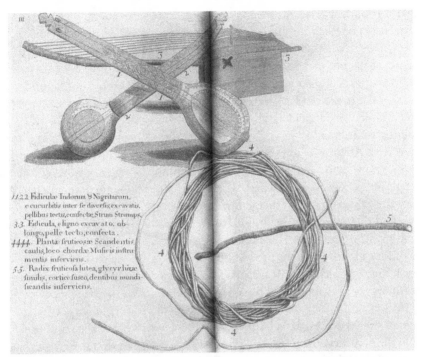

Illustration of instruments from Sloane, *A Voyage to the Islands,* vol. 1, plate 3. (David M. Rubenstein Rare Book and Manuscript Library at Duke University, QH109.J5 S6 1707 v.1 c.1)

appropriation and cultural theft of Black music that occurred in later centuries. Nonetheless, the musical texts remain extremely valuable because they provide insight into the performances that inspired them and what they may have sounded like.[26] As I will discuss further in the following chapter examining Baptiste's biography and the musical world in which he participated, Mr. Baptiste was likely a person of African descent himself. His notated compositions therefore offer insight into the experiences of free people of African descent who performed music from European traditions in the Caribbean.

One of the truly remarkable things about Baptiste's notation is the extent to which it documents the diversity of enslaved musical practice in late seventeenth-century Jamaica. Each of the pieces are titled according to distinct African nationalities, "Angola," "Papa," and "Koromanti," and they are also very different in character, musically. This shows that at musical festivals, people chose to gather with others from shared backgrounds whenever possible, a subject I revisit in chapter 5. As historian Richard Rath emphasizes in his groundbreaking work on the pieces, it is unclear whether or not the titles accurately reflect the cultural traditions of the performers whose music is portrayed. Yet, the very existence of the titles, coupled with the clearly distinct genres represented, underscores the degree to which African identities and musical practices were maintained in Jamaica. Rath examines whether or not the titles of the pieces—"Angola," "Papa," and "Koromanti"—properly correspond to the West African regions to which they refer. Each of the three areas was a location from which enslaved Jamaican laborers were trafficked, but Rath ultimately concludes that the regional affiliations are not completely accurate descriptions of the performers' origins, although the music transcribed *does* correlate, he argues, to distinctive western and central African musical practices. His chief claim is that the transcriptions "provide a unique glimpse into the process of creolization among enslaved Africans of known ethnicity."[27] Rath's analysis offers crucial insight into the performers' backgrounds and the possible meanings of the lyrics provided. However, I do not agree that the pieces provide enough evidence to conclude that the musicians gathered were collaborating across traditions. On the contrary, the titles, and other evidence suggest that they were not.

As I explain further in chapter 5, there is considerable evidence that enslaved people gathered with those of shared background in Jamaica at this time. In particular, John Taylor's manuscript corroborates Sloane's portrayal of music among enslaved Jamaicans in the 1680s. Taylor wrote that on Sundays and at Christmas, Easter, and other holidays when captives were relieved from duties, "they meet *those of one and the same countrey,* and feast, sing, and dannce in a confused manner, seeming all mixth men and women together."[28] Nevertheless, I share Rath's interest in exploring this musical gathering for what it can tell us about the dawning of Black musical innovation in the Americas. While musicians at the festival likely assembled into national groups, the fact that they were doing so alongside and in the midst of each other shows how the space of the musical festival became the rich soil from which manifold Caribbean arts erupted. While festivalgoers may have been keen to gather with people who shared a language and musical traditions, they may also have been curious to take in other performances. Musicians, too, would have been exposed at these events to new styles and repertoire, as were Mr. Baptiste, Sloane, and readers of Sloane's eventual publication.

One of the best ways to examine the pieces that Baptiste transcribed is to hear them. I invite readers to visit a website, *Musical Passage: A Voyage to 1688 Jamaica* (www.musicalpassage.org), that I co-created with historian Laurent Dubois and composer David Garner. The site presents recordings of the pieces to provide some sense of what they may have sounded like. Our recordings, and the notation itself, amount to preliminary interpretations of what would have been complex performances. Baptiste recorded beautiful melodies in notation, but he did not provide information about what instruments would have been used to play them. He also did not offer any clues as to the types of percussion instruments or dancing that would have accompanied some of the music. On the website, we offer multiple versions of the pieces so that listeners can get a sense of how different they may have sounded with various combinations of instruments. Ultimately, there is much we do not know about the details.

However, Hans Sloane did have a bit to say about the instruments and dance practices he witnessed during his time in Jamaica. In paragraphs leading up to the introduction of Baptiste's notation, Sloane offers generalizing descriptions that help us to imagine some of what might have occurred at the festival. He wrote that some enslaved revelers used rattles to accompany performances. Some wore them on their wrists and on their hands, "with which they make a noise, keeping time with one who makes a sound answering it on the mouth of an empty Gourd or Jar with his Hand." At times, celebrants tied "Cows Tails to their Rumps, and add such other odd things to their Bodies in several places, as gives them a very extraordinary appearance."[29] These short lines resemble descriptions of instrumentation and musical styles in early modern Africa that I discussed in chapter 1. Many African traditions incorporated percussive implements like bracelets, metal rings, shakers, and resonating gourds. These implements were designed to ornament body movement and to add intricate aural textures to a symphony of sounds created by musicians and dancers. The jug gourd that Sloane observed would have created just the sort of breathy, buzzy sounds that were part of many African traditions. The object may have been an adaptation, an attempt to reproduce a sound quality that came from instruments like the bala or others involving gourd resonators like the kalimba and mbira.

Sloane singled out strummed instruments for their prominence in Jamaica, and his book includes an engraving of two of these instruments, a type of harp and a banjo, as well as a third object that he identified as being used in Indigenous American performance. He wrote that "they have several sorts of Instruments in imitations of lutes, made of small Gourds fitted with Necks, strung with Horse hairs, or the peeled stalks of climbing plants or Withs. These instruments are sometimes made of hollow'd Timber covered with Parchment or other skin wetted, having a bow for its neck, the strings ty'd longer or shorter as they would alter their sounds."[30] The image of the banjo, the object in center view, is the first known representation of the instrument in the Americas. As Laurent Dubois argues, the banjo was an American creation based on several African instruments. He shows that the instrument became recognizable as a singular entity in American slave societies, partly because they were relatively easy to construct from natural materials in the West Indies.[31] Likely, banjos were played at the festival documented by Sloane and Mr. Baptiste, but other instruments may have been present as well.

The three pieces reflect variety on multiple levels. Not only do the titles convey distinct ethno-national identities, they also are markedly different from each other in terms of musical style and basic features. The first piece, "Angola," stands out from the others because it was written to be singable. (One of the Koromanti pieces has lyrics, but they are not clearly aligned with the melody provided.) In Sloane and Baptiste's era, the term "Angola" often was used to refer broadly to people from West Central Africa, including those from the Kingdom of Angola, the Kingdom of Kongo, the Kingdom of Loango, as well as other smaller kingdoms and societies in the region. So, while the title is "Angola," the music performed may have reflected any one of many traditions from this broader area. The piece opens with a dramatic vocal line that begins on a high note and descends rapidly in a short phrase, "Ho-baognion." The lyrics are then answered by a percussive melody in the bass line that drives the piece forward in motion, leading to a subsequent repetition of the lyrics. This call-and-response framework between voice and instrument repeats throughout the piece. When the treble melody shifts, the bass responds in kind. In the final two measures, the two parts join one another in a rhythmically dramatic resolution. The song's precise termination probably reveals the transcriber's hand, or that of another musical editor who sought to lend finality to the piece, and thereby fashion it for readers who would expect a distinct beginning and end. Whereas notated music generally terminates according to the composer's specifications, many vernacular musicians repeat and elaborate upon musical patterns indefinitely. As Rath puts it, in African traditions, "musicians end a piece when they are finished rather than when it is finished."[32]

"Papa" probably referred to the Popo people of modern-day Benin and Togo. The music, which is very brief, appears to be a simple sketch of a melody that was probably developed through repetition in its musical context. The final phrase of the short piece perfectly launches into the beginning again. Although the piece is squared off in a straight line in its written form, when played this way, it has a circular quality.[33] This might explain why the excerpt is so truncated—if it is meant to be repeated or varied in an indeterminate performance, the tune here might represent a bare bones musical idea that would be improvised upon during multiple repetitions. In contrast, the music gathered under the title "Koromanti" amounts to three completely different pieces of music, collected as parts of a whole representing Koromanti performance.

The length and variety of the Koromanti pieces reflects the significance of this identity and culture in Jamaica. "Koromanti" referred to Akan peoples from West Africa, an important demographic within Jamaica's enslaved communities and an influential nationality across many parts of the Atlantic world in the era of slavery.[34] The term came to have multiple meanings in the Americas, where "Koromanti" referred both to an originating departure point on the Gold Coast from which many Akan people were trafficked, and it also became a symbolic referent for Jamaican Maroons whose self-identifications involved references to Koromanti as language, culture, and nation. It is unclear in this document whether or not "Koromanti" referred accurately to music by Akan people or whether the term may have been suggestive of a broader West African identity or cultural practice that was coalescing in the nascent slave society.[35] The musical text is a remarkable early artifact of a set of traditions that went on to shape history and culture on parts of the island in profound ways.

"Koromanti" is made up of three individual pieces that change in both key and meter. The varied nature of this final section suggests that it aims to capture an extensive performance by skilled musicians who played in a variety of styles, perhaps in a single sitting. The three pieces sound notably different from one another when played. The first bears similarities to Renaissance-era lute music as a result of the arpeggiated notes and modulations from minor to major key and back again. Mr. Baptiste and the performers appear to have been drawing from multiple musical vernaculars throughout the notated examples and particularly within "Koromanti." The second section's dramatic and abrupt descending scales issued in minor tones would have required a virtuosic performer and a nimble instrument. The third section of "Koromanti" nests between the first two segments in tonal quality, but the arpeggiated note patterns recall the initial section. Sloane and Baptiste's record of the 1688 festival documents the incredible musical and cultural diversity present in enslaved performances in the Caribbean. Even the three Koromanti examples entail significant variety.

I have been focusing, here, on the musical attributes of the pieces. Yet, for many of the performers and listeners, there likely would have been a spiritual dimension to the events as well. Sloane seemed to hint at this when he wrote that performers "must clap hands when the base is plaid and cry Alla Alla," but what did he mean by that? The words "Alla Alla" raise the specter of Islam, suggesting that perhaps some of the performers were Muslim, and that they expressed traditional words of praise, a very likely scenario. Many enslaved West Africans were Muslim and there would have been adherents to the faith among celebrants.[36] Islam was present in the regions from which the Popo ("Papa") and Akan ("Koromanti") hailed. On the other hand, "Alla Alla" may have referred to ululation, a vocal practice common among women across many African traditions. Ululating is a way of participating in and encouraging and praising performers. It often accompanies dance and body movement.[37]

Europeans like Sloane struggled to grasp the nuances of indigenous African religions, and he skimmed over aspects of the performance that may have involved ancestral worship, spirit possession, or other divine elements. Sloane proclaimed that both Africans and Indigenous Americans in Jamaica had "no religion" but clarified that "Tis true they have several Ceremonies, as Dances, Playing, &c. but these for the most part are so far from being Acts of Adoration of a God, that they are for the most part mixt with a great deal of Bawdry and Lewdness."[38] Sloane seems to have been vaguely aware of the spiritual components of performance while refusing to acknowledge the acts as "religious." In reality, African religions were central to enslaved peoples' experiences, and to their musical practice. Sunday and festival performances had their own religious overtones, owing to European and African Christian practice, and other forms of ritualistic gatherings and traditions were key to the institution of African musical life in the Americas.

Religion, Ritual, and Mourning

Whereas enslaved gatherings held in the evenings, on Sundays, and on holidays were prominent events widely recognized by outsiders, performance and ritual imbued many corners of life. Musical festivities held in the evenings registered for colonial observers, but other practices escaped their notice or were misunderstood. On American plantations, African-born healers and mystics were important sources of knowledge and influence for Africans and Europeans alike. Traditional African medicine was, on the whole, more effective than Western medicine in the colonies. Even Hans Sloane, a rather self-aggrandizing physician and natural historian, recounted a surgery performed on him by an elderly African woman who removed a parasite from his infected foot.[39] He relied extensively on African and Indigenous knowledge in his writing about the region and in his medical practice, in which he treated Jamaican inhabitants from all backgrounds.[40]

Numerous African diasporic religions born out of the era of slavery blend medicinal arts with performance in ceremonious gatherings, from Vodou to Candomblé and Santeria. These American traditions have their roots in African faith systems, and also in the shared space of the plantation. Records show that converts to Myalism, a Jamaican faith practice first documented in the second half of the eighteenth century, joined the fold by partaking in a ritual that began with the use of medicine. Participants would then conduct a sacred dance before falling into a sleep-state induced by the herbs. Later, a priest performatively raised initiates from the dead using additional herbs, and the celebrations continued. Practiced alongside, and in conversation with a broader belief system known as Obeah, Myal priests offered antidotes to white violence and Christianity as well as African sorcery. Initiation rites engaged ritualistically with the subject of death and resurrection, a fact that speaks to the larger specter of mortality and suffering that shaped life across the plantation Caribbean.[41]

Enslaved people encircled frequently to mourn the dead, in ceremonies that I see as a haunting echo to the more celebratory gatherings that took place in the evening, on Sundays, and on feast days. The physically torturous conditions of enslavement led to high mortality rates, and Vincent Brown has argued that death and dying were not only facts of life in eighteenth-century Jamaica, they were central to the region's cultural development. In the colonies, food and clean water could be scarce while disease spread abundantly. On many Caribbean plantations, the funereal rituals of enslaved people were audible affairs that explicitly tied African religious tradition to performance practice in the Americas.[42]

The historic customs enslaved people brought with them across the Atlantic inflected Caribbean death rites. Songs would be sung in natal tongues and the deceased themselves represented an important link across space and time. These rituals and ministrations became important vehicles for the creation of communal memory. In an earlier chapter, I discussed mourning rituals in Loango, as portrayed by Nathaniel Uring, and Igbo lamentation remembered by Olaudah Equiano. Among the Igbo, Loango, and many other African nations, vocal lamentation and the offering of libations were key to burial practices.[43] Equiano's homeland in West Africa was far from the West-Central-central African nation of Loango, and yet the traditions bore similarities. This shared context proved important on plantations where people from various backgrounds were forced into community. On some plantations, the majority of Africans might might even have hailed from a single ethnic group.[44]

Music was an important component of funerals conducted by the enslaved. Describing burial rights in 1680s Jamaica, John Taylor recorded that "when those slaves die they make a great adoe at their burials, for haveing caryed them to the grave in a verey mournfull manner, all both men and women which accompany the corpse sing and howle in a sorrowfull manner in their own language." He explained that at the gravesite, mourners lowered the deceased into the ground and offered "cassava bread, roasted fowl, sugar, rum, tobacco and pipes with fire" as oblations for the journey ahead. Then the mourners ate and drank, "singing in their own language very dolefully." After the festivities, there were ceremonious goodbyes during which gatherers asked the newly departed to convey messages to their loved ones back home. Taylor wrote that the enslaved would ask their deceased companion to tell their loved ones where they were and that they were enslaved.[45] He and many other Caribbean documentarians from the period remarked that enslaved people believed that they would return home to Africa after they died.[46] Planters' had only a loose grasp of what cosmologies of death and dying might have meant for enslaved people, but their records foretell what was to become a lasting theme in African diasporic art and tradition. Still today, funerals are described as homegoing celebrations, and portrayals of flight, often across water, remain central metaphors in religious and secular arts across the African Americas.[47]

One of the things that distinguished American from African scenes of mourning was the commonality of suicide among those who were enslaved, a testament to the grave difficulties and sorrows that enslaved people endured.[48] Enslavers were so cruel, and so determined to maintain their profits that they attempted to caution against suicides by publicly dismembering the remains of enslaved people who chose to end their own lives.[49] By mutilating the bodies of the dead, they hoped to convince others that those who died by their own hand would not be whole in body, and therefore incapable of returning to Africa in the afterlife.

While African traditions of healing and religion were more often noted by outsiders in the context of illness and death in the Americas, there is no doubt that sacred rites were a part of sanctioned Sunday and festival celebrations as well. The frequent events provided cover for practices that may have otherwise been aggressively forbidden by planters. Fears of poisoning and sorcery concerned enslavers who knew that the large populations they held in captivity had every reason to want them dead. And indeed, as I will discuss further, drumming, dancing, and singing regularly accompanied revolt. Enslavers came to realize that musical festivals made it possible for distant parties to strategize attack and escape. In chapter 1, I showed that Europeans portrayed music as closely linked to militarism in Africa and argued that as these practices crossed the Atlantic with enslaved captives, they came to be perceived as far more threatening to Europeans.

Revolt, Revolution, Prohibition

Revolutionary uprisings across the Americas incorporated music, a fact that underscores the degree to which musical performance created a space of collective agency for enslaved communities. Unfortunately, enslavers became aware of the connections, as well, and they enacted measures to control gatherings, particularly in the Protestant colonies. One author writing in the early 1700s compared performances he observed in the Kingdom of Loango to performances in Jamaica on this very point. Nathaniel Uring described festive gatherings in Loango, explaining that young people met in the evenings to sing and dance. He wrote that "this Custom of Dancing is kept up amongst the Slaves in all our *American* Plantations. On *Sundays,* when they have Leave to visit their Friends, they get together in small Companies in the Streets under a Shade, and sing and dance till it is Night, and then retire, it being not allow'd for any Number of them to be together after the Watch is set." Uring explained the restrictions revelers faced in Jamaica, writing that "they are so strict, that if they see a single Negroe on a *Sunday,* that can't give a good Account of himself, he is generally chastised, and sent Home, and none allow'd to be abroad after the Watch is set." He added that to police the movements of those who wished to gather at night, "They have a Guard both of Horse and Foot in *Kingstown,* which mount on *Sundays,* and as soon as the Sun is set the Horse Patrol in small Parties round the Town, in order to prevent any Mischief that may happen by the slaves getting together."[50] In Uring's telling, even when enslaved people were allowed to gather, they had to do so in a manner sanctioned by enslavers and local authorities. The sacred space of the musical gathering was regulated by patrols in what appears to have been a tensely tolerated practice. In Loango, people were free to congregate at will and use the instruments they pleased, but in Jamaica, the embodied pleasures of performance and dance posed an audible threat to white control.

Uring's account of the effect of the formal restrictions on musical gatherings is an important documentation of some colonial governments' efforts to repress musical gatherings, as well as enslaved communities' persistence in pursuing them. Legal prohibitions against instruments and gatherings varied across empires, colonies, and even local jurisdictions. For example, describing restrictions in 1680s Jamaica, Hans Sloane wrote that "They formerly on their festivals were allowed the use of trumpets after their fashion, and drums made of a piece of a hollow tree . . . But making use of these in their wars at home in Africa, it was thought too much inciting them to Rebellion, and so they were prohibited by the customs of the island."[51] French regulations on slavery, issued in the 1685 *Code Noir,* expressly forbid gatherings of enslaved people from different plantations.[52] And yet, we know that drums and wind instruments survived in Jamaican musical tradition. And in the French Caribbean, enslaved people gathered with regularity, and many African drumming traditions survived. The regulatory laws were tools in the hands of colonial elites, who enforced them at their discretion. Restrictions certainly impacted enslaved Africans' abilities to gather and their choices in music-making, but they did not stop the music, nor the gathering. Typically, in the wake of uprisings, officials would respond by enacting strict regulations that would eventually be relaxed again over time. This pattern created a conflicting body of evidence in that many written restrictions and laws survive alongside numerous accounts of musical gatherings, including gatherings that were linked to acts of armed resistance.[53]

For example, in 1739, during the Stono Rebellion in South Carolina, around fifty enslaved people armed themselves and banded together to assassinate local planters, with plans of marching on to Spanish Florida where they hoped to claim freedom. Participants marched with banners and drums, inviting others to join them as they proceeded about ten miles through the countryside.[54] The revolutionaries were eventually intercepted and assassinated. News of the rebellion led to the creation of laws forbidding drums in South Carolina that stayed in effect until after the Civil War.[55] The event took place on a Sunday, which further raised fears about the role of Sunday gatherings in fomenting political unrest among enslaved communities.[56] Tacky's Revolt in 1759 Jamaica, a months-long uprising, was also planned to launch in coordination with the Whitsun holiday festivities.[57] The uprisings goaded a culture of paranoia among planters who lived in constant fear of organized resistance, and this played into their efforts to cast musicality and musical gatherings as insurrectionist. Even the fictionalized revolt depicted in Aphra Behn's *Oroonoko* (1688) took place on a Sunday.[58] By trying to prevent the music, colonial authorities took practical steps to dispel gatherings, but they also came to characterize the music itself, especially traditional African instruments and performance styles, as inherently threatening and dangerous.

The records of Haitian liberation repeatedly link performance to episodes of political empowerment and military strategy. In the 1750s, revolutionary leader and folk hero Makandal planned an uprising via mass poisoning. Although the plot did not come to fruition and he was put to death, Makandal's courageous story lived on in legend, circling around the Atlantic. One story published in England explicitly emphasized Makandal's musical prowess and his skill in sorcery and African medicine.[59] The characterization reflected many planters' perception that African music, (and especially religious music), was inherently threatening to whites. Decades later, when Makandal's successors launched their revolution in 1791 at a hilltop gathering known as the Bois-Caïman ceremony, music and dance were key to the Vodou rites that took place.[60] One instrument, the *lambi*, a Haitian word for conch shell, emerged as a symbol of revolution and empowerment. The shell was used as a horn, blown to gather troops and alert people to impending attack. Still today, the *lambi* looms large in visual iconography throughout the West Indies, with the image of a man blowing a conch shell emblematizing Caribbean liberty.[61] Given the prevalence of ivory horns in Atlantic African military performance, as I discuss in the first chapter, the conch shell may have been a convenient replacement for the traditional ivory, which was difficult for enslaved people to obtain in the Caribbean.

After the Haitian Revolution, planters throughout the Caribbean tried unsuccessfully to suppress news about the events because they feared it would inspire other uprisings. In 1805 Trinidad, enslaved performers were accused of planning an uprising because they sang a song inspired by Haiti's war for independence. The lyrics struck fear into the minds of local planters. The song, "St Domingo," was sung in French creole by musical dancing societies in Trinidad called "regiments" whose membership reflected the origins of the enslaved participants, many of whom were from other islands including Danish St. Thomas, Saint-Domingue, and elsewhere.

Pain nous ka mange	The Bread we eat
C'est viande beké	Is the white man's flesh
Di vin nous ka boué	The wine we drink
C'est sang beké	Is the white man's blood
Hé, St Domingo,	Hé, St Domingo,
Songé St Domingo	remember St Domingo

The St. Domingo song cleverly reimagined the Christian sacrament as a metaphor for Black resistance to white control. By playing with ritual concepts to threaten white enslavers, the Black liberationist anthem drew upon well-established links between performances of music, armed resistance, and African religion in the plantation sphere.[62]

The Haitian Revolution is often described as the "only successful slave revolt in history," and while there is some truth to the statement, it obscures a greater truth, which is that the potential for uprising, planters' fear of it, and Haiti's successful practice of it was part of a broader, ongoing project of Black liberation. The struggle for full emancipation was long and hard, and the results of other attempted uprisings were not always immediate. Yet collective organizing and armed resistance among the enslaved and free Maroon societies put constant pressure on the trenchant hierarchies of racial slavery and colonialism. Every time enslaved performers gathered to make music, or drew a conch shell to their lips, white people tensed in fear. The music held a power over listeners that constantly asserted the presence and might of those held in bondage. The Haitian Revolution was in many ways the beginning of the end of Atlantic slavery, but the relationship between enslaved resistance and musical practice had been long in the making.

European Writing and Enslaved Gatherings—A Feedback Loop

Given the fears that Europeans had about musical gatherings, why did they allow them to continue? This question points to a central tension in the story of the emergence of Black musical tradition in the Americas. On the one hand, there is a great deal of documentation suggesting that white elites took pains to suppress enslaved people's musical practice. On the other hand, there is an even greater amount of evidence that enslaved musical practices flourished despite these efforts. I interpret the incongruity as evidence of enslaved peoples' determination and persistence in creating opportunities for making music. Their efforts are the primary factor shaping the survival and growth of African diasporic music. In addition, travel literature—the sources at hand—and other works portraying plantation life helped circulate information about these performances and their regularity, ensuring that European migrants expected to encounter them when they arrived in the colonies. These works may even have contributed to enslavers and governing officials permitting these gatherings. Portrayals of African performance in written accounts were repetitious in discussions of American plantations, helping to further cement musical practices as central customs to colonial life.

As discussed previously, travel writing as a genre was in many ways a how-to guide for prospective colonial migrants. The books explained the finer points of sugar working, they included detailed maps, and instructed travelers about what to bring in their trunks. Read by kings and merchants alike, travelogues were imperative for those striving to build empires of state and capital. Works in the genre proliferated but there were a handful of narratives that remained especially popular and therefore influential. Hans Sloane's and Richard Ligon's descriptions of Sunday music were some of the most widely read by other British travel authors, and they were widely referenced and plagiarized by others.

It is clear that travel authors read one another's descriptions of enslaved performances because they frequently referenced earlier accounts, sometimes borrowing from them liberally without citation. I track these intertextual episodes to provide insight into authors' mutual influence. The accounts provide details about the nuances of some Sunday gatherings, but they are also in some cases clearly derivative and unoriginal. Richard Ligon came first in a long-chain of English-language authors who described Sunday activities; he did so about Barbados in his 1657 narrative:

> On *Sunday* they rest, and have the whole day at their pleasure; and the most of them use it as a day of rest and pleasure; but some of them who will make benefit of that dayes liberty, goe where the Mangrove trees grow, and gather the barke, of which they make ropes, which they truck [trade] away for other Commoditie, as Shirts and Drawers.
>
> In the afternoons on Sundayes, they have their Musicke, which is of kettle drums, and those of severall sises; upon the smallest the best Musitian plays, and the others come in as Chorasses: the drum all men know, has but one tone; and therefore varietie of tunes have little to doe in this musick; and yet so strangely they varie their time, as 'tis a pleasure to the most curious eares, and it was to me one of the strangest noyses that ever I heard made of one tone . . .[63]

In a book published in 1672, Richard Blome, cribbed extensively from Ligon's descriptions. Blome never traveled to the West Indies, but he was a printer and mapmaker eager to cash in on public appetites for travelogues. He wrote that

> Every *Sunday* (which is the only day of Rest, and should be set apart for the Service of god) they employ **either in . . . making Ropes . . .** or else spend the Day in Recreation, **as Dancing or Wrestling . . .** in their Dancing they use antick Actions, their hands having more motion than their feet, and their head than either; nor do the men and women dance together, but apart; the Musick to which they dance **being a sort of Kettle-Drums, one bigger than another,** which makes a strange and various noise, but **whether harmonious I leave to the Judgement of the reader . . .**[64]

The passages in bold are lifted directly from Ligon and they continued to reappear nearly verbatim in subsequent publications.

In some cases, the descriptions appear to combine original observations with repetition of earlier writers' comments. In 1708 John Oldmixon cited Ligon directly while adding new details and commenting on the differences between what they witnessed:

> Sundays are the only Days of Pleasure to the Negroes . . . the Generality of them dance, or **wrestle all Day,** the Men and Women together. In Mr. *Ligon's* time, the Men danc'd by themselves, and the Women by themselves, but 'is not so in ours. They have two Musical Instruments, like Kettle-Drums, for each Company of Dancers, with which they make a very barbarous Melody. **They have other Musical Instruments, as a** *Bangil*, **not much unlike our Lute in anything, but the Musick; the rookwa, which is two Sticks jagg'd; and a** *Jinkgobing*, which is a way of clapping their Hands on the Mouth of two Jars. These are all play's together, and accompany'd with Voices, in a most terribly harmonious manner.[65]

When Charles Leslie published a narrative about Jamaica in 1739, he cited Sloane but actually copied directly from Oldmixon (who had cited Ligon).

> They have a great many other remarkable Customs, which you may see very curiously described in the Introduction to **Sir Hans Sloane's Natural History of Jamaica.** Sunday Afternoon the generality of **them dance or wrestle,** Men and Women promiscuously together. They have **two musical Instruments, like Kettle-Drums,** for each Company of Dancers, with which they make a very barbarous Melody. **They have other musical Instruments, as a** *Bangil*, **not**

much unlike our Lute in anything but the Musick; the *Rookaw,* which is Two
Sticks jagged; and a *Jenkgoving,* which is a way of clapping their Hands on the
Mouth of Two Jars: These are all played together, accompanied with Voices,
which make a very terrible kind of Harmony.[66]

Did the authors borrow from one another because the practices they observed seemed to them so similar? Or because they were describing events
that they never truly witnessed? Travel authors generally composed their
narratives after their journeys, sometimes drawing from journals or letters written while abroad.[67] It makes sense that they would then consult
other descriptions of the region to jog their memory and add detail when
their own memories failed. Not only did travel writers' descriptions shape
travelers' views *before* their journeys, but they also reinforced those same
views upon return to Europe.

In my own experiences as a reader of Atlantic travel literature, over
time, it has grown easier to distinguish between content that has been
borrowed and that which appears relatively original. This is how I came
to uncover the convoluted borrowing between Oldmixon, Blome, and
Leslie, who cribbed from Sloane and Ligon. The erstwhile plagiarists were
simply joining the ranks of their forbearers. It is clear from their narratives that Sloane and Ligon also read other travel accounts before and
after their journeys. In the Preface of the first volume of *Voyage to the
Islands,* Sloane penned what is essentially a literature review of all prior
American histories and voyages. He cited multiple authors, describing
the great lengths he took to track down obscure manuscripts and foreign
language editions. He even criticized one author for plagiarizing an earlier
source in an ineffective and unconvincing manner.[68]

As the genre conventions of colonial travel memoirs became formulaic, authors continued to generate new works based on journey after
journey. Whether copying existing narratives' content or simply copying
their format, travelogues constructed colonial culture as much as they
described it. Jennifer Morgan explains the feedback loop these types of
narratives created, writing specifically about the harm caused by the circulation of stereotypes about Black women. She writes that "By the time
the English made their way to the West Indies, decades of ideas and information about brown and black women predated the actual encounter. In
many ways, the encounter had already taken place in parlors and reading
rooms on the English soil."[69] This is also true of European encounters
with African music. Travel authors' acts of copying and plagiarism shaped

perceptions of African music in slave societies far and wide. Furthermore, as mentioned above, the repetitious and formulaic portrayals of Sunday and festival gatherings may well have contributed to these practices continuing, despite enslavers' fears of African music-making. Yet enslaved Africans' persistence played an important role as well. When Europeans traveled to plantation colonies they expected to encounter musical performances by enslaved people, and encounter them, they did.

Colonists also seemed to consider the events worthwhile for winning favor among those they held in bondage, and often there was a paternalistic character to planters' endorsement of musical practice. Whereas in antiquity peasants might have been subdued by "bread and circuses," Caribbean overlords offered rum and molasses to their captives.[70] This was especially true of the more lavish holiday gatherings. Some enslavers sought to discourage escape and resistance by encouraging musical festivities and occupying the enslaved with food and spirits. Others prohibited gatherings because of the same concerns. The practice of slavery produced many such paradoxes: enslavers feared revolt so intensely that some of them restricted music and others encouraged it with jugs of kill-devil rum. And planters were so eager for the labor and knowledge of African captives that they portrayed them as unworthy beings fit for enslavement. While enslavers fine-tuned their ideologies of race and brutish practices of plantation management, their captives were busy crafting and implementing their own strategies for survival. By instituting musical performance as integral to the rhythm of daily life in the colonies, they ensured a space of their own in which strangers could be brought into community, knowledge could be cultivated and shared, and time could be well spent.

The foundation of musical life under slavery must not be understood as an accident of history, or even worse, as something that planters "allowed." Rather, the legacies of African music in the Americas must be appreciated as the product of an intentional, collective effort. Where there were opportunities to gather to make music, enslaved people took them. And where there were none, they created them. Indeed, the organization of daily life in plantation colonies generated possibilities that enslaved communities took advantage of. The recognizability of gatherings—their prominence and notoriety—helped to formalize them as an accepted part of plantation culture. By carving out space for performance in the social order of plantations, enslaved people instituted conditions that would allow for the growth of an enormously influential artistic and cultural tradition: Black music. The following chapter narrows in again, focusing on the biography of Mr. Baptiste, who transcribed the musical notation documenting the 1688 Jamaican festival in Hans Sloane's narrative. Mr. Baptiste's story, and the publication of his transcriptions in Europe, underscores the breadth of enslaved musical gatherings' influence on Atlantic culture. The musical performances were key to the formation of African diasporic traditions, but they also shaped artistic practices and cultural discourses well beyond the space of the plantation.

4 Race and Professional Musicianship in the Early Caribbean

In Search of Mr. Baptiste

Who was Mr. Baptiste? What kind of musical background enabled him to produce the pieces he published in Hans Sloane's Jamaican travel narrative? Zooming in on this remarkable musician's life makes it possible to reconstruct the complex cultural sphere that emerged in and characterized the colonial Caribbean, where Spanish, French, and British territories were intimately interconnected. Baptiste's life and music also illuminate the experiences of free people of color who performed European genres in the plantation sphere in the late seventeenth and early eighteenth centuries. Encounters between enslaved and free musicians of all backgrounds eventually led to the invention of new Caribbean musical forms that blended techniques and attributes from multiple performance traditions. Examining Baptiste's background also helps us to understand how professional musicians helped to circulate musical ideas around the circum-Caribbean and the greater Atlantic world.

In his narrative, Hans Sloane mentioned Mr. Baptiste only in passing and offered just one cryptic explanation of his undertaking, writing that "Upon one of their Festivals when a great many of the Negro Musicians were gathered together, I desired Mr. *Baptiste,* the best Musician there to take the Words they sung and set them to Musick, which follows."[1] The author praised Baptiste as "the best musician there," but it is not clear whether or not he meant that he was the best musician in all of Jamaica, or if he was the best musician at "one of their Festivals when a great many of the Negro Musicians were gathered." There are no other clues about his identity in the published work or in Sloane's voluminous personal archive. In this chapter, I examine Mr. Baptiste's identity by exploring other records gathered in Jamaican archives. Reconstructing his life allows me to offer a more detailed portrait of musical life in late seventeenth-century Jamaica, and to show how questions of race, class, and freedom status shaped the broader world of musical performance on the island.

As mentioned briefly in the preceding chapter, I, along with Laurent Dubois, and David K. Garner, came to believe that Mr. Baptiste was probably a free person of African descent as we created our digital project on the musical records in Sloane's book.[2] We observed that the pieces were so distinct from one another that they must have been created by someone rooted in the Caribbean who would be equipped to meaningfully distinguish African traditions. An outsider trained exclusively in European genres would not have had the necessary familiarity to create nuanced and contrasting works like the five pieces discussed in chapter 3.[3] So, we wondered, who created this fascinating and complicated record of early Jamaican performance? Eventually, I traveled to Jamaica, where I uncovered records in the Jamaica national archives that support the notion that Mr. Baptiste was a musician of African descent, and one who was familiar with the traditions of enslaved people in the Caribbean.[4]

The stakes involved are considerable, because if Baptiste was a colonist like the interloper Sloane, who was briefly in Jamaica serving as physician to the island's governor, then his notations are more likely to cloud rather than to illuminate the story of the enslaved musicians who went unnamed in Sloane's two-volume tome. But if Mr. Baptiste was himself a person of African descent, and perhaps more importantly someone whose musical training took place in the Caribbean, then he, too, can be considered part of the African Atlantic musical legacy. Perhaps he even ought to be celebrated as a composer of written music in that tradition.

Whoever Mr. Baptiste was, as the author of the music printed in Sloane's *Voyage to the Islands,* his perspective on African Atlantic music is important because his cultural fluencies, or lack thereof, help us to understand the musical record he left behind. His story also allows me to sketch the broader musical world in the Caribbean to which enslaved captives contributed. Until now, I have focused largely on the musical production of Africans, whether in Africa or on American plantations. Questions about Baptiste's biography draw our attention to the Atlantic circulation of free people of African descent, especially those from Catholic and Iberian contexts, and their influence on musical society in Africa, the Caribbean, and Europe.

There was a substantial population of free people of African descent in the Caribbean and the broader Atlantic world who became professional musicians. This class of performers is especially well-documented in the Iberian empires, where enslaved and free men were trained in liturgical settings from the earliest eras of imperial expansion, becoming performers and composers like the sixteenth-century Afro-Portuguese musician Vicente Lusitano.[5] In the eighteenth-century French Caribbean, the singer Minette starred on the operatic stage in colonial Haiti (Saint-Domingue) and Guadeloupe-born violinist and composer Joseph Bologne, the Chevalier de Saint-Georges, dazzled audiences in France, while the African-born and formerly enslaved Joseph Emidy performed, conducted and composed both in Lisbon and in Cornwall.[6] Throughout mainland North America and the Caribbean, African-descended violinists came to dominate the profession during this same period.[7]

There is a growing awareness among scholars that cultural exchange between Africans and Europeans began in earnest during the Middle Ages, which challenges the common misperception that African influences on European music came about primarily through the transatlantic slave trade.[8] A figure such as Mr. Baptiste represents a crucial link between earlier periods of African-European exchange and the subsequent musical forms of the Americas. His legacy brings into sharper focus the connections between musicians of African descent working in Western genres and those who made equally significant contributions as performers of wide-ranging vernacular music. For every Saint-Georges, Baptiste, and Lusitano who left their mark on written records of European music, there were hundreds of artists who shaped Atlantic music by creating and circulating music of diverse genres anchored in non-Western performance. By transcribing and disseminating enslaved performers' musical practices, Baptiste created a written trace of musical circulations that extended far beyond the printed page.

Race in Seventeenth-Century Jamaica

The legacy of racial classification, and its connection to the history of slavery gives me pause around my effort to establish Baptiste's heritage. To "pin down" his background—an expression that recalls the practice of preserving ecological specimens—would be to echo the fictitious biological theories of race born out of the ties between Enlightenment science and plantation slavery.[9] And yet, Baptiste's cultural heritage is central to the story of the music he left behind, and his racial identity is important for increasing our awareness of the role and influence that African-descended musicians had on Caribbean cultures in his era.

In Baptiste's Jamaica, race-based slavery was a growing practice, but race was not yet the firm method of categorization that it would become in the British colonies by the end of the eighteenth. In the 1680s, when Baptiste composed music for Sloane, class, freedom status, religion, education, and property ownership were more determinate categories than phenotype. That said, these social markers largely correlated to race, meaning that there were far more wealthy, free, propertied white people than non-white people. And to be sure, non-white people experienced racial harm during the era; practices of race-based slavery and colonial dispossession are the most egregious examples.[10] Largely speaking, though, free people of color in Jamaica had more social and economic mobility in the late seventeenth century than they would a hundred years later. Racialization became increasingly rigid as the sugar economy boomed, and eventually, white Jamaican planters systematically disenfranchised and disempowered free people of color, whom they saw as a threat precisely because of their growing wealth and influence. It was in the 1730s that Jamaican authorities began a concerted effort to impose a strict racial caste on the island.[11]

Sloane's use of the honorific "Mr." may be what caused some modern readers to assume that the musician was white, but Sloane would have considered a free person of African descent with a Western education differently than someone who was enslaved.[12] There also would have been a noticeable gap, at the time, between "Creoles" (people native to the Americas) of all backgrounds and the African-born. In Sloane's introductory narrative he describes the demographics of Jamaica's inhabitants, drawing divisions in this way: "The Inhabitants of *Jamaica* are for the most part *Europeans,* some *Creolians,* born and bred in the Island *Barbados,* the Windward Islands, or *Surinam,* who are the Masters, and *Indians, Negros, Mulatos, Alcatrazes, Mestises, Quarterons,* &c. who are the Slaves."[13] Free people of color were absent from his descriptions although they would have been present on the island to some degree, though perhaps less visibly as a distinct social group. The omission could indicate that Sloane folded free people of African descent into the larger milieu of "Creolians," many of whom were from more established colonial outposts like Suriname and Barbados.[14] The late seventeenth-century Caribbean was a remarkably fluid place where people of many different empires, identities, and language traditions commingled in colonial settings that saw frequent changes in imperial rule and governing practices.

One of the records I found in the Jamaican archives that likely refers to Baptiste's life describes him as "negro," and while we do not know how he self-identified, his heritage is very relevant today.[15] Centuries of racial injustice mean that people of African descent are vastly underrepresented in histories of Western music. African-descended musicians have contributed to and participated in musical traditions and practices stemming from Europe for at least a millennium, but their legacy has been obscured by the insistent privileging of canonical composers at the expense of what was always a multifaceted and demographically diverse tradition. To me, Baptiste as a historical figure stands in for a much larger community of Caribbean and Atlantic performers whose practice transcended African, European, and American genres and identities.

Biographical Possibilities

Although some records I found in Jamaican archives support the likelihood of Baptiste having African ancestry, they offer frustratingly imprecise clues about his larger biography. During my investigation, I searched a lengthy time period, from British conquest in 1655 to 1730. I hoped not only to find Mr. Baptiste but also to better understand the demographic composition of communities on the island to ascertain the likelihood of free African-descended musician being in Sloane's proximity. I uncovered just four records that reference anyone by the name "Baptiste" during this seventy-five-year span. This alone was surprising because records documenting colonists' lives—from land patents to wills, estate inventories, and vital records in parish registries—are fairly extensive. This means that wealthy and even middling Jamaican planters' names enter the record repeatedly, so much so that I began to recognize by sight a handful of names across indexes in my quest to find Mr. Baptiste. I believe that at least one, if not all of the four documents I uncovered at the Jamaica Archives in Spanish Town are likely to be connected to the Baptiste commissioned to write music.[16]

The four traces of a Baptiste appear in two clusters. The first two items, a marriage record and a land patent, are clearly connected to one another.[17] In 1689 a man named John Baptisto married a woman named Rachel Geanego in St. Andrew's parish. Just nine years later, in 1698, a land patent was issued to a man named John Baptist and a woman, Hannah Jennico. Significantly, the second woman, Hannah, has the same last name (although spelled rather differently) as the woman, Rachel, that the earlier Baptisto wed. The land patent, which is for 54 acres in the Parish of Vere, is a rather confusing document for several reasons, all of which seem to be important clues. It was unusual for a woman to be listed in a property record alongside a man; if she married, her name would not be included. And if a woman was widowed and the inheritor of her husband's estate, then no man would join her as co-heir. In this case, both a woman and a man were listed, which means that the two individuals were not married. So, what might their relationship have been? And how were they connected to the Baptisto and Geanego from the marriage registry? To make matters yet more unclear, the land patent actually refers to two different men named John Baptist. The first, who died in 1695, left no heirs. His land, these 54 acres in Vere, was purchased (for the exact sum of his estate—9 pounds) by John Baptist and Hannah Jennico. One possible explanation is that the second John Baptist was the illegitimate son of John Baptist, Sr. This would explain the shared name, the interest in the property, and the lack of rightful inheritance. Or, the second Baptiste may have been away at sea or abroad and Jennico served as proxy.[18] Was Hannah Jennico possibly Rachel's sister? If both Rachel and Baptiste had died, it would make sense that their extended family might be eager to protect a claim to the homestead.[19]

If the Baptist on the land patent was an illegitimate heir of mixed-race parentage, he may have wished for a white woman to share the claim to the property to protect his investment. Or perhaps she had money, and he had an interest in the property (or the opposite). The plantation in Vere was not large and it was not in a particularly desirable region of the colony, confirming that the parties involved were not among the island's well-to-do. A Jamaican law on the books at the time stated that indentured servants who came to Jamaica and concluded their four years of service would be granted fifty acres by the government. Perhaps the plot of land was such an allotment that had grown to include a few additional acres.[20] Many questions and possibilities are raised by the land patent, none of which lead to certain conclusions. Unfortunately, I was unable to locate the original inventory of Baptist the elder's estate, which may hold further clues if it still exists.

The first cluster of records coincide with Sloane's time in Jamaica, but there is nothing about the purchase of the property nor the individuals involved that suggest a musical connection. By contrast, the second set of documents seem to plausibly document the life of a professional musician. A 1714 naturalization record refers to "John Baptista a negro" who lived in Port Royal, just across the bay from Kingston.[21] The port city had previously been a hotbed of Caribbean commerce and revelry, but it had been largely destroyed by a massive earthquake in 1692. Just three years after the naturalization was recorded and Baptista claimed the rights of an Englishman, an estate inventory appears for a man with the same name.[22] Because these records appear so closely together, this Baptista seems likely to be the same individual. The man died with an estate worth roughly nineteen pounds. He had little more than a trunk, nine ounces of silver and some gold to his name at his death, but he did have a remarkable wardrobe, including two full suits, eighteen shirts, seven cravats, four additional pairs of breeches, and eight waistcoats. Unless he was a tailor, this strikes me as potentially the wardrobe of a performer, who would need costumes for the stage.[23]

One of the two witnesses to the estate inventory of Baptista's belongings was John Wolmer, a wealthy goldsmith and merchant who is still remembered prominently in Kingston today.[24] He founded the first free school on the island by bequeathing a large portion of his estate upon his death in 1729.[25] Notably, the Jamaican law that was passed in 1736 to manage the educational trust from Wolmer's estate did not impose any restrictions on student demographics. From its founding, Wolmer's School was open to boys and girls of all classes, creeds, and color.[26] While it does not tell us much about Baptiste, this fact underscores the degree to which some African-descendant Jamaicans had access to limited education during the eighteenth century, even as free people of color became increasingly subjected to legal restrictions and racial violence.[27] The connection between Baptiste and Wolmer also document the likelihood of a free person of color having close ties to a prominent white Jamaican during the era.

Only one of the four records shows that a Jamaican Baptiste had African ancestry, the naturalization record from 1714 that names "John Baptiste" as "negro" and gives him the rights of a native-born British subject. What foreign territory was Baptiste from? Could the naturalization record have served as freedom papers for previously enslaved individuals, or was Baptiste a free person from an "alien" territory, as the document indicates? The spelling of his name presents possibilities that are as inconclusive as much of the other evidence. While Sloane uses the name "Baptiste," there is much variation across the four surviving records. The spelling of names in the era was notoriously inconsistent, and in Baptiste's case even within the same record I encountered these variants: Baptist, Baptista, and Baptisto. While there is no discernible pattern across the two clusters of documents, the names Baptisto and Baptista introduce the possibility that the musician may have had Spanish or Portuguese roots rather than French ones. (Baptisto could be an Anglicization of Bautista and Baptista is a Portuguese surname.)

Jamaica had been a Spanish territory before English conquest in 1655 and it was very close in proximity to both Cuba and colonial Haiti

(Saint-Domingue). The proximity between these territories meant that there was constant traffic between the English, Spanish, and French empires in the Caribbean basin. Because of the centuries-long connections between Africans and the Portuguese, there was a considerable population of Lusophone Africans throughout the Atlantic world, enslaved and free.[28] Describing enslaved communities in Barbados in the 1640s Richard Ligon noted that "some of them, who have been bred up amongst the Portugalls, have some extraordinary qualities, which the others have not; as singing and fencing . . . their voices, I have heard many of them very loud and sweet."[29]

While much remains unclear about Baptiste's biography, surviving records support the likelihood that he was a person of African descent. The records also show that he was an emigre to Jamaica, and it is likely that he traveled from elsewhere in the Caribbean. Baptiste clearly was not a wealthy planter, and was instead a person of a person of middling or low status. Given these likelihoods, as well as the implications of his surname, Mr. Baptiste probably had a relationship with the Catholic church, which would explain his musical training.

Catholicism and Caribbean Tradition

If Baptiste was from a colonial society controlled by one of the seaborne empires of Spain, Portugal, or France, then he likely would have been trained as a musician in the Catholic Church.[30] It was common for musicians in Europe and the Americas to receive musical educations as boy choristers. This type of training generated a professional class of musicians who would then grow up to be tutors and performers themselves, sometimes but not always in the church. Such opportunities were especially attractive for families of modest means who needed their children to be fed, clothed, and educated. The model traveled to American cathedrals where free young men of color and also enslaved people were given musical educations in similar roles.[31] This type of background would make sense for a Caribbean musician like Baptiste who could read and write Western notation and seemed to have familiarity with African genres. It is also possible that Baptiste hailed from the Kingdom of Kongo, where African and European music was practiced in a syncretistic manner in liturgical settings, and where Kongo people were educated in European languages and traditions as Catholic priests.[32]

Even though Catholics faced prohibitions in England in the seventeenth century, Sloane's tenure in Jamaica coincided with a public resurgence of the religion on the island because of King James II's reign and because its English governor, the Duke of Albemarle was himself Catholic. The Catholic faith was already, of course, practiced in Jamaica, but more discreetly. The Spanish government had an important diplomatic agreement with Jamaica known as the Assiento, which allowed for a compound of Spaniards to live on the island in order to conduct the slave trade. The leader of the Assiento in the 1680s, Don Juan Castillo, reportedly built a chapel on his compound that could hold 300 worshippers and installed several priests and clerics to lead the church.[33] One could imagine Sloane interacting with a church musician through his intimate connections with the devout governor and the broader milieu of officials such as Castillo. Albemarle's brief term of leadership was not remembered positively by local planters who resented both his Catholicism and his intention to promote Christianity among enslaved people, which was more common in Catholic colonies. At the time in Jamaica, enslaved people who became Christians could claim freedom after professing the faith for a set period, but this practice was later abolished.[34]

Early histories of Jamaica document the story of an influential African Catholic priest on the island, who played a role during the English conquest of the island. His existence was later questioned and nearly erased by twentieth-century historians of the church who doubted that early modern Afro-Caribbeans would have had church educations.[35] More recent scholarship, however, reaffirms the prominence of Afro-Caribbeans across a number of professions and trades.[36] Mr. Baptiste's story and the story of other influential Africans in the Atlantic world present important correctives to damaging narratives. In many ways, Western scholars are just now returning to a conceptualization of African and diasporic history that was more widely accepted across Europe during the earliest eras of European trade and travel in Africa and the Americas.[37]

Jamaica's Music in 1688

In 1688, around the time Mr. Baptiste transcribed the African music Sloane witnessed, Jamaica had only been in English control for about thirty years. Before that, it was held by the Spanish, and neither empire had yet brought the island into peak agricultural production. Rather than the wealthy sugar plantation society that it was to become over the course of the eighteenth century, the island was in this moment fairly sparsely populated by buccaneers, a handful of wealthy landowners and far more struggling planters, a growing population of enslaved people, some free people of African descent, holdovers from the Spanish rule, a host of poor laborers, some indentured, from England, Ireland and elsewhere, as well as a population of Indigenous Caribbeans, including Arawak and Mosquito people, and Jewish people hailing from a variety of locales. The vibrant center of life on the island was on its edge, in the town of Port Royal, located on a finger that stretches from the mainland, creating a sheltered harbor between the port city and Kingston.[38]

Jamaica's bustling entrepôt was infamous for its entertainment and debauchery. Known at the time as the "wickedest city of the West," Port Royal was a popular stopover for seafarers because of its brothels, taverns, and "music houses." For example, Englishman John Taylor explained in his unpublished memoir that "in the eavenings many young sparks and the common sort resort to musick houses to devert themselves, for the port indeed is verey lose in itself . . ."[39] In London during the same period, the term "music house" referred to a tavern where music was played and also an establishment that hosted public concerts. Music houses became popular in the 1670s in part because of the ongoing effect of the prohibitions on theatrical performances that had taken place during the interregnum, when the British monarchy was briefly replaced with the Commonwealth of England. Theatrical productions involved a great deal of music and after the plays stopped, musicians needed to find work elsewhere. Taverns became informal hosts to performances and eventually, once musicians could be paid to entertain openly again, the music house emerged as a concert venue.[40] Many royalists fled to the colonies during the Commonwealth era and helped to populate colonial settlements in Barbados, Jamaica, and Virginia; surely a good number of professional musicians were among the migrants.[41]

Richard Ligon was one such royalist and avid amateur musician who brought his theorbo (and his strong opinions) with him to Barbados in the 1640s, as discussed in chapter 2. Barbados was the first English colony to develop a successful plantation economy in the Caribbean, and its trajectory held influence over England's eventual expansion into Jamaica. While Ligon wrote extensively about African music, he was less impressed with the music of the planter class. He found their musical fare so wanting that he suggested that the locals try to persuade the performers of the Black-Friars theatre to move to the island and enliven the music scene. Offering the briefest of clues about the circulation of music among colonists, he explained that "they with some supplies may come from *England,* both for Instruments and voyces, to delight that sense, that sometimes when they are tir'd out with their labor, they may have some refreshment by their ears; and to that end, they had a purpose to send for the Musick, that were wont to play at the *Black Fryars*, and to allow them a competent salary."[42]

On the whole, little information has surfaced about the musical practices of colonists in the early British Caribbean, but a notice in the *Jamaica Courant* in 1721 advertised an importation of instruments and music: "Just come from England, and to be sold at the Printers, a choice Collection of the Newest Songs, with Notes, engrav'd on Copper Plates, Also Instruction Books, with Lessons for the Violin, Harpsichord and Flute; New Sets of Minuets, Rigadoons, and Country-Dances; likewise good Violins and Flutes."[43] The wealthy would also have entertained guests at dances at their homes and this, too, would have required musicians, both amateur and professional. Charles Leslie, writing about Spanish Town in 1739, Jamaica's oldest city and seat of the island's government, emphasized the lavish parties of the elite, noting that "Several wealthy Merchants reside there, and most Gentelman of Estates have Houses in it, and live after a very gay manner . . . they have frequent Balls, and lately have got a Play-house. . . ."[44] These balls and the theatre would have employed many musicians. Leslie wrote that while there was little in the way of formal education in the colony at the time, rather, the sons of planters would attend "dancing-schools" and that the young ladies "dance a great deal."[45] These anecdotes suggest that there would have been high demand for musicians to entertain the island's elite in domestic ballrooms and beyond.

Mr. Baptiste may well have been someone who played for high society gatherings that the notoriously bacchanalian governor, the Duke of Albemarle, hosted. Such a performer would have had a foot in multiple worlds. He might have spent an afternoon giving music lessons to a planter's heir then set out in the evening to play for a lively ball. On another night he might have gigged in a music house or caroused among various classes in a tavern. If such a person had been born in the Caribbean, in Cuba, perhaps, he might have had a Spanish Creole father who married a free woman of color. A struggling young family might have sent this young man into the church to be trained as a chorister and learn the trade of music. On the streets of Veracruz or perhaps Jacmel or Santo Domingo, he would have made merry from a young age at Christmas festivals where enslaved people gathered and performed. His ears would have been filled from childhood with multiple languages, and he may have spoken several himself. He could have grown up to travel around the region, perhaps as part of an entourage of a wealthy trader or even as paid entertainment on a ship. He might join up with a successful buccaneer for several months at a time, then disembarked to make money with his violin. While it is impossible to substantiate such a background for this Mr. Baptiste, it is significant that it seems plausible. Such imagining and speculation brings to light multiple possible early Caribbean musical biographies, all of which enrich our understanding of musical life in the period and the role of African-descended performers within it.[46]

Baptiste the Composer?

From Baptiste we have just a few, relatively brief musical gestures rather than fully realized works, but they amount to far more than mechanical transcriptions. He may have set out to accurately portray in notation what he witnessed aurally, but the pieces—intentionally or not—are necessarily very different from the performances that inspired them. The constraints of Western notation, and the conventions of European music mean that the printed works are highly mediated portrayals of performances that exceed the capacities of the page. So much detail is left out that these notations probably only sparsely resemble the performances on which they are based. In my earlier work on Baptiste's transcriptions and other examples of notated transcriptions of African Atlantic performance, I parsed the limitations of musical notation, even going so far as to suggest that transcriptions like Baptiste trapped and distorted enslaved Africans' performances, enacting further racialized violence.[47] I still believe in the validity of this critique, yet, over time, my understanding has shifted toward a spirit of possibility. Particularly, as I collaborated with contemporary musicians in Jamaica and elsewhere on performances of Baptiste's transcriptions, I came to appreciate further what the pieces can make possible in the present in terms of memorializing and revivifying histories of enslaved people and their music.[48] The politics surrounding Baptiste's compositions are complex, both in terms of their historical significance as well as what they signify for audiences today.

The published pieces ultimately reflect multiple acts of creation. First and foremost, there is the music that enslaved Jamaicans performed, and which gave rise to Baptiste's notations. In my home discipline of literary studies, we acknowledge than any act of adaptation across genre or medium is a creative act. This means that a translator of a poem is as much a poet as the original author, and I understand Baptiste's pieces similarly.

Another way to think of Baptiste would be to consider him an arranger of traditional music. Following Stephen Blum's *Grove Music* definition in which he defines "composition" to include any act of music making, whether written, aural, or derived from standardized, pre-existing tradition, both the enslaved performers and Baptiste created original "compositions."[49] I would argue that if these artists made compositions, then they were, by definition, composers, thus making Mr. Baptiste one of, if not the earliest Black American composer to be recognized by name in the historical record.

Considering Mr. Baptiste to be a composer is a bit of a devil's bargain. To do so decenters the artistic agency of the enslaved African performers, while it helps to demonstrate the creative legacy of a free person of color. This tension is at the heart of the challenges inherent in studying the colonial past. Figures like Mr. Baptiste emerge into view mercurially, with sparse biographies, whereas enslaved performers often are unnamed entirely in the historical record. By contrast, Sir Hans Sloane has a marble bust standing in the Enlightenment gallery at the British Museum, where he is flanked by the spoils of empire. The idea of a "composer" is itself freighted with Western Enlightenment notions of creativity and individuality. Because of this, music scholars rightly have been working to put pressure on the centrality of composers, with the larger goal of making evident the fact that artistic production is always fundamentally collaborative. These efforts are making important inroads, but as of yet, canonical composers (largely white and male) continue to dominate Western musical education.[50]

Mr. Baptiste, as an adaptor, arranger, or interpreter of African performance, authored three compositions that because of their publication in a prominent volume have gone on to have an outsized influence on our understanding of early African diasporic music in the Caribbean and broader Atlantic world. For this reason alone, he ought to be considered a published composer in the modern sense. No, he probably would not have used the term, nor would Sloane, but he remains the creator of the written notation. "Composition" is ultimately a Eurocentric way to conceptualize and champion musical production. The performance traditions in which African-born enslaved people participated placed value upon musical knowledge and innovation differently. Nonetheless, it remains important to articulate the historical significance of early Black musicians' artistic contributions for modern audiences.

Mr. Baptiste's music documents the influential role of enslaved performers of various backgrounds who revolutionized Atlantic music in the context of stark inequity and oppression. That is a story that must be woven into the already well-established trajectories of music history. The historiographic methods and formal categories we use to do so must adjust and adapt to new archives and also to values and practices inherent in early modern African and African diasporic performance. While Mr. Baptiste's biography remains largely mysterious, the possibilities raised in trying to uncover his story reveal a rich and multifaceted musical Caribbean in the early modern period. European immigrants, African captives, Indigenous Americans, and traveling mariners were all making music in the region. Their performances extended from rural plantations to seaside taverns, urban festivals, and domestic ballrooms. Professional musicians were among these performers, including free people of color who turned to musical trades for social and economic mobility. The following chapter will continue to examine musical and demographic diversity in the context of Caribbean musical life by looking at how the space of the enslaved musical gathering served as a site of both musical preservation and innovation throughout the eighteenth century.

5 African Traditions and the Evolution of Caribbean Festival Culture in the Eighteenth Century

By the dawn of the eighteenth century, enslaved musical gatherings in America's plantation colonies had become well-established as spaces in which enslaved Africans performed numerous traditions originating from their home continent. As the century wore on, these festivals evolved to include genres and practices that were born in the Americas. In this chapter I show that African national musical traditions continued over a long period of time, but also that these performances coexisted with emergent diasporic practices. My research suggests that it was in the 1770s, roughly, that uniquely Caribbean traditions rose to prominence in public festivals in the region. But even then, African traditions continued to a remarkable degree. In other words, Caribbean musical gatherings were at once the site of African cultural expression among specific national communities as well as key spaces for cross-cultural encounters that gave rise to uniquely American practices and identities.

Given the eventual emergence of Caribbean performance genres that involved a departure from preexisting African, European, and Indigenous American practices, it is easy to assume that the process of "creolization"—as scholars have termed it—was straightforward and swift.[1] The truth is that second and third generation colonial inhabitants—enslaved and free—had different experiences from survivors of the Middle Passage and other émigrés, and in many slave societies, these groups of people lived alongside one another. Records show that captives sought out and purposefully renewed natal traditions in the Americas to every possible extent that they could. In this way they circulated knowledge that they brought with them, built upon it, and shared it. It was their children, and their children's children who created creole traditions by developing multiple fluencies in African, European, and American ways of life.

In American settings plagued by disease and deadly overwork, enslaved populations did not grow because of natural increase—a term used to describe the growth of populations due to childbirth rather than human trafficking. Mortality rates were high for all captives but especially for infants and children. To offset substantial and continual human loss, planters customarily purchased newly trafficked captives to replenish their human labor source.[2] With death and disease so rampant, particularly in sugar-producing regions, African-born people arrived en masse throughout the seventeenth and eighteenth centuries. For these large populations of native-born Africans, being trafficked into slavery did not result in an immediate break with their traditions or identity.[3]

The historical record is clear that whenever possible, enslaved Africans took pains to reunite with those of shared background.[4] In fact, the Sunday and feast day gatherings discussed in chapter 3 made it possible for people who shared a language and similar traditions to spend time together.[5] The length of Sunday and holiday events afforded enslaved laborers the opportunity to assemble from distant plantations and to commune with those who shared their languages and cultural beliefs. As discussed in the previous chapters, Hans Sloane and Mr. Baptiste took pains to record the distinctiveness of African traditions in their collective record of a Jamaican musical festival in the late 1680s.[6]

A century later, colonists continued to document musical practices among the enslaved by distinguishing their instruments and practices according to African national origin. Jamaican planter William Beckford made note of his appreciation for "Caramantee flutes" and a type of mouth bow he described as a "bender" from Whydaw, in a work published in 1790.[7] Another travel memoirist, John Stedman, had observed the same instrument in 1770s Suriname, using the spelling, "benta."[8] The fact that documentarians of the Caribbean were observing and specifying distinct African instruments and practices in disparate spaces underscores the degree to which African identities and practices continued prominently in the ever-evolving space of American slave societies.

Enslaved Africans chose to gather with those of shared nation whenever they could, but the realities of life under slavery meant that there were outside forces restricting these practices. People were intentionally separated from their kin. Planters and officials forbade the use of certain instruments and policed enslaved gatherings. Over time and at uneven rates, these forces contributed to a process of change. I wish to emphasize that these changes were uneven and they were never totalizing, but they did take place. Importantly, I want to stress that the emergence of uniquely Afro-American cultures did not depend on the erasure of African traditional practices; rather, new traditions grew alongside African practices that were kept up continually as survivors of the Middle Passage came to the colonies.

Musical Diversity in John Stedman's Dutch Suriname

Writers like Stedman and Beckford described a complex world where people from many backgrounds lived alongside one another. Memoirist John Stedman, in particular, painted a detailed portrait of plantation society in the 1770s, a time when Africans continued to be trafficked across the Atlantic, but also when Caribbean arts began increasingly to flourish and to circulate as something identifiably unique. For modern readers, Dutch Suriname and British Jamaica may seem distant and unconnected from one another, but at the time, the two colonies were part of a plantation complex that created intimate connections between islands and landmasses as a range of empires jockeyed for power in these colonial spaces. Indeed, research by Kristina Gaddy shows that African Atlantic musical practices documented in Suriname were also practiced in South Carolina in this period.[9] Suriname had briefly been held by the English in the 1660s, after which many planters from the region migrated to Barbados and Jamaica as part of early English settlement of the islands. South Carolina would later be settled by many planters from Barbados.[10]

John Stedman was himself multicultural, the son of a Scottish father and a Franco-Dutch mother, who found himself in Suriname working for the colonial government as a mercenary soldier. He spent his later years in England, where he published an influential memoir, *Narrative of a Five Years Expedition against the Revolted Negroes of Surinam* (1796). Stedman's travelogue was well-timed to coincide with rising public interest in debates about slavery in Britain. His work appealed both to advocates of slavery and to abolitionists, and his book was translated into multiple languages. The narrative featured numerous illustrations, including several well-known images depicting slavery that were engraved by the poet and graphic artist, William Blake.

Stedman's records are especially valuable to researchers because in addition to the published account, his original, un-edited manuscript survives, as well as the journals he kept during his travels, several paintings composed in situ, and a collection of African musical instruments.[11] These various documents and objects allow scholars to examine the process by which travel authors' recollections were edited and transformed for a public readership. As Richard Price and Sally Price discuss in a scholarly edition of the original manuscript, there are significant differences between the two versions. They explain that Stedman was displeased with many of the changes, which came primarily from the pen of a ghost-writer hired by the printer to revise the original draft. The published work sanitizes many of Stedman's descriptions, especially those concerning his portrayal of slavery and sexual encounters. Because of this, I exclusively cite the manuscript descriptions of the narrative in this book.[12]

As I observed through my own examination of the extant manuscript, the eventual publication also changed Stedman's representations of African music. The manuscript, now housed at the James Ford Bell Library at the University of Minnesota, seems to have been prepared by a professional copyist, whose handwriting is distinguishable from Stedman's. Stedman wrote in his own hand to add specific directions about the way musical notation and illustrations should appear in the manuscript. He oversaw the musical materials carefully, including the production of an illustrated chart of instruments that I discuss below, and an excerpt of song that I examine in the following chapter.[13]

Most importantly for the story of African Atlantic music, Stedman's portrayal of the Dutch colony illustrates the coexistence of African national traditions as well as emergent creole practices. The author was uniquely exposed to a very wide range of society during his time in Suriname. He attended balls conducted by free Black people in the colony, visited with the highest echelon of colonial officials, cohabited with an enslaved woman named Joanna, and he fought in battle alongside freed Black rangers while working to suppress Maroons. His descriptions of musical life span these diverse spaces, but the written record he left behind is not without troubles.

Stedman was deeply complicit in the racial hierarchy of colonial Suriname. He worked toward the government's efforts to suppress Maroons, self-emancipated enslaved people and their descendants who established independently sovereign states in remote areas of the colony.[14] He also engaged in exploitative sex with numerous enslaved women, including a long-term partner named Joanna, with whom he had a son, Johnny. Their coupling seems to have been contractual in nature, yet Stedman also portrayed their domestic life as a romantic partnership. The truth may fall somewhere in between. Stedman idealized what he described as their courtship and "marriage," which was not in fact a legal union, but rather a local custom that provided male colonists with sexual and domestic labor. Joanna's experiences and her perceptions of the relationship are impossible to ascertain because of the one-sidedness of Stedman's account. We do know that she was vulnerable to exploitation by Stedman, and fundamentally trapped in the system of slavery that left her with few options for independence and economic mobility.[15] When she had the opportunity to leave Suriname and become Stedman's lawful wife in Europe, she ultimately declined. Eventually, Stedman left Joanna and their child behind when he departed the colony, although he maintained a paternal relationship with Johnny, who came to live with Stedman's new family in Devon, England, after Joanna's death.

Stedman's connections with Joanna, her family, and her community opened doors to the social world of the enslaved and free Black people of Suriname. The journals he kept record many details about their life together that were left out of the published works, including descriptions of evening entertainment. He noted that on one evening "Free negroes have a ball," and on another, "I slip out to see a curious mulatto ball." He wrote that on his son Johnny's first birthday, "I treat the captains' &c., and drink his health. We sing and play, and the negroes dance a banjar." Stedman's statement that Africans in Suriname "dance banjar" or "baniard," are interesting because they seem to refer both to the instrument, the banjo, and a specific dance or genre.[16] Kristina Gaddy has uncovered further that "banyar" is an Afro-Surinamese dance tradition involving instruments, spirituality, and fashion.[17] Stedman also had a fiddle with him that he seems to have played at some gatherings.[18] He was a late-night carouser always looking for a good time, willing to party and dance with whoever was having fun. His journals and the narrative illustrate that many scenes of entertainment included white Europeans, free people of color, and enslaved captives.

Despite his cavorting ways, the ugly truth of slavery bleeds like an open vein throughout Stedman's narrative, even in passages that attempt to make light of the realities of plantation life. He visited one plantation at which an enslaver had recently purchased captives from Loango. The planter, a Mr. De Graav, "gave a Holy day to all the Negroes of his Estate, and there I had the opportunity of seeing the diversions peculiar to the People." He took pains to describe the "*Loango-Dancing,* which was performed by the *Loango*-Negroes, Male and female, and not by any others." About their gatherings he wrote that "these Dances which are to the sound of a Drum, and to which they stricke time by Clapping of hands." He explained that the performances "are more like a play, divided in so many Acts, which lasts hours together."[19] The observations reveal that Loango captives gathered as a group in a plantation setting. Stedman differentiated their performances from others that he witnessed, which I interpret as evidence that African affiliations and performance genres maintained coherence in Caribbean plantation societies where a diversity of peoples lived.

Stedman's portrayal of Loango performances turned to disparaging and racializing characterizations when he described the musical participants' physicality. He wrote that the dancers did not become fatigued but instead became "more Active and Animated, til they are bathed in a lather like Post Horses, and their Passions wound up to such a degree, that Nature being overcome they are ready to drop into Convulsion." By comparing dancers to animals, Stedman dehumanized Loango performers, framing their activity around his expectations and preferences as an outsider, European witness. Indeed, he observed the performance alongside "Europeans and Creole ladies" who found what they saw humorous, apparently taking a "hearty laugh" at the events.[20]

Not only did Stedman's language mediate the events for his eventual readers, but it also seems likely that the presence of observers cast a pall over activities that were not fully reserved for the Loango in this case. This is to say that while some enslaved Africans were able to carry out their customs in the Americas, the scene of slavery and colonialism interfered in ways great and small. Although the community probably took pride and pleasure in participating in a sacred tradition, they were also encircled by mocking witnesses who seem to have been accustomed to the events but nonetheless looked on with belittlement. The tacitly accepting but critical presence of the onlookers was of a piece with larger efforts by white colonists to codify performances through narrative description.

"Grand Balls" and the Emergence of Diasporic Traditions

Over the course of the eighteenth century, struggling island economies evolved into wealthy colonies because of the success of the sugar trade. Alongside, the character of enslaved gatherings changed, as well. While there continued to be events, especially on plantation grounds, that involved survivors of the Middle Passage performing in and among their own national communities (Such as the Loango gathering on Mr. de Graav's plantation discussed above) there were also many public events that combined African genres with new diasporic forms and European genres. Especially around high holidays like Christmas and Mardi Gras, the space of the enslaved musical festival swelled to include colonists and enslavers, free people, and the blend of traditions and languages that came to characterize the Caribbean. Elaborate public festivals combining music, dance, and costuming still thrive today across the region. Bermudans have Gombey, Haitians have Rara bands and Carnivale, New Orleaneans have Mardi Gras and Super Sunday, and Bajans have Crop Over. These are among many African Atlantic festival traditions that all have their own fascinating and unique histories. Here, I intend to emphasize their common roots in the enslaved musical gatherings that became a cultural institution in the plantation Caribbean.[21] In the late eighteenth century, these festivals brought creole styles and expressive genres to center stage.

The festivities were visually resplendent affairs, not simply audible ones, and evolutions in style, taste, and tradition were particularly evident in the realm of material culture. Some forms of costuming in festival gatherings had strong ties to existing African traditions, whereas others were à la mode. Accessories like feathered head adornments, animal tails, material objects of the divine, and masks drew from traditions founded on the African continent.[22] Through entrepreneurial efforts, some enslaved and free people attained a modicum of economic mobility, enabling them to acquire eye-catching textiles and wares. African-descended women, in particular, drove fashion trends on both sides of the Atlantic during this period.[23]

Public celebrations on high feast days presented an ideal opportunity during which to display one's finery. At "grand balls" in Suriname, John Stedman observed that women donned "their best chintz petticoats" and their dance partners wore "fine Holland trowsers."[24] Some revelers coordinated their dress to compliment the dances they enjoyed. Stedman noted that "the Negroes dance Always in Couples, the men Figuring and Footing, While the Women turn Round like a Top, and their Petticoats Expand like a Circle which they Call *Waey Cotto*." These beautiful wide skirts are now known as Koto ("Cotto") and have become a traditional Surinamese clothing proudly celebrated as iconic to the region's heritage.[25] Stedman's description suggests the Koto fashion may have emerged as a complement to the dancing traditions at public balls. He also emphasized the length and high-spiritedness of the celebrations, writing that "so indefatigable are they at this diversion, that I have known the drums continue beating without intermission from Sun Set on Saturday Night, till that Celestial Orb Again made its Appearance on the Monday Morning following, being mostly Accompanied by Cheering, Halloing, and Clapping of Hands." The events stimulated the senses, with the sounds of drumming continuing constantly, and dancers swirling apace.

Suriname was not the only colony in which revelers sported fashionable dress during festival celebrations. A range of pictorial records and narrative accounts document similar practices in many other regions of the plantation Caribbean. Jamaican Set Girls, whose traditions I discuss further in the following chapter, for instance, were troops of performers who combined fashion with dance and musicianship in public displays at Christmas parades, beginning in roughly the 1770s. In 1790s St. Vincent, one writer commenting on Christmas festivities observed that "the negroes (with a very few exceptions) were all dressed in pattern cottons and muslins, and the young girls with petticoat on petticoat; and all had handkerchiefs, put on with fancy and taste, about their heads." So taken with the merriment, the writer, William Young, Jr., felt that "In England, no idea of 'jolly Christmas' can be imagined, in comparison with the three days of Christmas at St. Vincent's. In every place is seen a gaiety of colours and dress, and a corresponding gaiety of mind and spirits; fun and finery are general."

Christmas merriment in St. Vincent clearly blended European, African, and Caribbean forms. Young observed men playing a bala as women danced along in an African style, and he also saw enslaved couples dancing minuets in the English style. He witnessed a "mumbo jumbo" performance involving a masked performer on stilts, that an editorial footnote identifies as a practice particular to the Mande people of West Africa, or as Young writes, "the Mandengoes." Many of the enslaved islanders attended services at the Roman Catholic church on Christmas day, a testament to the widespread influence of Catholicism and Catholic festivals in the region, and on St. Vincent in particular, given that it had formerly been a French colony.[26]

An engraving that portrays a festival scene in St. Vincent further illuminates the presence of European, African, and Caribbean styles in festival merrymakers' dress and comportment. The image does not portray a Christmas gathering specifically, but it is closely associated with the performances that William Young, Jr. observed. The published image was developed from a drawing by Agostino Brunias, the Anglo-Italian artist famous for his portrayals of West Indian life, and a friend to the Young family. The plate notes that the picture was in the possession of the elder Young. William Sr., who had been born in Antigua and was at one point governor of the island of Dominica. After his death, Young, Jr.

Engraving derived from an artwork by Agostino Brunias
entitled "A Negro Festival drawn from Nature in the Island
of St. Vincent." Found in Edwards, *History, Civil and
Commercial,* vol. 2, facing p. 184. (John Carter Brown
Library, D801.E26h)

traveled to the region to inspect the family's many plantations, and
these travels formed the subject of his published memoir. In the image,
white and Black revelers share the stage, with degrees of luxury evident
in participants' dress. A shirtless, dark-skinned man sits to the side, playing a drum. Other details echo what we know about enslaved festivals
at the time. Women perform labor in the scene, with market women selling fruits and vegetables, and other women dance and play tambourine.
The engraving documented the presence of white onlookers at what the
caption names as a "Negro Festival." It also idealizes the racial and class
mixing of the late eighteenth century-Caribbean, sanitizing the oppressive
social hierarchies constraining life for free and enslaved Black people in

the region while reflecting the demographic diversity inherent to Caribbean festivals.[27]

The Young family were prominent advocates for slavery who believed that the institution should be reformed but not abolished. William Jr.'s writing drips with a romantic view of the circumstances of enslaved people's lives, and as Sarah Thomas has argued, the Brunias artwork echoes these same types of mischaracterizations of slavery that grew prominent in response to abolitionist agitation. Mia L. Bagneris adds that while Brunias' depictions of plantation life do serve the interests of planters on one level, they simultaneously engage diverse aspects of Afro-Caribbean life with seriousness and regard. As both scholars make clear, scenes of musical merriment were increasingly co-opted by proslavery advocates who argued that the practice of slavery was not the morally corrupt, violent practice that abolitionists were proving it to be in this period.[28] Reformers pointed to musical festivities as evidence that enslaved people were content, even "happy" with their condition. They acknowledged that some enslavers were cruel and the practice had flaws, but they sought to protect their economic investments in the institution and their way of life.

Musical Gatherings and the Trope of the "Happy" Slave

When discussing scenes of musical merriment in the late eighteenth century, many planter-authors attempted to present themselves as benevolent paternalists in the face of growing abolitionist criticism. From the earliest eras of slavery, writers had questioned the morality of the practice, and many witnesses documented violence and inhumanity, wittingly and not. But in the second half of the eighteenth century, as both enslaved uprisings in the Caribbean and abolitionist activism in Great Britain began to shift public discourse, descriptions of plantation life tended to engage debates about the institution more explicitly. John Stedman took up these issues repeatedly in his narrative, and while he recorded abuse and violence against enslaved people, he ultimately advocated a reformist view like his contemporary, William Young. Reformists argued that slavery was necessary for the economic health of the region but acknowledged that it should be practiced more humanely. Stedman explicitly portrayed enslaved musical gatherings as evidence that some captives were contented with their condition. Indeed, he opened the description of "Grand Balls" by writing, "But to Proceed with My Description of a happy Slave."[29] In so doing he drew upon tropes that would spread like wildfire when blackface minstrelsy boomed decades later in the antebellum United States. Minstrelsy rose to popularity between the 1830s and 1850s, at roughly the same time that the abolitionist movement took flight in the U.S. In other words, discourses surrounding debates about slavery on both sides of the northern Atlantic increased existing appetites for portrayals of plantation music.

White supremacists eventually twisted the remarkable story of African diasporic music under slavery into a racist narrative of passivity and contentment. As Stedman's writing makes plain, stereotypes linking musical performance in enslaved communities to "happiness" were long in the making, with roots running deep in the travelogues that portrayed African Atlantic performance dating back to the dawn of the colonial era. No author better countered this popular misrepresentation than Frederick Douglass, who devoted an early section of his 1845 memoir to dismantling what was, by that time, a long-standing trope. Speaking of his own experiences with music while enslaved, he wrote that "I have often been utterly astonished, since I came to the north, to find persons who could speak of the singing, among slaves, as evidence of their contentment and happiness. It is impossible to conceive of a greater mistake. Slaves sing most when they are most unhappy. The songs of the slaves represent the sorrows of his heart; and he is relieved by them, only as an aching heart is relieved by its tears."[30] More than half a century earlier, John Stedman had witnessed festivals in Suriname as an outsider looking in and painted a scene of mirth and happiness. But the event he described involved far more than musical merriment.

The event he wrote about was a high-fashion affair full of drink and dance, but it was also a place wherein survivors of the Middle Passage became newly enfolded into Caribbean life under slavery. Stedman expressed astonishment at the "Good nature and even with a Degree of Good Manners these Dancing Societys are kept up." To illustrate his perception of enslaved peoples' enthusiasm for the events, he crafted a glib anecdote drawing from the experience of a survivor of the Middle Passage. He wrote that "I have known a Newly imported Negro/for want of a Partner/Figure & Foot for near the Space of 2 Hours to his Shadow Against the Wall." Stedman's characterization, offered with equal parts lightheartedness and derision, reproduced stereotypes about African peoples' love of and aptitude for music and dance discussed in chapter 1. His anecdote highlights the cavern between his perception of the events and what they may have meant to those who participated as insiders or as newcomers to the tradition of the enslaved musical festival.

His observation raises questions, also, about the different experiences of performers well-acclimated to life in the colony and the experience of new arrivals.

What might these balls have meant for survivors of the Middle Passage who found themselves confronting a foreign social order in the late eighteenth-century Caribbean? Stedman observed the strong pull that enslaved people felt toward the festivities, and his illustrations and descriptions document the persistence of Popo, Loango, and Koromanti musical tradition in the colony. But here he portrayed the African-born reveler, new to the island, in isolation. The dancer had just survived the miserable Atlantic crossing, and likely even more terrors on the way to and from the slave holds. To hear and to be drawn into music-making with similarly situated peers must have been a welcome, but possibly also disorienting experience, with or without a partner. Stedman characterized the solitude of African captives crudely, with a literary cliché about a person dancing with their shadow, but the observation caused me to reflect on the experiences of newly arrived African captives who encountered diverse and foreign musical performances from the margins.

When trafficked to the Americas, Africans clung to experiential traditions. The specificities of the musical practices they encountered in the colonies may have been foreign, but they were far less foreign than the enslavers' ways. By taking part in musical gatherings, enslaved people were welcomed into diasporic African community. Whether new to the Americas or creole-born, participants helped to formalize traditions that became recognizably Afro-American. Evening gatherings, Sunday celebrations, and holiday festivals made possible the birth of countless diasporic traditions. In turn, these events became spaces of empowerment and institution-building in the Americas, as the riches of multitudinous and interconnected ways of life took root in a new land.

Charting African Instruments

John Stedman's narrative included a chart of African musical instruments of Suriname. This chart illustrates the fact that distinctive African traditions coexisted alongside musical forms that were recognized as "creole," which meant that they were developed in the Americas. For instance, Stedman distinguished different types of drums as Loango (5, 7), Papa (6), and Creole (4, 8). He also used the term "creole-bania" to refer to what we now know as a banjo, the iconic instrument of early African America.[31]

1. Qua-qua (wooden "sounding-board" struck with pieces of iron or bones)
2. Liemba-toetoe (nasal flute)
3. Ansokko-bania (xylophone similar to the one constructed by Macow in Ligon's narrative)
4. Great creole drum
5. Great Loango drum
6. Papa drum
7. Small Loango drum
8. Small creole drum
9. Coeroema ("wooden cup . . . covered with sheep-skin" beaten with sticks)
10. Loango-bania (sansa, mbira, or similar instrument)
11. Callebash (resonator used to amplify the loango-bania)
12. Saka-saka (gourd rattle filled with pebbles)
13. Conch (not used to accompany dancing, more of an alarm)
14. Benta (mouth bow)
15. Creole-bania (banjo)
16. Trumpet of war (used for military purposes)
17. Horn (used to call slaves to work on the plantation)
18. Loango too-too (type of flute)

In narrative descriptions accompanying the chart, Stedman explained the construction of the instruments, the sounds they made, and how they were used. I summarize this information in a numbered list provided to create a shorthand reference of the names he ascribed to the instruments as well as basic information about their use. As Richard Price and Sally Price discovered, Stedman actually collected these instruments, and a small handful of them survive today in the Museum Volkenkunde in Leiden, the Netherlands.[32]

The chart helps to provide a visual catalogue of objects central to African Atlantic genres. Indeed, the illustration includes numerous instruments that I touch on in *African Musicians in the Atlantic World,* The "trumpet of war" (16) and the horn used to call enslaved workers to fields (17) compares to the instruments that I discuss in African military contexts in chapter 1. In that same chapter, I also discuss resonating gourds like the "Callebash" (11) and the "saka-saka" (12), a gourd rattle filled with pebbles. The conch shell (13) was used to sound alarm, which as I discussed in chapter 3, is known as an emblem of the Haitian Revolution. The "Ansokko-bania" is not unlike the xylophone that Macow constructed in Barbados in the 1640s, a scene central to chapter 2.

The chart records nuanced characteristics of African instruments from slave societies in the late eighteenth century, but like a lot of the records

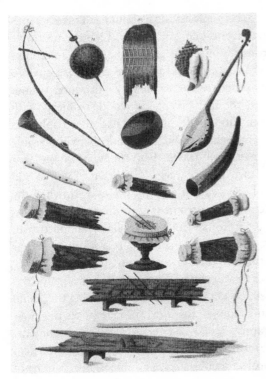

"Musical Instruments of the African Negroes," found in Stedman's *Narrative* (London, 1796), opposite p. 289. (Newberry Library, Chicago, G 987.84)

discussed in this book, the images translated the material objects of African musical production for European consumption, resulting in a distortion of reality. Like travel authors who relied on reader's familiarity with the sounds of Western music to explain African performances, the illustrator made use of viewers' visual associations with European instruments to communicate details about the African instruments. For example, the banjo in the chart has a sharp pin extending from its base, of the sort that would be used to position a cello, or in Stedman's day, a large viol between the legs so that it could be bowed upright. (Banjos are not played upright, they are plucked and strummed while holding them horizontally.) The banjo depicted here features a headstock that is scrolled in the manner of a violin. The surviving instrument object, now housed in a museum in the Netherlands, does have a beautifully curved headstock, but it does not resemble a scroll, nor a violin.[33]

When I first viewed the image, I noticed that the instruments' rough edges have the effect of primitivizing and thus also racializing the objects. Yet, when studying the image further, I also began to understand that the artist's mischaracterizations convey information about each instrument's material construction, playing technique, and sound. Like the narrative descriptions that borrow from readers' musical familiarity to communicate novel sounds, the visual representations in the chart use cues to indicate how the instrument's design relates to the way it produces sound. The artist portrayed many of the instruments as wooden objects with splintery edges. These instruments would not have had sharp splinters jutting out at their bottom because that would have made them impossible to play. The graphic artist may have drawn them this way to render it visually obvious that certain instruments were constructed of wood, and in the case of specific items, hollowed out and bottomless. So, while the chart does not accurately depict the instruments, the illustrator seems to have attempted to render them in some detail. A less elaborate portrayal, for instance, might not have presented so many different kinds of drums in ways that make them distinguishable for European audiences.

The artist appealed further to a European visual vernacular by arranging the instruments in the vein of a botanical chart. By echoing the visual culture of natural history and ecology, the illustration exposes the close ties between early ethnography, racial discourse, and Enlightenment-era science.[34] Stedman's careful catalogue of Afro-Suriname musical instruments and practices project a colonialist and imperialist pattern of extracting knowledge from non-European peoples while also characterizing them as primitive and exotic. Giving themselves the right to name, organize, describe, and to presume to understand African and Indigenous ways of life, authors and collectors like Stedman helped build a Western knowledge tradition that would engage but not empower systems of knowledge production like the one sustaining musical life among the enslaved peoples of the Americas. These various systems of belief and habits of taste remained in tense dialogue in the plantation sphere, where a diversity of peoples battled within a strict racial hierarchy to be free, to make art, to come together, and to individuate. Such struggles spurred change and also resistance to change as enslaved people and their descendants practiced traditional forms of music and invented others. Again, we see that the space of the enslaved musical festival, a tradition established so early in the trajectory of plantation culture, was crucial to the maintenance of African forms and the emergence of diasporic tradition. The following chapter looks closely at surviving excerpts of musical notation documenting this period to offer a richer sense of the character of performances that spanned public festivals, scenes of labor, and more intimate occasions.

6 Songs from the 1770s

A Musical Moment

THIS FINAL chapter presents the opportunity to listen more deeply to some of the music discussed throughout this book. After the publication of Baptiste's transcriptions in Hans Sloane's 1707 volume, nearly eighty years passed before other examples of notated African diasporic vernacular music began to enter the historical record.[1] Suddenly, in the 1770s, a significant handful of notated transcriptions representing enslaved performances emerged. This chapter draws some of these records of musical life into conversation with one another, examining them for what they can teach us about early Black music and Caribbean life under slavery.

Brought into conversation, here, for the first time, I assemble these works as a compilation album or anthology documenting an influential decade of early Caribbean music. Each individual tune presents a window into a world of musical practice that was diversified and expansive. I focus on bringing the musical artifacts into conversation with one another and interpreting each musical text for what it can teach us about the lives of the enslaved and the public discourses they created through performance. The records offer a rare window into lived experiences, moments in time in which individuals assembled into collectives to celebrate, to parade, and even to criticize their condition and the colonial regimes under which they lived.

The transcriptions also allow us to probe the specifics of how music was actually performed at the time. Some of the songs include documentation of instruments used, or they describe where and when performances took place and who their audiences were. Much of the other material examined in this book noted general characteristics of musical events and episodes, but these handful of transcriptions offer deeper insight into the

way performances were conducted and also what they meant to performers and audiences. Lyrical content, in particular, opens up a window into
the popular discourses of the enslaved.

These musical records are also significant because they can be used
by modern ensembles and composers who wish to incorporate histories
of enslaved people into living repertoire. Without these historic works,
it would be difficult to reflect the significance of African Atlantic music
in the eighteenth century in a concert. While there are untold number
of Western European scores surviving to be performed, just a precious
handful survive to document the vast traditions of enslaved musicians of
the period. Here I intend to introduce a sampling of these works to new
audiences, while providing information and context about their specific
settings and meanings.

Each of the songs I have chosen to examine in this chapter is a remarkably unique artifact that illuminates the social world—and life in late
eighteenth-century plantation colonies more generally—in which it was
performed. A song from Barbados begins our musical tour with a discussion of music and labor and the roots of African diasporic work songs.
Then, I turn to a short excerpt of vocal music from John Stedman's narrative of Suriname that reflects tensions between the enslaved, Maroons,
freed people of color, and the colonial government. Stedman's song introduces the subject of "rangers," or enslaved men who were recruited into
colonial armed forces. Rangers are the subject also of a song from the
period in Jamaica. That song is part of a lengthy and diversified collection of tunes gathered under the title "Jamaican Airs." Both the Barbados work song and the Jamaican Airs survive in manuscript and were
never published in their own era. The Jamaican Airs include work song,
popular song, ritual music, and a lengthy portrayal of music composed by
Jamaican Set Girls, groups of women who performed during Christmas
celebrations. The chapter concludes with an examination of the Set Girls'
influential performance practices, which are emblematic of women's rise
to prominence in the musical sphere at the close of the eighteenth century
in the British West Indies. Around this same time period, women were
also assuming prominent roles on theatrical stages in the French colonies.[2]

There are probably many factors that contributed to the contempora-
neity of these 1770s sources. As I discussed in the previous chapter, when
British abolition boomed, so did portrayals of enslaved people's experiences, culture, and music. European appetites for descriptions of plantation life may have contributed to the generation of these sources. The
period may also have marked an evolution in Caribbean arts and culture,

a belief echoed by other scholars working on the era. For instance, in his research uncovering the "Jamaican Airs" transcriptions, Devin Leigh suggests that during the late 1760s and early 1770s, cultural influence among the enslaved shifted from the African-born survivors of the Middle Passage to those born in the Caribbean, and their distinctive ways of life. Leigh cites the example of the Hanover Plot, which was one of the first documented uprisings led by enslaved people who were American rather than African-born to support this notion.[3] Beyond Jamaica, the decades between the 1760s and 1780s were a time of great change in the cultural sphere of colonial Saint-Domingue because of the founding and rapid rise of the theatre. African-descended performers eventually ascended to great acclaim on the stage in Saint-Domingue during this period.[4]

Based on my own research I am inclined to agree that the 1770s were a decade of both change and publicity for Caribbean arts and politics. Hopefully future research can discern further the extent to which this period marked a shift in culture as well as a shift in documentation of culture. Regardless, the significant records that survive from the 1770s present a rare opportunity to assess diverse musical practices in conversation with one another.

Barbados "Work Song"

A manuscript transcription from Barbados explicitly addressed the condition of enslavement, offering rare insight into the perspectives of captive laborers. The music is, to my knowledge, the earliest surviving example of an African diasporic work song in notation, and it invites reflection on the work song genre as a whole, challenging and expanding our understanding the role of music in the context of plantation labor. The song survived in the collected manuscripts of abolitionist Granville Sharp, who transcribed the melody from another abolitionist named William Dickson.[5] Dickson lived in Barbados from 1772 to 1779, serving as secretary to then governor of the island, Edward Hay. After witnessing slavery in the West Indies, Dickson became an outspoken critic of the institution. He wrote two books on the subject, *Letters on Slavery* (1789) and *Mitigation of Slavery, in Two Parts* (1814). The first is both an antislavery political tract and travelogue detailing his years in Barbados, written in epistolary form to a governing official that Dickson hoped to persuade against slavery. In the letters, Dickson described music with some frequency, although the song he later shared with Granville Sharp was never discussed explicitly in the published works.

"An African Song or Chant." A work song sung by enslaved people in Barbados, observed by William Dickson, and written down by Granville Sharp. (Gloucestershire Archives, United Kingdom, D3549/13/3/27)

Dickson's writing about the music he heard in Barbados provides some context for the song he transcribed in England. He was a rare documentarian of early Caribbean music because in comparison to his peers, he seems fairly aware of the limitations of his position as an outsider witness. For instance, he wrote that when he first arrived to Barbados, his curiosity led him to attend enslaved gatherings, "to mix with such nocturnal meetings, both in town and country, when sometimes, I did not know an individual present." He mocked other colonists for being fearful of enslaved gatherings, explaining that the "only mark of even disrespect I ever experienced, was, that, on my going up, the music sometimes, has ceased–a modest hint for an intruder to withdraw."[6] Dickson's awareness of the impact of his presence on musical gatherings underscores the degree to which in many cases Sunday and holiday affairs were a space for the enslaved to gather exclusively amongst themselves.

Dickson also differentiated between what he encountered in urban centers compared to rural plantations, explaining that the festival gatherings in town were more cheerful because of the better living conditions of urban captives in comparison to the enslaved people who labored on plantations. He made the point to address those who would falsely assume, because of the merry celebrations in town, that slavery was a pleasant condition (offering an implicit retort to the "happy slave" trope discussed in the previous chapter).[7] Even in late eighteenth-century Barbados, rural gatherings continued to be a predominantly African space, although in urban environs gatherings grew to include a more diverse array of participants of enslaved, free, African, European, and Creole of all backgrounds.

The abolitionist Sharp would have been very interested in what Dickson presented—a seemingly authentic tune documenting the experience of slavery, from the perspective of enslaved people, while at labor. We do not know much about the context in which the music was passed from enslaved performers to Dickson and later to Sharp. Presumably Dickson overheard the music and chose to commit it to memory and document it in his own papers. Dickson probably sang the music to Sharp, who then composed the notation. In the headnote to the music Sharp explains that the "African song or chant" was "taken down in notes by G. S. from the information of" Dickson. It remains unclear when the two met to discuss the song, but given what we know about the biographies of the figures, their encounter probably occurred between the years 1785, when Dickson returned from Barbados, and 1814, when Granville Sharp died.[8]

These years coincide with an era when concerns about slavery rose to a fever pitch in Great Britain. Formerly enslaved writers and lecturers were giving accounts of their experiences in greater numbers, actively cultivating the slave narrative genre. For instance, Olaudah Equiano's influential autobiography was first published in 1789.[9] The Barbados song echoed what many British abolitionists were preaching widely, that slavery was an inherently violent practice, and that those who participated in it were morally bankrupt. The song effectively illustrated the cold calculus of the system, which evaluated the worth of enslaved people's lives in financial terms. Abolitionists in Britain published their own songs about the experience of slavery during the era—sentimental ballads that often portrayed mourning mothers and victims of violence.[10] Given the features of the song and the broader abolitionist appetite for stories and music about slavery, it is somewhat surprising that the music was never published in print.

> Massa buy me he won't killa me Oh
> Massa buy me he won't kill a me Oh
> Massa buy me he won't kill a me Oh
> 'For he kill me he ship me regulaw
> 'For I live with a bad man oh-la
> 'For I live with a bad man Obudda-bo
> 'For I would go to the Riverside Regulaw

The song's lyrics are worth examining in detail because they portray rhetorical perspectives of enslaved laborers. In what follows I attempt to interpret the possible meanings of the song's two verses, while making note of unresolved ambiguities. The tune was led by a solo voice, who performed the verses. A chorus of co-laborers would respond in refrain, using a vowel sound transcribed as "a" and explained as "like the French *ai* or English a." In the first verse, the vocal narrator explains that "Massa buy me he won't killa me," which I would paraphrase as "because my master bought me, he won't kill me." The suggestion is that no master would destroy their costly "property." Barbadian musician, Roger Gibbs, has recorded the song and published it on YouTube and nominated it for a UNESCO documentary heritage award.[11] When we discussed the lyrics, he explained that in his interpretation "Massa buy me he won't killa me" is a kind of boasting, in which the singer signals their worth—yes, through the economy of slavery—but with a threatening overtone. The singer essentially cautions their enslaver that if they treat them badly, causing them to die, then they would lose profit. Gibbs, a seasoned Calypsonian, points out that many Barbadian and Eastern Caribbean folk songs rely on innuendo to veil political critique and sexual themes. Songs in the tradition often feature humorous or biting messages that operate beneath the surface of lyrics that otherwise read as fairly innocent or compliant with social norms.

The work song participates in a broad Black Atlantic lyrical tradition of conveying multiple meanings at once. Some of these meanings remain covert, like the full significance of the first verse's concluding line, "'for he kill me he ship me regulaw." The manuscript includes annotations that attempt to clarify some of the localized language in the song. Some of these explanations are helpful, like the gloss on the word written as "for" as meaning "Before he would kill me, he would. . . ." On the other hand, Sharp incorrectly assumed that some of the regional inflections of the words had Hebrew roots, as John Rickford and Jerome Handler have explained.[12] The meaning of "ship me regulaw" is unclear, but it may mean that the master would either sell or hire out the enslaved singer before killing them.[13] The subtleties remain vague, but the second line reiterates, to some degree, the message from the opening that cautions or boasts that the enslaver will not kill the person that they have purchased.

A second verse revisits the subject, taking matters further into the hands of the enslaved singer. The vocalist asserts that "'For I live with a bad man oh-la . . ." meaning that "before I would live with a bad man, I would go to the Riverside Regulaw." The implication may be that before the singer would consent to live with someone who treated them badly, they would go to the "riverside regulaw." The mysterious word "regulaw," repeated twice in the song, shades the possible meaning here.

Does the singer mean that they will steal away? Or, is the implication, that by going to the riverside, he or she will cross over into death?[14] Crossing bodies of water symbolizes death in many African diasporic traditions, a subject I will return to below. Barbados has no major rivers, so the song's meaning may be entirely symbolic, or it may have originated from a different region. Enslaved people were often trafficked across multiple colonies during their lifespans, which contributed to the circulation of songs and practices.

The subject of suicide and death course through the song, no matter how the lyrics might be interpreted. Living with a "bad man" would impose the threat of mortality, and also the narrator-as-singer implicitly threatened those who would dare to treat them wrong. The singer's over-arching message that "if you treat me wrong, you will suffer because you lose me," was no emancipatory anthem, but the lyrics nonetheless worked within the logic of slavery to proclaim and to affirm the value of the lives of the enslaved. Saidiya Harman has written influentially about the challenges inherent to interpreting records of enslaved people's lives for acts of resistance. Writing specifically about enslaved peoples' decision to engage in dance and musical performances that were prohibited on nineteenth-century U.S. plantations, she argues that it can be difficult to "make any claims about the politics of performance [under slavery] without risking the absurd" when considering performances that were conducted "in the face of the everyday workings of fear, subjugation, and violence."[15] The Barbados work song emblematizes the tensions inherent in performing political possibility under the constraint of enslavement. And yet, the lyrics presented a rebuke to violent enslavers that remains veiled under a seemingly compliant narrative in the song.

The performance context further emboldened the meaning of the Barbados work song's lyrics. To vocally criticize enslavers' violence while ostensibly submitting to the task of forced labor replicated the practice of veiling politicized messaging in embodied compliance. The song expressed an unwillingness to tolerate abuse, a fact underscored when a chorus of co-laborers would reply with a resounding collective voice. The melody of the chorus beautifully complements the verses, but not in echo. The chorus follows the established musical architecture of the song but in a way that resonates with the name "chant" that is inscribed in the manuscript. To chant is to voice in unison, in solidarity and collective will. This song was clearly that. By singing the song, enslaved laborers would remind their perpetrators of their worth. We do not know whether or not the song, when performed, was rendered with humor or gravitas, but the lyrics and performance context do their own work of criticizing slavery from the voices of enslaved people in the documentary record.

Work songs took place in an oppressive sphere shaped by physical fatigue and repetitive motion as well as the critical presence of enslavers and overseers. Because of this, performers' choice of tempo, volume, and subject matter amounted to far more than musical preferences. These gradations were at times acts of resistance, aggression, and also potentially a way to envelop co-laborers in a private space of collective expression. While overseers may have been watching and listening, singing created a cocoon of sound and belonging that distracted laborers from the work and the watching. There were probably other times when overseers were not present and the singing may have signaled activity from a distance, allowing laborers to sound like they were working while at rest. By considering the complex social environments in which songs were performed we can begin to have a richer understanding of the meanings generated by and reflected in performance practice.

Here, authors of slave narratives can offer further insight into the social collectivity formed among the enslaved while at work. Solomon Northup, who was enslaved in the antebellum United States after having been born free in New York, wrote about the ways that he and his peers in the fields would collaborate on strategies to ease their toil. Together, they orchestrated the appearance that they were doing what they were asked to do while instead working to preserve their strength and well-being. Northup was tasked with the role of "driver" on cotton and sugar plantations. This meant that he had to carry a whip and use it on his friends and community in the fields if they were not working fast enough to meet the wishes of the white overseer. He described learning to wield the whip with "marvelous dexterity" to make it seem as though he was striking his friends, who would "squirm and screech as if in agony, although not one of them had in fact been even grazed." Later, Northup's friends would complain loudly, within earshot of their enslaver that Northup had been treating them very badly. In this way they collaborated to appease their enslavers while creating their own space in the fields, to the extent that they could.[16]

Work songs like the one from Barbados also may have helped enslaved laborers create the impression that they were hard at work. The song's message, when framed by the performance of labor, worked within the constraints of the plantation as a site of productivity, to assert the will of the enslaved. One enslaver who wrote about work songs in colonial Louisiana in the 1770s fretted over the degree to which the music-making impeded laboring. He wrote that when he happened upon enslaved laborers singing while working he would say to them, "Courage, my boys, I love to see you merry at your work; but do not sing so loud, that you may not fatigue yourselves, and at night you shall have a cup of Tafia (or rum) to give you strength and spirits."[17] Some enslavers wanted their workers to make music that would bolster their productivity, but also feared that if they enjoyed the music too much, or took up too slow a tempo, that it would hamper the exploitative agenda.[18]

Work songs loom large in the historical imagination of slavery in the antebellum U.S. South, but they were less central to the characterization of Caribbean slavery in the seventeenth and eighteenth centuries. That doesn't mean that work songs were not part of the musical landscape of the region at that time, but colonists and enslavers who chose to write about music in the Caribbean rarely, if ever, commented on the practice. Noting the relative absence of descriptions of work songs prior to 1800, Dena Epstein points out that while the documentary record of first-generation enslaved Africans performing work songs under slavery in the Americas is slim, the genre has long been assumed to have African origins. She compares this to the mid-twentieth-century debates among musicologists about the origins of jazz and gospel music. Scholars of Black music had to "prove" the African influence upon these genres in the face of perceived European musical dominance. Work songs, perhaps because of their association with commoners and labor, were not treated with the same scrutiny, even though many musical cultures of Europe have work songs of their own, such as the waulking songs of Scotland, in which women sing while preparing traditional fabrics. All of this is to say that the genre of "work song" has a history of its own, one shaded by the politics of labor and the labor of Black peoples especially.[19]

When work songs *were* documented in the eighteenth-century Caribbean, they tended to concern the practice of singing while rowing boats. John Stedman repeatedly commented upon the music of enslaved laborers who rowed barges and tent boats that passed up and down the Commewijne River in Suriname.[20] Scholar Ana Maria Ochoa has also written about the importance of boat rowers' music and sound in colonial Colombia. These rowers, known as *bogas,* were free men of mixed African, Indigenous, and European ancestry whose labor fueled commerce and communication along vast river networks in the region. The songs of boat rowers have faded in the historical memory of music and slavery, but these types of performances had great influence because of the significance of riverine travel, which connected the maritime Atlantic to the innermost territories of the Americas. The impact of rowing music compares in some respect to the role of railroad workers' in shaping many popular U.S. genres in the early twentieth century. Railroad camps generated the spread of many iconic American genres rooted in the Black experience, from boogie woogie, blues, ragtime, to country. Similarly, boat rowers, their sound, and role as information conduits along vital trade networks influenced the development of Caribbean and Latin American music. The rowers' song was an important part of the soundscape that could be heard by many different kinds of people as the vessels passed from place to place and from river port to ocean front.

Work songs of railroad laborers and prison "chain gangs" in the twentieth century helped generate the impression that the genre was dominated by adult men, but records in the eighteenth century highlight the singing of women and children while at labor. The Barbados manuscript does not specify the laborers' identities, which leads me to conclude that the singers probably were of mixed genders.[21] One of the few references to work songs in Africa that I have encountered from the period portrays a group of women in Segou, Mali, who sang while spinning cotton. Traveler Mungo Park was taken in by a friendly woman who took pity on his poor condition. In his 1799 travel narrative he explained that while he slept in a corner of the room, the woman and her female family members stayed up late into the night spinning cotton.[22] The women composed the lyrics on the spot, improvising references to Park's presence among them. He explained that "They lightened their labour by songs, one of which was composed extempore; for I was myself the subject of it. It was sung by one of the young women, the rest joining in a sort of chorus. The air was sweet and plaintive."[23]

The music of the women from Segou raises questions about African traditions that may have influenced performances of work songs on plantations. Perhaps work songs were more prominent in the period in the context of domestic labors that took place in the home and among families rather than in more public spaces on farms.[24] Music accompanies childcare in many cultures. Lullabies are a well-known example and while they are often cast in a sentimental mode, they are above all, a work song that accompanies women's labor in breastfeeding and caring for infants and toddlers.[25]

In the Caribbean, both women and children sang work songs while processing sugar. In a narrative published in 1790, William Beckford, son of a wealthy family of enslavers in Jamaica noted that women would sing at night while grinding raw sugar cane at the mill. This was dangerous, time-sensitive work and the songs were probably important for keeping the women alert while fatigued during a long night's effort. Beckford claims that the practice of singing work songs in which one voice leads and a chorus follows (like the Barbados song in question) was generally only practiced by women.[26] Dena Epstein argues that Beckford's observation was not echoed in other sources from the period, however I note than in my own reading there seems to be some truth to the impression that work songs were especially common in the context of women's labor. Also, because women led agricultural work in parts of Africa and were also prominent as field laborers on American plantations, it may be that the practice was uniquely shaped by women, whose influence was slowly erased over the centuries as male laborers became the face of the genre in the nineteenth and twentieth centuries, especially in the United States.[27]

Children also sang work songs in connection to sugar labor. For instance, in the 1828 novel, *Marly; or, A Planter's Life in Jamaica*, which was written anonymously by a planter from the island, enslaved children are portrayed as singing songs to stir mules tasked with turning the sugar mill. This episode sheds light on the dangers children faced as they were forced to work around dangerous machinery with large animals. Their work songs may have helped occupy the children while also serving to keep the mules alert and active.[28] Records from the Newton plantation in Barbados provide insight into children's roles on sugar plantations, documenting that at Newton in the late eighteenth century, young people were broken up into distinct "gangs" according to age and ability, beginning from around four years of age. The term "gang," which was also used in the manuscript music in question, had a long history as a term used in Barbadian plantation management.[29]

Most descriptions of work songs point out that a single voice or small group of voices would lead, followed by a chorus involving a larger group. This call-and-response pattern made it easy to sing the music repetitively while also performing other tasks. There was a utility in work songs, in that they helped people perform at a pace and in unison, when necessary, like for the boat rowers of Suriname and Colombia, but the work songs also lessened the burden of the work by bringing a measure of pleasure and entertainment to difficult tasks. In a 1745 narrative about Nevis, author William Smith explained specifically how the pattern was deployed in sugar fields, a likely scenario for the Barbados manuscript source. He did not clarify whether the entire group of workers was composed of men, but he did note that men with deep voices sang the verses together.

He wrote that "The Negroes, when at work, in howing Canes, or digging round Holes to plant them in, (perhaps forty persons in a row) sing very merrily, i.e. two or three Men with large Voices, and a sort of Base Tone, sing three or four short lines, and then all the rest join at once, in a sort of Chorus, which I have often heard, and seemed to be, *La, Alla, La, La,* well enough, and indeed harmoniously turned, especially when I was at a little distance from them."[30] The call-and-response pattern deployed in work songs compare to the formal characteristics of other iconic genres of African diasporic expression such as sermons and spirituals.

Indeed, the Barbados song shares with spirituals many features: structure, tone, and even themes. In spirituals, themes of rivers and bodies of water (which often signify crossing into death and baptisms), are threaded through mournful tunes in minor tones traditionally performed with melodic intensity and longing. Afro-American spirituals emanating from the nineteenth century are vast and diverse. It would be reductive to say that all of them were sorrowful and sung in minor tonalities, but a great many were. W. E. B. Du Bois famously theorized the U.S. Afro-American spirituals, calling them "sorrow songs" in *Souls of Black Folk* (1903). He was a graduate of Fisk University, whose Jubilee Singers have been at the vanguard of preserving the historic repertoire of Christian hymns inflected with enslaved experiences.

The spirituals were not typically work songs, and yet they bear some similarity with the Barbados piece, particularly if sung slowly. My interpretation of the music has been influenced by Roger Gibbs's performance, in which he leans into the sorrowful possibilities in an evocative manner. As a modern Barbadian musician specializing in Calypso, Gibbs's interpretation reflects many traditions, probably including spirituals and work songs from the U.S., many of which are performed and recorded with frequency.[31] Another recording of the song, from a CD released by Colonial Williamsburg, draws from the sound of "chain gangs" by incorporating the rhythmic percussion of work tools.[32] The performance is at a faster tempo than Gibbs rendition, and the song features a group of male voices. We should also consider how the presence of women's and possibly children's voices might have shaped the song's execution and meaning. Without knowing the specific tasks that accompanied the music, estimating an appropriate tempo is difficult, yet the available recordings offer an opportunity to consider divergent possibilities for what the music may have sounded like in its era. These renditions also invite modern audiences to reflect on historical performers experiences and political sentiments about slavery. The Barbados work song is but a single musical text, and yet examining it raises myriad questions about the role of music in the context of plantation labor. The song also asks us to reconsider the historical arc of the work song genre in a broader African Atlantic context that brings African and African-descended women and children to the fore.

A Musical "Specimen" from Suriname

John Stedman, who was prolific in his attention to the various musical practices of Suriname's enslaved and free inhabitants, also composed an excerpt of notation that he described as a "specimen" of African vocal music. His phrasing recalls natural historical collecting of the sort that Hans Sloane practiced in Jamaica a century earlier. As with Sloane, Stedman's use of scientific discourse to address matters of African diasporic culture dovetailed with the mores of Enlightenment-era racism. Stedman's efforts to systematically catalog African instruments and to provide a "specimen" of song invokes the argument that cultural and what we now understand as racial difference is determined by biology rather than humanity.[33] Stedman's use of the term "specimen" speaks volumes about a larger effort by white Europeans to confer scientific knowledge via arts criticism. He introduced the music by explaining that their "Vocal Musick is like that of some birds, melodious but without Time," explicitly comparing African performances to sound-making in the animal kingdom. In fact, Stedman's narrative included just one other excerpt of notation, and it portrayed birdsong.

The musical transcription comes before a lengthy discussion of literary works by Phillis Wheatley Peters and Ignatius Sancho. Stedman wrote favorably about their accomplishments, but the section as a whole, titled "General Description of the African Negroes," racialized and objectified Africans in cultural and physical descriptions that toggle between complementary and degrading. As with many of the sources consulted in this book, white authors' practice of sitting in judgment over Africans' artistic abilities helped to fabricate ideals of whiteness and Western academic superiority, even when authors used these modes of description ostensibly to defend Africans from criticism. On the whole, I find Stedman's musical excerpt to be less revelatory than others discussed in this chapter because he so clearly produced *his* version of what he deemed to be the African music of Suriname. I believe his "specimen" to be a composition that he created to mimic or exemplify some of the musical characteristics he witnessed, rather than a transcription of a song that he heard.

Because Stedman's unpublished 1790 manuscript survives alongside the much-revised 1796 two-volume publication, we have essentially two different, but related documents to analyze, and both are historically significant in their own respects. As I discussed in the previous chapter, I rely primarily on Stedman's unpublished manuscript, because it presents a more unvarnished representation of his recollections, but the revised manuscript also helps us to understand the expectations and interests of publishers and audiences.[34] There were changes, too, to the musical transcription and its framing in the published volume. The visible differences in handwriting between the copyist and Stedman allow us to see that Stedman inserted the musical notation and the lyrics into the original manuscript himself, carefully overseeing the musical aspects of the narrative.[35]

But although Stedman oversaw the inclusion of the musical material, the published version makes significant changes to the presentation of the transcription. In the manuscript, Stedman compared the vocal music to "birdsong" and described a call-and-response musical pattern that is characteristic of many African diasporic genres, including work songs like the Barbados example. He wrote that the music "is not unlike that of some Clarks reading to the Congregation, One Person Pronouncing a Sentence Extempory, which he next hums or Whistles, when all the others Repeat the Same in Chorus, another sentence is then Spoke and the chorus is Renew'd a Second time & So ad perpetuum. As a Specimen of it I will try to Put the following Note[s] to Musick Supposing a Soldier going to battle taking leave of his Mistress."[36] The published version of the narrative presents a slightly altered version of the same information,

Musical notation from Stedman's *Narrative* (London, 1796), p. 259. (Newberry Library, Chicago, G 987.84)

adding that the vocal music Stedman described was "much practiced by the barge rowers or boat negroes on the water, especially during the night in a clear moonshine; it is to them peculiarly animating, and may, together with the sound of their oars, be heard at a considerable distance."[37] Some might read the new passage to indicate that the transcribed song was itself sung by boat rowers, but I believe instead that the song is a generalized composite of characteristics that Stedman associated with the vocal music of the enslaved population in Suriname, and boat rowers in particular. He distinguished vocal music from instrumental performances and dance, and discussed them separately. This suggests that singing may not have been a prominent feature of festival and dance music involving instruments.

Stedman's explanation that the song "supposes" a soldier going to battle causes me to wonder *who* might have sung this song in Suriname. A soldier? Someone singing in the voice of a soldier? If this is a song of enslaved boat rowers, why would they be singing a love song about a soldier leaving for battle? Stedman's days in Suriname were filled with concerns about battle, and indeed he traveled on tentboats to and from military fronts. Tentboats were sometimes rowed by sailors although they were more commonly rowed by enslaved laborers.[38] Stedman probably composed a melody meant to generally reflect tunes (and perhaps even a specific song) that he remembered from his years in Suriname. He may have authored lyrics reflective of the themes that he experienced and observed in the colony at the time.

The revised version of the musical excerpt in Stedman's published narrative adjusts details from the manuscript and adds new ones. He specified that the song imagines the perspective of a "ranger" rather than simply a soldier. Rangers were enslaved men who had been recruited by the colonial military to join their fight. In exchange for their service, they were promised emancipation and a small garden plot. Because European

Musical notation from John Gabriel Stedman's 1790 manuscript, p. 662. (James Ford Bell Library, University of Minnesota, 1790fSte)

troops were so poorly skilled in the warfare tactics practiced expertly by Maroon troops, the Dutch government was in need of more experienced soldiers. The recruits were offered a crude choice: gain your freedom and run the risk of dying in battle, or from disease or starvation in the jungle, or remain enslaved.[39] Stedman's song portrays the perspective of a ranger who must say goodbye to his lover, "Amimba," before departing for war. Stedman fought alongside rangers in battle, and he was acquainted with a wide-variety of African-descended people in Suriname, enslaved and free.

The melody calls to mind the sort of love song that might be performed in honeyed tones from a balcony in a stage musical. Situated right in the center of a typical vocal range of either a man or woman, the notes feel warm to sing and they sound somewhat sad and longing because of the minor tonality. The notation is easy to follow and the song is straight-forward and pleasant to sing. Curved lines indicate how to elide specific groups of notes and fermatas at the end of the phrases advise performers to hold the ending notes longer than the given values—an explicit license to interpret the music liberally. These details add to the song's playability. The original manuscript presents the lyrics only in Sranan Tongo, the creole language of Suriname, but in the published version, the words are translated for English readers. Stedman considered himself accomplished in Sranan Tongo, but Richard Price and Sally Price note that some of his translations "tend to be at once over-literal (relying too heavily on cognates) and subjectively embellished."[40] The translations further indicate that the song was editorialized to be more easily performed by English readers.

The song participates in European musical tropes, but it also enacts some of the characteristics of African diasporic music in Suriname that Stedman and other observers documented. The call-and-response pattern of vocal improvisation that Stedman described appears in the song's structure: the second half of the tune is essentially a re-working and elaboration of the first half. Also, the triplets at "Me lobby fo fighty me mano," attempt to capture intricate rhythms he described as "melodious but without time." Stedman was schooled in a musical tradition that placed value on formalizing and regulating rhythmic patterns, whereas many vernacular traditions privilege the varied motifs of spoken language, especially in singing.

The rhythmic pattern Stedman penned in the manuscript became notably simplified in the published 1796 version. The manuscript presents three triplets per phrase, whereas the edited print edition includes only two. The publisher might have wanted the rhythm to sound "exotic" but familiar enough that it could be executed in English drawing rooms with relative ease, or perhaps Stedman decided to revise the composition after producing the manuscript. In either case, Stedman's "specimen" of vocal music documents European publishers and audiences growing appetites for music purporting to record plantation melodies.

The "Jamaican Airs"

The "Jamaican Airs" epitomize the growing trend of recording enslaved people's performances in Western notation. The transcriptions were written by an anonymous author—an enslaver living in Jamaica—who, like Hans Sloane a century prior, sought to portray musical variety. If Stedman composed one very particular sort of tune, the "Jamaican Airs" attempted to portray a breadth of genres and performance contexts. This manuscript collection includes eleven different pieces of music that range from popular dance tunes to sacred rites. Scholar Devin Leigh brought "Jamaican Airs" to light after chancing upon them when researching the manuscripts of Jamaican planter Edward Long. Intrigued by the music, Leigh went on to uncover the complicated history of how the music came to be tucked away in the manuscript archive of the influential Caribbean documentarian. Leigh has made the entirety of the "Jamaican Airs" manuscript material available online, in a curated exhibit on the *Early Caribbean Digital Archive*.[41]

A devout racist and pro-slavery advocate, Edward Long came from a wealthy family who had deep roots in the Jamaican plantocracy. His lengthy *History of Jamaica,* like Sloane's tome from the prior century, loomed large in the literary discourse on slavery and West Indian politics.[42] Still today, Long's book is widely read by scholars, and his records have an outsized influence on our understanding of the period, particularly from the point of view of British colonial elites. The anonymous author of the transcriptions must have been an associate of Long, who planned to incorporate the sheet music in a revised edition of *History of Jamaica.* The planned volume was never published, and as a result, the compositions languished in Long's manuscripts, which now reside in the British Library.

The "Jamaican Airs," which were probably written between 1770–76, comprise several musical scores as well as narrative descriptions. Devin Leigh learned that these descriptions were published in a Kingston periodical, the *Columbian Magazine,* in 1797.[43] However, the magazine only included the author's written portrayals, probably because it would

A page from the Jamaican Airs. "Ranger Song," discussed below, is identified as "Air IV" at the bottom of the page. (British Library Board, C. E. Long papers add. MS 12405 f338v)

have been impractical to print the notations. In light of these details, the anonymous author likely sent the manuscript to Long with hopes that the notations could be included in the planned revision of his magnum opus on Jamaica.

The anonymous author organized the "Jamaican Airs" into three parts. The first, "Tunes in General Use," includes an assortment of popular music in Jamaica at the time. These tunes range from country dances that would be played on fiddles to humorous songs on the subject of plantation life, such as "Guinea Corn," which tracks the stages of farming, from hoeing and planting to harvesting and eating crops.[44] Another untitled song tells the story of a local woman who suffered from alcoholism. The second section, "Airs Used by Distinct Sets," documents the original compositions of women's performance troops who paraded during Christmas festivals. These so-called Set Girls crafted a unique, and much commented on tradition that combined fashion, dance, and vocal and instrumental music. These musical transcriptions offer a rare window into women's roles as composers and musical innovators. Most earlier records of musical life from slave societies portray women as participants rather than performers of public vernacular music, but the 1770s seem to have been a turning point when women performers took center stage more prominently and in a greater variety of roles.

The Jamaican Airs' final section, "African Music," features two tunes attempting to portray Myal performances—an African diasporic religion discussed in chapter 3 that involved ceremonious rites combining herbal medicine, dance, and song. I believe these final "African" songs were not composed by the anonymous author. They were not mentioned in the original *Columbian Magazine* publication, and in the manuscripts, the final two African pieces are written in an entirely different hand, one that resembles Long's other writing. Long is the earliest documentarian of Myalism in the written record, so it makes some sense that he may have been the author-transcriber, or at least collector of the two final pieces.[45] Perhaps he wished to round out the anonymous author's collection of popular music with tunes that he perceived to be more closely tied to traditional African practices.

For the purposes of this chapter, I have chosen to focus specifically on the Set Girls' numbers and the "Ranger Song"—one of the popular numbers from "Tunes in General Use"—because they complement the other transcriptions I assemble here. The Myal music, and indeed all of the Jamaican Airs, deserves careful study.[46] Given the fact that Edward Long degraded African spiritual and musical practices to an abhorrent degree, his records of Myal musical practice should be analyzed cautiously, and ideally with the guidance of practitioners and experts of Afro-Jamaican religion.[47]

As a whole, the "Jamaican Airs" provide a sense of the lively and diverse musical landscape in late eighteenth-century Jamaica. They document the continuity of African traditions on the island, as musicians and celebrants continued to gather in evenings and on feast days in keeping with the practices instituted by enslaved communities in the seventeenth century. In the "African Music" section, the author (who here may be Long) notes the combination of song and dance on occasions when "Negroes of each tribe or nation assemble in distinct groups with their several instruments." Reflecting the coexistence of distinctly African and Afro-American traditions, the Jamaican Airs also document performance practices that were unique to enslaved communities in the Caribbean, including Jonkanu and Set Girl troops. Both of these traditions are well-known to researchers, but the recently uncovered Jamaican Airs notation record their prominence earlier than historians have generally dated these practices.

The Jamaican Airs also provide further evidence that uniquely Caribbean musical forms and genres were traveling around the region.[48] The anonymous author believed, for instance, that the "Calemba" came from "Curracoa" (probably Curaçao).[49] We now know that eventually Jonkanu circulated beyond Jamaica and took root in the Bahamas, and among the Garifuna in Belize and Central America (the Black Amerindian Garifuna were expelled from their homeland in St. Vincent in 1797).[50] At the same time, African traditions also continued to be practiced widely in these regions. The Jamaican Airs therefore portray practices that echo the diversity of the musical life that John Stedman documented during the same period in Suriname. These details are important because they help bring clarity to how and when Caribbean and broader African diasporic traditions began to cohere in American slave societies.

Ranger Song

Like Stedman's transcription, the Jamaican Airs includes a tune associated with rangers. In this case, however, the song mocked rangers from the perspective of enslaved people subject to their oversight. Rangers in Stedman's Suriname were generally enslaved people who were offered their freedom in exchange for their labor as soldiers in the fight against Maroons. But in Jamaica, rangers were themselves Maroons, who had been contracted by the government to assist in the capture of runaways.[51]

The Maroons of Jamaica had lobbied to preserve their independence by various means, ultimately entering treaties that protected their interests in exchange for assistance in tracking and returning people who fled plantations. The idea was to discourage the enslaved population from joining Maroon communities in the island's dense mountainous regions. This resulted in tensions and between Maroons and enslaved communities. The anonymous author of the Jamaican Airs wrote that both white colonists and the enslaved reviled the Maroon rangers.[52]

The fact that two songs about rangers survive in the very limited written record raises the possibility that the subject may have been something of a common theme for popular songs across parts of the greater Caribbean. Perhaps the individual examples were part of a discourse that sprung up in response to colonial authorities' attempts to coerce African descendants into service on behalf of white enslavers. Rangers were traitors of sorts, caught in a web of conflicting loyalties emblematic of the lose-lose situation many people faced in if they chose to seek independence by self-emancipation. For many people living in slave societies, ostensible "freedom," achieved through escape or other means, often resulted in the loss of community, kin, and safety. For instance, all of the self-emancipated slaves who lived to tell their tales in slave narratives of the nineteenth century had to sacrifice loved ones in order to claim freedom. Mary Prince, born in Bermuda, and author of an 1830 memoir, endured this fate. She was able to claim freedom after traveling under captivity to England but never again saw her family in the West Indies because of her choice.[53] The history of Maroon societies in Jamaica, Suriname, and elsewhere offer a counter-vision of enslaved community, independence, and resistance. The Ranger Song, however, preserves the painful reality that freedom for some tightened the chains of others. Yet the bitter truth is met with sardonic wit and biting criticism from enslaved collectives who sung the song as a "jeu d'espirit," according to the anonymous author of the "Jamaican Airs."

The transcription of the Ranger notation offers little more than a melody and simple guitar accompaniment, but the description anchoring it reveals the social significance of the song, and how it was performed in group settings. The transcriber did not include lyrics, explaining, "The words to this tune, were very few, hinting at their employment and sung as a 'jeu d'esprit,' especially when a ranger happened to be within hearing." A "jeu d'esprit" is a witty social commentary, here performed specifically to roast rangers when they dared to patrol near a gathering of enslaved workers.[54] The Jamaican Airs' author was impressed by the

verbal takedowns he witnessed, writing that they far exceeded British tal-
ents for lampoon and that Jamaican lyrical performances could "seldome
convey more poignant expressions of contempt." As with the Barbados
work song, "Ranger Song" unabashedly presented social criticism in the
disguise of an otherwise jaunty melody. The songs document the political
discourse of the enslaved and the ways that people worked in collectives
to publicize social critique amid tense racial and colonial hierarchies.[55]

A "rattling accompaniament" embellished performances of "Ranger
Song," in which participants created percussive sounds using a local
plant. The anonymous author describe the technique in this way: "A
dried pod of the Barbadoes pride, held at one end, between two fingers
of the left hand, resting the other against the thumb, and struck smartly,
by passing the back of the fingers of the right hand in a quick succession,
from the forefinger to the little one, over the pod, and repeating the stroke
twice, with the inside of the thumb, was the rattling accompaniment to
this air."[56] The Barbados Pride is a flowering plant that produces a slen-
der bean pod that apparently could be rapped and shaken to create a
percussive sound. The quality of the sound hearkens back to those
explored in chapter 1 in the context of early modern African and African diasporic performance. Rattling and shaking sounds were iconic, and
used in many genres of the era, and here we see how enslaved Barbadians
made use of found materials to achieve aesthetic ideals rooted in African
tradition that they helped transform and reimagine in the Americas.

"Ranger" also hints at the circulation of European traditions and aesthetic conventions in the Caribbean, and their practice among enslaved
communities. The melody reminded the anonymous author of a sonata by
English composer John Garth, and it bears resemblance to generic Anglo-
European tunes.[57] "Ranger" appears to be an archetypal artifact of the
creolization that has long fascinated scholars of the Caribbean, in that
the song involves elements that reflect characteristics that we associate
with African and European tradition, respectively, while being rooted in
the sociopolitical discourse of the plantation Caribbean. Yet, as I hoped to
emphasize in the opening chapters of this book, and work by other scholars also urges, European-African cultural exchange began shaping African
Atlantic music long before this cultural moment.[58] For a long time, the
creolization thesis that so dominated Caribbean cultural history seemed
to imagine African and European musical tradition as impermeable con-
tainers that arrived to America in pure, unadulterated form, where they
began to mix and blend in the context of plantation societies. Without
knowing the origins of the "Ranger" melody, or what it sounded like

when performed there is no reason to assume the melody has European origins. When vernacular performances are documented in notation it becomes tempting to read and hear them through a Western-centered lens. As interesting as these notated examples are, they have stark limitations when it comes to fully imagining what the performances sounded like and what they meant to those who partook in them.

Jamaican Set Girls

The festival performances of the Jamaican Set Girls also involved a diverse blend of modalities that reflected multidirectional cultural exchange in the African Atlantic world. Participants banded into troops to parade during Christmas festivities, and their performances were highly anticipated by Jamaicans of all stripes. The troops coordinated songs and dances, and they promenaded around towns and through rural hillsides, stopping frequently to grace bystanders with performances. The activities seem to have had had a sororal, if not competitive character. As scholar Linda Sturtz has explained, the urban "sets" were somewhat more lavishly styled, but countryside troops were no less regaled in spirit. In cities, sets engaged fiddles, tabors, and pipes, to accompany them whereas in more rural areas more traditional instruments like horse teeth, goombay, and other drums were common.[59] The troops paraded through their own communities and also into the receiving halls of the island's elites. There, they often would be fed food and drink in exchange for the entertainment.

Set Girls developed an entertainment spectacle that was at once fashion show, orchestrated musical and dance performance, and festival parade. The groups were highly coordinated, from head to toe, with each member donning a detailed costume in striking color. In some areas, like in Montego Bay, the troops were known as "red" and "blue" sets, but among the performers documented by Long and the anonymous author they were described as the "Velvet," "Garnett," and "Golden" ladies. Velvet is a luxurious fabric, or a lustrous shade of black, whereas garnet is a precious stone and a rich shade of red. Golden, too, is a hue signifying wealth, precious metal, and sunshine. These terms speak to the aesthetic ideals of the tradition, which heralded feminine fashion and finery.

The women built on processional practices of masquerading and costuming that had long been a part of African Atlantic festivals, both in Africa and the Caribbean.[60] Set Girls also performed in parallel to Jonkanu, a Christmas performance tradition predominated by bands of male celebrants, one of whom would dress up as a central character, sometimes called "Junkano" or "John Canoe." In Jamaica, the figure's costumed evolved, originally involving tusks, horns, and an elaborate mask. Eventually, performers came to wear an elaborately constructed hat, designed as a miniature house or ship. The Jonkanu festival characteristics varied across regions and over time, and the tradition remains diversified. The celebrations continue to take place in Jamaica, the Bahamas, and among the Garifuna in Belize and Central America. Jonkanu is one of the most well-documented, and oldest Afro-Caribbean festival traditions that survives to the present day, although in modern Jamaica, the festivities are less prominent than they once were, and the Set Girl tradition that was once such a key part of seasonal Christmas festivals does not survive in its original form.[61]

Reports of the Set Girls' activities can be found scattered across sources from the period, in illustrations, travel accounts, and periodicals. The "Jamaican Airs" manuscript offers a unique window into the practice by documenting the Set Girls' music in notation alongside narrative description. The author wrote about the performances he witnessed in some detail, providing a sense of how and in what context the tunes were animated in live performance. Remarking on how expensive and refined the sets' costumes were, the author reproduced the pro-slavery trope, discussed in the previous chapter, that linked musical expression to "happiness" in portrayals of slave societies, especially in the late eighteenth and early-to-mid nineteenth centuries. To the trope, he added an impression that enslaved Jamaicans were not only happy, but wealthy enough to purchase finery. Like many other documentarians of African Atlantic performances of his day, he appeared charmed by performances that he also attempted to control and deride through his own narrative performance of superiority:

> I cannot help remarking, in proof of the wealth and happiness of the Negroes in this country, that, at this season of the year, and particularly on the first of this month, I saw great numbers pass by my window dressed in a stile of expence which the generality of people in England will scarcely believe, attended with music. A *set* of them (for by that appellation they distinguish themselves) was in the house while I was writing the foregoing. They consisted of about thirty young women, with white beaver hats, ornamented with blue ribbands, & brown and white, and black ostrich feathers. They wore short gowns, of fine printed callico, of the same pattern, and were attended by fiddles and a tabor and pipe; some of them were acquainted with the housekeeper, and, upon the strength of that, familiarly entered the hall, and danced for half an hour, were regaled with cake, wine, &c. and then pursued their diversion; many

such sets, some of them still better dressed, where at the same time parading in different parts of the town; I am convinced there were some scores, whose cloathes and ornaments, upon this occasion, did not cost less than from ten to fifteen guineas.

The author emphasizes the costliness of the Set Girls costumes, and also the "familiarity" with which they entered the halls of the island's elite. White paternalistic critique of Black women's sartorial self-expression has a long history. In the modern United States, for instance, similar condescending tropes came to the fore in public discourse in the 1980s and 90s when poor and working-class Black women were widely stereotyped as "welfare queens." The stereotype demonized women for the perceived extravagance of their fashion choices, hair and nail styling, and expensive cars. The anonymous author's descriptions foretell these racist narratives, in which white observers appear enraptured by the women's finery and aesthetic prowess, while also troubled by the belief that the women were reaching beyond their station.[62]

White reactions to Black women's aesthetic invention and self-fashioning reveal the sociopolitical power behind practices that were too often dismissed and misunderstood by outsiders. Scholars Elizabeth Dillon, Linda Sturtz, and Sara E. Johnson all emphasize the political valence of Jamaican Set Girls' activities in their work on the historical practice. Dillon argues for the significance of self-fashioning, claiming that the choice to parade in "showy finery" was a critique of the logic of slavery which confined Black people to their "suitability for labor." By deliberately engaging in luxury, she argues, they undermined those who would have them do nothing but work and exist for the benefit of the planter class.[63] Linda Sturtz contends that the Set Girls, and the musical bands that accompanied them in procession through the streets of Jamaica at Christmas established a "de facto Pan Africanism" that seeded radical political formations that generations later would echo in the work of Marcus Garvey and others.[64] In her work on the Set Girl tradition, scholar of the French Caribbean Sara E. Johnson focuses on a band of Haitian Set Girls that formed in the wake of the Haitian Revolution as planters and their households fled to nearby Jamaica. This influx of enslaved and free people left a significant cultural and political influence on Caribbean culture. Johnson urges that to fully understand the "counterplantation aesthetic" in the era of Black revolution in the Caribbean, it is vital to incorporate a "transcolonial" methodology that reveals the circulation of people and ideas across space in the region. The Haitian Set Girls found a way to maintain their French Caribbean identity and bonds even while embracing a local Jamaican practice.[65] Indeed, as Johnson's work underscores, the Haitian women's troop exemplifies broader processes by which regionalized diasporic practices spread, like the "common wind" that Julius Scott identifies in the era of the Haitian Revolution, which set aflame anticolonial and antislavery sentiment across the Atlantic world.[66]

Details from the "Jamaican Airs" help explain precisely how the Set Girls orchestrated such an influential and innovative program of performances, year after year. In preparation for the festivities, each Set would compose music specifically for the yearly occasion. The author explains that, one of the women in the troop, "having determined on the words to be used by them at their next festival, and adapted an air of her own composition," would sing the tune for a "negro musician until he can execute it with facility on his violin: Most of the sets employ a fiddler so instructed to accompany them in their procession."[67] The anonymous author recorded a rare detail about women's musical authorship, and the anecdote also helps explain how musicians composed and circulated novel tunes through aural transmission. Often, musical traces that entered the historical record were the product of extensive circulation. These pieces typically had already become popular before they were written down, as with "Ranger" and other melodies recorded in the "Jamaican Airs." But the Set Girl pieces represent the genesis of a musical idea and the pedagogical practices by which performers instructed musical collaborators in original music during this period.

The anonymous author must have been a particular fan of the Garnet Set because he describe their mid-1770s performances at some length, recounting a tragedy that befell the troop. He included two of their anthems, the first from Christmas 1775 and the second from 1776, in the series of Set Girls' tunes. The two pieces are markedly distinct in tone and subject, which has to do with the fact that the Garnett ladies suffered "a heavy loss" in 1776 when a merchant, whom they had paid to procure "printed linnens, all of the same pattern" in England, drowned during the sea crossing. The ladies lost an associate, and importantly for the performance, they lost precious funds as well as the planned costumes for the 1776 celebrations. The lyrics to the 1776 tune address the subject of their misfortune:

Garnet Ladies have a heavy loss,
   Huzza! For Garnet, we have a heavy loss.

Last year this time, we have a merry day,
This year we have a heavy loss.

The anonymous author explained that "In memory of this gentleman, or their own loss, they were mourning in their procession, during the holy days." The Garnet Set appears to have folded the unfortunate experience into their act.

The musical transcriptions present basic melodies that complement the lyrics provided for each set, but much is left to be imagined. The tunes generally indicate a lively feel, and a very danceable beat with flourishes that resemble fiddle tunes for country dances. The melodies entail repetitive patterns that would enable a chorus of set girls to chant along. Many of the melodies could be expanded upon in solo voice, fiddle, or pipe, as the anonymous author suggested. The Garnet Sett's 1776 number is as upbeat as the other tunes, but the melody does modulate towards a minor tonality ever-so-briefly, suggesting, possibly, the mournful occasion.[68]

Drums and pipes were common in military bands, and indeed the Set Girl genre as a whole often entailed martial elements. Matching costumes alluded to military uniformity, given that they were strictly coordinated among all group members. Some troops overtly nodded to soldiering, like performers from St. Elizabeth parish, documented by Monk Lewis decades later in 1816.[69] One of these Sets wore red for English and another wore blue for Scotland. Military marching bands were prominent in the local soundscape.[70] Here I would like to note suggestive similarities between these historic troops and performance traditions across the Americas that emerged centuries later. In the United States, for instance, cheerleaders, women's drill teams, and pep groups combine military aesthetics with dance and fashion, and at Carnivale in Haiti, Rara groups parade in finery, and baton twirlers entertain.[71] The Atlantic circulation of processional performances that combine feminized fashion, dance, and music suggest that the Set Girls may have influenced performance practice more widely than what was documented. Or more certainly, their traditions exemplified broad African Atlantic festival practices. Notably, in the case of Set Girls, we can identify a unique tradition in which women moved from spectators and dancing celebrants, to center stage.

The nuances of the Set Girl tradition also serve as a reminder that musical performance is always about far more than simply making or listening to sounds. But the audibility of the sounds helped define community during the performance by enfolding listeners and observers into a shared experience of observation and celebration. By working in large sets

"Queen or 'Maam' of the Set-Girls," 1837, from Belisario, *Sketches of Character.* (Yale Center for British Art, Paul Mellon Collection)

of women, the Set Girls also established their own internal audience. Just by their own number, they were a crowd and could spark a party through their dancing, song, and cheering. This is important for understanding the significance of festival performances to enslaved communities and to the broader world. Festival performances created a gathering ground, and a shared space of belonging that was rooted in the social world of the enslaved, and later, their descendants.

These songs from the 1770s offer key insights into the musical lives of diverse peoples, at a time when sugar colonies were at the height of their wealth and violence, and also at the precipice of their downfall, as antislavery movements in colonial Haiti, the British Isles, and the United States sparked aflame. From these songs, we learn that enslaved people authored subtle political critiques of slavery when singing while at labor. We also learn that rangers, formerly enslaved men pressed into colonial service, became the lyrical subject of popular songs. And finally, we learn of the multidisciplinary performance practices of enslaved women in Jamaica, who established the Set Girl tradition.

The 1770s were a turning point both musically and politically, as second-generation enslaved people in the Caribbean produced a blossoming of public performances and a subtle turn away from traditional African genres toward identifiably American arts. The era represented an uproarious pinnacle of Caribbean public performance. For every song that survives in transcription, there must have been scores passed from ear to ear, and coast to coast, shaping modern music, far and wide. Eighteenth-century representations of African Atlantic music, in both musical notation and literary narration, helped to set a precedent for what followed in the nineteenth century, when blackface minstrelsy rose to prominence and white composers peddled sheet music purporting to reflect the experiences of the enslaved. But the transcriptions surveyed in this chapter did far more than simply racialize early Black music; they also document the degree to which the performances in enslaved communities circulated around the Atlantic world.

The temporal arc of *African Musicians in the Atlantic World* closes here, but enslaved Africans continued to arrive in the Americas well after the 1770s, and the musical circulations across and between Africa, the Americas, and Europe continued as fervently as ever in subsequent decades and centuries. The epilogue will consider the afterlives of musical performances during slavery by following the journey of a single song across voices, generations, continents, and archives.

Epilogue
Listening for Tena

How can narrative embody life in words and at the same time respect what we cannot know? How does one listen for the groans and
cries, the undecipherable songs, the crackle of fire in the cane fields,
the laments for the dead, and the shouts of victory, and then assign
words to all of it? Is it possible to construct a story from "the locus
of impossible speech" or resurrect lives from the ruins? Can beauty
provide an antidote to dishonor, and love a way to "exhume buried
cries" and reanimate the dead?
                    —Saidiya Hartman, "Venus in Two Acts"

WHEN I began the research journey that led to this book, I
wrestled with the idea of archival silence. It seemed that so much had been
lost and obscured when it came to the story of music and slavery. In the
end, I put aside my worries in order to examine what I could, choosing
to pay closest attention to the stories that seemed most irrecoverable: the
experiences of survivors of the Middle Passage. To explore their musical
lives, I tuned into the documents and other artifacts that have formed the
basis for this book. I also listened to a song by an enslaved woman named
Tena. Her story hummed in the background of all this work. Enslaved in
the state of Georgia in the 1820s, Tena was among the last generation of
survivors of the Middle Passage in North America. She sang a song in an
African tongue that was preserved in unexpected ways, and her story ties
the world of the early modern Caribbean to the plantation United States,
and to twentieth-century entanglements between Africa and America.

The research journey that I document here is a mournful, unpredict-
able, terribly beautiful concert that occasions the opportunity to listen to
one woman's life—the song she chose to sing, and the words she refused
to speak.

I first encountered Tena's music in a copy of *The American Songbag*
(1927), a mammoth collection of folk songs compiled by the poet and
orator, Carl Sandburg. The anthology is a relic of Sandburg's moment,
a time when folklorists, academics, and populists like himself turned

JUNGLE MAMMY SONG

Margaret Johnson of Augusta, Georgia, heard her mother sing this, year on year, as the mother had learned it from the singing, year on year, of a negro woman who comforted children with it. The source of its language may be French, Creole, Cherokee, or mixed. The syllables are easy for singing; so is the tune. It may be, as provisionally titled, a Jungle Mammy Song, in the sense that all mothers are primitive and earthy even though civilized and celestial.

Ah yah, tair um bam, boo wah, Kee lay zee day, Nic o lay, mah

lun dee. Nic o lay ah poot a way, Nic o lay ah wah mee— Ah

yah, tair um bam, boo wah, Kee lay zee day, Nic o lay. mah lun dee.

Tena's song in Sandburg, *The American Songbag*, p. 455 (New York, 1927).

to the cultural productions of the working class in order to conjure an American past.[1] Tucked away in the huge volume of 280 songs, I happened to notice "Jungle Mammy Song." From the racist title, I assumed the piece to be a holdover from minstrelsy and the stereotypes the genre helped to popularize.[2] But looking more carefully, I saw that the music was not a stage number at all. The lyrics were in an unfamiliar and untranslated language, and the headnote explained that "Margaret Johnson of Augusta, Georgia, heard her mother sing this, year on year, as the mother had learned it from the singing, year on year, of a negro woman who comforted children with it." I deduced that the tune had been remembered and passed down by a white Georgia family whose children were cared for by the singer. This explained the presence of the mammy iconography in the title.

Given the non-English lyrics, I immediately wondered whether or not the woman who originally sang the song had been a survivor of the Middle Passage, or perhaps a member of an enslaved community maintaining strong African traditions. With Augusta being so close to the Georgia Sea Islands and Gullah communities, that seemed plausible. If the singer had been enslaved when she sang the music, then this was a unique artifact, one far more interesting than Sandburg's racist title would suggest. As this book addresses in several chapters, notated examples of early African Atlantic music—and particularly music by enslaved women—are exceedingly rare.

The piece from the *American Songbag* recalled all the familiar problems of archival erasure. The singer's memory was disparaged and commodified in the pages of the book, her true story disregarded and untold. I wondered, though, could the music itself—its sounds—teach me something about the song and its singer, what it might have meant to her, and what it might mean to honor her legacy? As I took up the task of trying to encounter the music in a different way, I began a process that would ultimately lead me to discover traces of Tena's biography across voices and continents and archives. I did not know her name at the time, but I would come to learn that, and more.

Listening through Performance

Some say that lullabies are really about soothing those who sing them, rather than the children who listen, and I wondered if this song helped to soothe the singer as she cared for other people's children. I wondered if she might have sung it to her own children as well. Knowing how often families were separated, and how often children perished under slavery, I considered that singing such a song might have brought up tender memories, perhaps of her own mother, or a child she mourned. Was the song a source of pain, of comfort, or even humor? Or, was it simply a way to shush pestering children or pass the time? I did not know.

At the time I discovered the song, I happened to be teaching a singing class to young girls at a nonprofit arts organization, the Walltown Children's Theatre, which is located in the heart of an historically Black neighborhood in Durham, North Carolina. Known for its excellent dance program, the theatre also provides arts-based aftercare for school children, as well as music classes. The leadership, faculty, and clientele of the community-centered organization is predominately Black and Latinx. I decided to share the song with my students, curious to explore the music in community with young people. I had heavy research questions about the song and the broader history of Black women's labor on my mind when I showed up to class, but the girls in my singing class instantly lightened the mood and took a playful approach to the music. They were all between the ages of 7 and 12. I chose not to share Sandburg's racist title with the students, but I did tell them that the song was sung by an African or African-descended woman to children in her care, and that she had probably been enslaved. When I shared the foreign lyrics, Spanish speakers in the class chuckled at one of the words that sounds phonetically similar to a curse word in Spanish. We all wondered what "lundee" and "bam boo" might have meant. We had no translation whatsoever, but thinking through the musical possibilities together brought the sounds to life.

During the class I made a recording of the young singers performing the song. We were working on learning music by ear and I wanted them to be able to hear what they sounded like as we tried to get on the same pitches—after all, it was a singing class. But later, when I listened to the recording at home, I heard their "errors" quite differently. I came to understand their missed notes as novel interpretations demonstrating the process of oral circulation in action. (To hear this recording, and other audio excerpts connected to the history of the piece, please listen to a podcast episode that I produced about Tena's story for the *C19 Podcast* series.)[3] In the recording, the girls' pitch slides downward throughout the song, as if their voices are determined to find a more comfortable key. They reach unison on certain notes and stray and wander on others. Their performance exemplifies music as a process, and how a single tune can evolve and yet stay recognizably the same as it circulates across voices and time.

Hearing a multi-vocal performance of the song, learned by ear, lifted the music from the page, placing it into the vernacular realm, where it could be interpreted anew. I do not wish to romanticize aurality over textuality, but the conditions in which we encounter music profoundly influence our understanding of it. Transforming historical transcriptions into audible performances can be a powerful way to de-privilege white and Western-centric understanding in our efforts to hear the past. Acts of listening and singing create opportunities for engaging historical musical sources in collectives. Rather than the singularity of a researcher analyzing a printed document and singing to herself without an audience, by interacting with the song across generations and categories of difference, bringing our voices and our ears into living contact with the historical source, we can participate in a method of interpretation that is perhaps more akin to the musical mode. Needless to say, I learned a lot from the students, and not just in terms of Tena's song. Sharing music with young people and being part of the Walltown Children's Theatre artistic community taught me how to think about music and dance as an empowering space of possibility and collectivity.

After learning the song with the students, I published an essay in an online journal of experimental history called the *Appendix*. In that piece, I described my experience with the students and reflected on using performance as a research method, writing that "though she remains distant and opaque to me, hidden among the silences of history and the words framing her performance in the book, her music is frequently in my ears and on my mind. It may be that knowing her song means simply that, to know it . . . The song, then, is not a portal into an understanding of a particular woman's story, but an opportunity to witness something that her voice made known. Rather than repackaging the music and its creator like Sandburg did, this time. I'd rather just listen." Though I concluded that essay with an insistence on the value of listening to the historical subject, I had no idea at that time that her story would continue to speak.[4]

To my great surprise, several months later, I received an email from a descendant of the family Sandburg had referenced in the description. I followed up with a phone call to the woman and learned that the family called the song "Tina's Lullaby." The descendant had no idea where Sandburg had learned the music or that he had published anything about it at all. She then told me the family's oral history about the song and Tena. My hunch was right—the family had enslaved her, and she was said to have lost a child, a boy who died during the Middle Passage. For nine generations they have passed down Tena's music, along with a handful of details about her biography. The descendant shared with me details about her family's ancestry which helped me undertake archival research to verify some of their claims and uncover other details, about Tena's life. I use the spelling "Tena" because that is how her name appears in historical records. I also learned from the family that in 1961, a scholar had researched Tena's song and purported to discover her African origins. The descendant was searching the internet for the scholar's article (which was locked behind paywalls) when she chanced upon my writing.[5]

Listening to the Past

The white family's transformation of Tena's music into a kind of sonic family heirloom is a troubling story of its own, one that speaks to white listeners' possessive claims to Black performance in the wake of slavery. As with Sandburg's framing, the family narrative was shaped by the mammy stereotype, which romanticized Black domestic laborers for many white audiences, and white Southerners, especially. As a white Southerner myself, I am all too familiar with the cultural narratives that drove the descendants to characterize Tena and her song in this way. My own family has participated in the peculiar brand of racism that shades white Southern historical memory. Indoctrinated from an early age in the Lost Cause narrative, I, too, was taught sanitized and romanticized history lessons about the "Old South." Later, I came to understand that profound racial injustice formed the bedrock of the world I grew up in, a rural Southern city along the Texas-Louisiana border. In my research, I turned to questions that would help me make sense of the worldview I inherited, and to better understand and to honor the experiences of enslaved people and their descendants, who shaped my life and my culture. My background is part of what compels me to try to tell Tena's story in a way that does greater justice to her legacy and that of women like her. Women whose care and time and energy, and even music were taken up like possessions that could be owned and exchanged and inherited by families like mine. I recognize that it is impossible to root out the violence from the story, to cast it aside. I am as bound up in it as Tena was.

I have been able to corroborate the basic facts of the white family's oral history concerning Tena, but other details about her life circumstances come from their intergenerational recollections.[6] Working with two streams of information—the archival and the oral—I have been able to sketch a tentative biography, filling in gaps with speculations informed by what we know about slavery at the time. Tena probably was born on the African continent in the late 1700s or early 1800s. She was trafficked to the Americas at a time when the international slave trade was illegal, and because of that may have been smuggled through the Caribbean or the Gulf of Mexico before eventually being sold in Charleston to a man named Alexander Spencer (1756–1831).[7] The sale took place sometime before 1831, which is when he died.[8] Spencer was a Scottish immigrant, and a merchant who lived in Augusta, Georgia. According to the family, he purchased Tena for his daughter, to help take care of her two young children. They lived together in one household, which included Alexander Spencer, his widowed daughter Isabella Bones (later Coskery), and sixteen enslaved people. They were, along with Tena: Lewis, Charles, Jack, Celia and her child James, Henry, Washington, Mary, young Lewis, Clarissa, Maria and her three children, and Tamar.[9]

Tena reportedly never learned to speak English and communicated using her own unique set of hand gestures, a curious fact that has survived in the memories of the Spencer descendants. The Spencer family claims that she was a mother and that her only child, an eleven-year-old son, died during the Middle Passage. They also remembered her as tall and very beautiful—the slave trader who sold Tena said that she had been a princess in Africa.[10] When caring for the children, Tena sang a song that became etched into their memories, and that they chose to pass down to their children and grandchildren. Descendants of the Spencer family recall that Tena lived in the family's household long enough to provide child-care for two generations, but I have been unable to confirm that. Despite my best efforts, I do not know when or how Tena died, who her family or intimate connections may have been, nor whether or not she lived to be emancipated.[11]

Just one document clearly bears Tena's name—an estate inventory of Alexander Spencer from 1831. In the document, Tena's name is listed alongside all the other enslaved people that Spencer owned, along with their ascribed financial values. The sum next to Tena's name is five dollars. Why was Tena valued at just five dollars, and what might that tell us about her or her enslavers? All of the other enslaved families and individuals in the household were valued at well over one hundred dollars. At the time, young children, the infirmed, disabled, or elderly often were assigned the smallest prices upon sale.[12] I don't have reason to believe that Tena was particularly elderly at this point in her life, especially since the Spencer's claimed that she took care of two subsequent generations of children, but I do know that she did not speak English, which may have detracted from the financial value ascribed to her labor. Or, she may have been intentionally devalued because the surviving heirs did not intend to sell her.[13] These details insist that we remember that Tena's enslavers imagined and exploited her life as capital, and that within this cruel framework they also portrayed her as being of little value.

Tena disappeared from archival records after 1831, as did so many enslaved individuals, whose lives surface in documentation only when those who claimed to own them died or sold them.

But although the textual record of Tena's life is slim, she did not vanish. Her song traveled long after her life ended, even making its way back to the African continent and to communities that may have been her homeland. The preservation of Tena's existence in song tells us something about the way that her voice was heard, and the way that it rang out, perhaps, amid the comparative silence of her inability—or refusal—to speak her enslaver's language. As the Spencer descendant suggested to me in a reflective moment during our phone call, perhaps Tena's choice not to speak was her way of saying "you may own me, but you don't own my mind." Indeed. How ironic, then, that the family held on so tightly to the song for so many years. Was the sound of Tena's song like a burr that attached itself to the memories of her enslavers, traveling across eras and continents, determined to seed her story across the decades? But along with the sounds, her silence traveled too, a profound opacity that seems to frustrate those who would presume to understand, including, I must admit, myself.

Listening for Tena in Africa

Let us listen to yet another a trace of Tena's song. At some point in the 1950s, the Spencer descendants became curious about Tena's African origins, prompting them to contact a local librarian, Ruth Bartholemew, at Paine University, an historically Black college in Augusta. Bartholemew then wrote to Hugh Tracey, an influential British musicologist and immigrant to South Africa who founded the journal *African Music* and the International Library of African Music (ILAM). His legacy is in some ways on par with a figure like Alan Lomax in the U.S. in that he was a white scholar who helped to promote the study of Black music while building significant collections. Lomax and Tracey both benefited, to some degree, from racializing Black music, and Tracey did so in apartheid South Africa.[14] Tracey eventually wrote an article about the song and recorded a radio broadcast about Tena's story.[15] The circulation of Tena's song and story across the broader region prompted response from Africans who claimed connection to her through shared heritage, a point I will return to.

After receiving the letter (now lost) from Ruth Bartholemew about Tena's song, Tracey asked that the family record it so that he could hear the lyrics and tune. The family obliged, sending him a version of the song sung by family elder, Margaret Louisa Johnson. She was the granddaughter of Margaret Clarissa Bones Wright, one of the children that Tena took care of.[16] Eighty-year-old Mrs. Johnson probably heard Tena's song from both her mother and grandmother, meaning that the recording she sent to Tracey is just one generation removed from a first-hand witness to Tena's performance. The way the family sings the song today sounds remarkably similar to the performance in the 1950s recording, and noticeably different from the way the song was presented by Sandburg in notation and his recorded performance.[17]

After hearing the music, Tracey attempted to determine Tena's origins in Africa, an effort very much in tune with anthropological studies of African American culture of his day. After analyzing phonemes within the Johnson family's version of the lyrics, he ultimately concluded that Tena had been from a Bantu-language culture in Eastern Africa, and crafted a Chimanyika translation of the song, placing Tena's origins in Zimbabwe or Mozambique. While I do not place a tremendous amount of faith in his methods, I do think it is worth considering that Tena may have been from Eastern Africa.[18] Although most enslaved people in the U.S. came from West and West Central Africa, Tracey's hypothesis about Tena's origins remains plausible, if somewhat unlikely. In the years just prior to the end of the legal trade, ships containing captives from "Mosambique" were advertised in the *Charleston Courier*.[19] The name Tinashe, which in Shona means "God is with us," is a common name in the region.[20]

Tracey's proposed lyrics imagine a children's song or folk song that tells the story of a child who has been sent as a messenger to a nearby village. Here is Tracey's proposed English translation and explanatory note from his article on the subject:

Yes, I ran quickly to his father, the Chief.
Indeed, I have sent a messenger.
Where shall I go straightaway?
then I will go straightaway.

A small child has been sent by his *Tenzi*, the headman of the village, and no doubt, a senior relative or *Bambo*, to take a message to some nearby village and the child who conveyed the Tenzi's instructions now asks for another mission. As a child's verse this would be in keeping with many a folk song of the region.[21]

Tracey's interpretation of Tena's song as a "child's verse" shares similarities with other songs of enslaved people that survived to the present day by being passed from families to their children. For instance, a Gullah family from South Carolina, the Dawleys, preserved a song sung by their enslaved ancestor. Their efforts to locate the origins of the song in a village in Sierra Leone were documented in the film, *The Language You Cry In* (1998).[22] Both the Dawleys' song and Tena's song share similarities with another musical heirloom which was preserved by the family of W. E. B. Du Bois. In his landmark book, *The Souls of Black Folk* (1903), Du Bois explained the origins of music passed down among generations of his family. The family learned the song from Du Bois's great-great grandmother, who had been trafficked into slavery by the Dutch. He described her experience of enslavement and the song's origins: "black, little, and lithe, she shivered and shrank in the harsh north winds, looked longingly at the hills, and often crooned a heathen melody to the child between her knees . . . The child sang it to his children and they to their children's children, and so two hundred years it has travelled down to us and we sing it to our children, knowing as little as our fathers what its words may mean, but knowing well the meaning of its music."[23] Scored into the minds of youngsters who eventually grow old, songs like the Dawleys', the Du Bois's and Tena's serve as a portal to ancestral pasts, and as a means of memorialization. In an observation that gave the Dawley documentary its title, an elder named Nabi Jah, leader of the community-of-origin in Sierra Leone, explained why he believed the Dawleys' song survived in America. He said, "You can speak another language, you can live in another culture, but to cry over your dead, you always go back to your mother tongue—the language you cry in."[24] The Dawleys' song, as interpreted by Nabi Jah, is a mourning cry that bears the legacy of all the love and intimate bonds that the Dawley ancestor lost when she was torn away from home under slavery.

An African elder also entered the record to interpret Tena's song. After Tracey's radio show was aired, an editor from an anticolonialist newspaper contacted Tracey to ask if he could print a story about Tena based on Tracey's research. The *African Mail* was published in Lusaka, Zambia, which was at the time part of colonial Rhodesia. After the publication of Tena's story in the *African Mail*, a reader from Kusungu wrote a letter to the editor. This person, W. Kasiwira, challenged Tracey's interpretation of Tena's song, writing that "Mr. Tracey . . . may have made mistakes because it was not his language." Kasiwira claimed to have spoken with an elder woman in Malawi who offered an alternate translation of the lyrics. This woman claimed Tena as an ancestor of her people in Nyasaland and said that these were the true words to Tena's song:

Eya tarumba bamboo wace Dazi
Yai ndiye kuti mai muranda
Ndikhale kuti kwari O!
Kdikhale kuti mai oye.

(Be praised father of Dazi [name];
I can go nowhere, mother,
Poor I am where can I stay? Perhaps if can—
Where can I stay, mother?
Nowhere.)

The Malawian elder offered a haunting translation that seems to recall Tena's displacement, as a survivor of the Middle Passage, living under slavery in a foreign land. *Where can I stay, mother? Nowhere.* The child in the lyrics also echoes the displacement of the diaspora, and the wandering of the song's meaning across the eras. We can no more verify this translation than we can verify any of the other details of Tena's life and song. And yet I know that it is true. I heard the mournfulness in the song myself.[25]

Tena's lullaby ultimately traveled all the way across the Atlantic Ocean, back to Africa, in a poignant return that raises new questions about how to interpret her history. Bringing new questions and new methods to historical study allows for a shift in perspective, so that even when our research fails to unearth and reveal stories and lives that have been lost, it can still reorient our own engagement with the world. In fact, it may be more important to tune into the things that we don't know and can't know than those that we do know. Many aspects of Tena's personal history are lost, yet there is a world of meaning yet told in her song.

The story of Tena's lullaby also teaches us that just because someone's life and experiences do not appear to be accurately reflected in traditional sources, or even in public historical memory, it does not mean—not at all—that they did not leave a tremendous legacy. Those legacies may be experienced in sound, in performance, in image, in practices of care, in religious expression, in landscape, in so many modalities that shape our lives, but that we need creative research methods to understand. I hope, in this book, to have shown the value of bringing sound to bear on our engagement with slavery's past. I also hope to have illuminated the musical lives of enslaved people, and how they came to found artistic traditions. People whose names we do not know, but whose songs we know by heart, whose techniques and innovations proliferate, and whose stories have been preserved in the archives of sound in abundant and curious ways. The sounds of the African Atlantic past are not irrevocably lost, rather they are ever-present.

Notes

Introduction

1. Ligon, *A True and Exact*, 48–49. All direct citations are drawn from the 1657 edition. I examine Macow's musicianship extensively in chapter 2. On Ligon's biography, see Kupperman, ed., *A True and Exact*, 1–35.

2. Martin Munro also questions how researchers might study sound for a deeper understanding of slavery's past in Munro, *Different Drummers*, 215.

3. Black music as we conceptualize it today certainly would encompass the performances of all enslaved Africans. However, not all enslaved Africans would have thought of their own music as "Black music," nor would they have thought of themselves as Black, or perhaps even as musicians. Eventually, of course, Blackness came to signify the shared history and culture of descendants of enslaved Africans, as well as the experience of being racialized and subjected to racism by white Europeans and their descendants. But many enslaved Africans in the early modern period conceptualized their identity differently, and categories like "Black," "African," and also "music," as we understand them today, were different then. For this reason, when I use the term "Black music" I mean to refer to a modern discourse *about* the music of the African diaspora, its history and present.

4. On minstrelsy and portrayals of slavery, see Thompson, *Ring Shout;* Morrison, "Blacksound"; Lott, *Love and Theft;* Lhamon, *Raising Cain;* and Radano, *Lying up a Nation.*

5. See Jones, *Staging Habla de Negros.*

6. On white performances of African dance in colonial Haiti, see Prest, "Pale Imitations."

7. In *Lying up a Nation*, Radano argued that "beyond a minor assembly of historical fragments and passing references, there is, quite simply, no documentary evidence of North American slave musical practices from the eighteenth century," 51. He viewed documents from the eighteenth-century to be reflections of white racism rather than artifacts of Black musical expression.

8. Across generations, many Black intellectuals have turned to the subject of music and slavery when theorizing the Black experience in the Americas. For instance, see Douglass, *Narrative of the Life of Frederick Douglass,* 12–15; Du Bois, *Souls of Black Folk,* especially chapter 13, "Of the Sorrow Songs"; Hurston, "How It Feels to Be Colored Me"; Baraka, *Blues People;* Glissant, "Cross-Cultural Poetics" in *Caribbean Discourse;* Gilroy, *The Black Atlantic;* Moten, *In the Break;* and Nourbese-Philip, *Zong!.* The Fisk Jubilee Singers have kept repertoire connected to nineteenth-century slavery in the United States alive on the stage for well over a century. On the Fisk Jubilee Singers, Hurston, Du Bois, and debates about Black musical authenticity, see Gilroy, *The Black Atlantic,* 87–92.

9. See Johnson, "On Agency"; and Brown, "Social Death and Political Life in the Study of Slavery."

10. On the politics of historical memory, see especially Trouillot, *Silencing the Past;* and on the limits of academic methodology in the study of slavery specifically, see Fuentes, *Dispossessed Lives,* 1–12.

11. The term "history from below" came from mid-twentieth century leftist labor historians of Britain who sought to revolutionize the study of history to privilege the stories of common, working-class people.

12. The following several notes draw together contributions from the field, focusing on works that stand out to me as particularly relevant to the study of music and slavery in general, and my project in particular. Field-defining contributions from musicology are Southern, *The Music of Black Americans;* and Epstein, *Sinful Tunes and Spirituals.* Epstein's book has been especially influential for this book because she turns to the broader African Atlantic world, and especially the Caribbean, to expand the temporal scope of Black music history. Both books, however, focus primarily on the nineteenth century. See also the bibliographic compilation by Southern and Wright, "African-American Traditions in Song, Sermon, Tale, and Dance, 1600s–1920." Of a similar generation, Olive Lewin had a field-defining impact on the study of Jamaica's traditional music, and she also emphasized ties to the era of slavery. See Lewin, *Rock It Come Over* and "Traditional Music in Jamaica."

13. Nonwhite scholars have faced many barriers in academia which reduced the amount of scholarship on early Black music. Many publications that did emerge have not been well-preserved in academic libraries and thus remain difficult to access. An anthology, Coester and Bender, *A Reader in African-Jamaican Music, Dance and Religion,* has been particularly useful to me in learning about and accessing scholarship by early twentieth century scholars and practitioners such as Astley Clerk, Ivy Baxter, and others. Also, see an annotated bibliography published in 1981 by Robert M. Stevenson, "A Caribbean Music History."

14. The following have been helpful to my understanding of early modern African music: Sublette, *Cuba and Its Music;* Charry, *Mande Music;* and Thornton, *A Cultural History of the Atlantic World* and *Africa and Africans in the*

Making of the Atlantic World. For an expansive introduction to many aspects of diverse African music traditions and histories, see Agawu, *The African Imagination in Music.*

15. Although they are more abundant than earlier sources, I find that nineteenth century sources on Black music can be difficult to work with because they are so strongly inflected by the racist tropes emanating from minstrelsy and other racist discourses. For scholarship addressing Black music history in nineteenth-century contexts, see Floyd, *The Power of Black Music;* White and White, *The Sounds of Slavery;* Abrahams, *Singing the Master;* Thompson, *Ring Shout;* Radano, *Lying up a Nation;* Roberts, *Black Music of Two Worlds;* May, *Yuletide in Dixie;* Smith, *Listening to Nineteenth-Century America;* Stoever, *The Sonic Color Line;* and a forthcoming book by Matthew D. Morrison on "blacksound."

16. Studies addressing performance traditions during the era of slavery in the Caribbean include multiple works and editorial projects by Kenneth Bilby, such as Bilby, "Surviving Secularization"; Handler and Frisbie, "Aspects of Slave Life in Barbados"; Roberts, *A Response to Enslavement;* Dewulf, "From the Calendas to the Calenda" and *From the Kingdom of Kongo to Congo Square;* Johnson, *The Fear of French Negroes,* chapter 4, "French Set Girls and Transcolonial Performance"; Lingold, "Peculiar Animations"; Cummings, "'They Are Delighted to Dance for Themselves'"; Sturtz, "The Sett Girls and the Pedagogy of the Streets"; Cowley, *Carnival, Canboulay, and Calypso;* Dillon, *New World Drama;* McDaniel, *The Big Drum Ritual of Carriacou;* Prest, "Parisian Palimpsests and Creole Creations"; Ryan, "'The Influence of Melody'"; Leigh, "The Jamaican Airs"; Fuller, "Maroon History, Music, and Sacred Sounds in the Americas"; Cooper, "Playing against Empire"; Hill, *The Jamaican Stage;* Dubois, "Minette's Worlds"; Fouchard, *Le Théâtre à Saint-Domingue;* and Camier, "A 'Free Artist of Color' in Late-Eighteenth-Century Saint-Domingue."

17. Work on the Iberian Atlantic world, colonial Latin America, and Brazil illuminates the contributions of Atlantic Africans, such as Fromont, ed., *Afro-Catholic Festivals;* Valerio, *Sovereign Joy;* Voigt, *Spectacular Wealth;* Jones, *Staging Habla de Negros;* Dewulf, "Rethinking the Historical Development"; Budasz, "Black Guitar-Players"; Ramos-Kittrell, *Playing in the Cathedral;* Allende-Goitía, "The Mulatta, the Bishop, and Dances in the Cathedral" and *Las Músicas Otras;* Quintero, *Rites, Rights and Rhythms;* and Le Guin, "One Fine Night in Veracruz."

18. The following incorporate an Atlantic world frame to address musical performances connected to slavery from earlier eras: Rath, *How Early America Sounded* and "Drums and Power"; Fryer, *Rhythms of Resistance;* Munro, *Different Drummers;* Skeehan, "Black Atlantic Acoustemologies and the Maritime Archive"; and Floyd, Zeck, and Ramsey, *The Transformation of Black Music.*

19. Scholarship on the history of the banjo has brought welcome attention to the story of African Atlantic music. See Dubois, *The Banjo;* Gaddy, *Well of Souls;* Winans, *Banjo Roots and Branches;* Conway, *African Banjo Echoes in Appalachias;* and Gura and Bollman, *America's Instrument.*

On public writing and media, see the multifaceted work of musician and researcher Rhiannon Giddens; luthier and historic banjo specialist Pete Ross; and writer John Jeremiah Sullivan, whose articles include "Death Rattle: Searching for the Old Jaw Bone" and "Talking Drums," among others.

20. Music historians working on Black artists performing genres rooted in European traditions include Powers, *From Plantation to Paradise?*; and a forthcoming book project by Maria Ryan on enslaved and free performers in the late-eighteenth and early nineteenth century British Caribbean, as well as forthcoming doctoral research on music in Jamaica by Wayne Weaver. Forthcoming work by Henry Stoll looks to a range of musical practices in postrevolutionary Haiti.

21. Examples include Smallwood, *Saltwater Slavery*; Hartman, "Venus in Two Acts"; Fuentes, *Dispossessed Lives*; Morgan, *Laboring Women*; Aljoe, *Creole Testimonies*; and Smith, *Black Africans in the British Imagination*.

22. For studies of musical notation of non-Western performance in travelogues and other early modern records, see Wood, *Sounding Otherness in Early Modern Drama and Travel*; Goodman, "Sounds Heard, Meaning Deferred"; Bloechl, *Native American Song at the Frontiers of Early Modern Music*; Woodfield, *English Musicians in the Age of Exploration*; Tomlinson, *The Singing of the New World*.

23. Mary Louise Pratt's bellwether study *Imperial Eyes* articulated a framework for understanding the role travelogues had in creating the imperial ideology. On slavery and colonialism in the Caribbean specifically, see also Hulme, *Colonial Encounters*.

24. Literary historians Nicole Aljoe and Cassander Smith have charted a path for my work, in particular, by recovering the stories and expression of Black Atlantic individuals from within the pages of African and West Indian travelogues written by Europeans. Aljoe uncovers "embedded slave narratives" in white-authored colonial sources and Smith argues that it is imperative and indeed possible to consider the "material world beyond the text" in order to account for the "physical presence of black Africans in the early Atlantic world." Aljoe, *Creole Testimonies*; and Smith, *Black Africans in the British Imagination*. Cécile Fromont also argues that documented encounters between Europeans and Africans in the pre-colonial era may be understood as "spaces of correlation" that do not presume postcolonial understandings of power. Fromont, *Art of Conversion*, 16–19. Many other works on the Atlantic world and colonial Americas seek to recover subaltern perspectives from white and elite-authored works. For example, see Parrish, *American Curiosity*; Iannini, *Fatal Revolutions*; Wisecup, *Medical Encounters*; Dillon, *New World Drama*; Cohen, *The Networked Wilderness*; and Skeehan, *Fabric of Empire*, among others.

25. For example, see biographical work on enslaved individuals, such as Paton, "Mary Williamson's Letter, or, Seeing Women and Sisters in the Archives of Atlantic Slavery"; Reed, *The Hemingses of Monticello*; Jessica Millward, *Finding Charity's Folk*; Dunbar, *Never Caught*; Sweet, *Domingos Álvares, African*

Healing, and the Intellectual History of the Atlantic World; and Lindsay and Sweet, eds, *Biography and the Black Atlantic.*

26. I join other cultural historians of sound who turn to aural experience to illuminate histories both of the Americas and early modern global contact. See especially Rath, *How Early America Sounded;* Gautier, *Aurality;* Eyerly, *Moravian Soundscapes;* Vazquez, *Listening in Detail;* Finley, *Hearing Voices;* Smith, *Listening to Nineteenth-Century America;* Wilbourne and Cusick, eds, *Acoustemologies in Contact;* and Wood, *Sounding Otherness.* On the historical situatedness of sonic perception, see also Geoffroy-Schwinden, "Digital Approaches to Historical Acoustemologies."

In the field of Black studies, methodologies of sound have also been integral to theorizing and historicizing the arc of Black music and thought in the recorded era and earlier, see especially Moten, *In the Break;* Brooks, *Bodies in Dissent;* Brooks, *Liner Notes for the Revolution;* Weheliye, *Phonographies;* Jaji, *Africa in Stereo;* Chude-Sokei, *The Sound of Culture;* Meintjes, *Sound of Africa!*

27. Christopher Small's term "musicking" has also been key for my understanding of music as a complex, lived experience that is collectively creative and diversely experienced. Small, *Musicking.* Novak and Sakakeeny, *Keywords in Sound,* is useful for parsing the theoretical impact of sound studies on multiple fields, including music.

28. For an in-depth primer on African music that distinguishes African and European conceptualizations of music theory, history, and practice, again see Agawu, *The African Imagination,* especially pages 27–35.

29. In this, I take up the call issued by scholar Diana Taylor, who argued for a turn to the "repertoire" in lieu of textual records and material artifacts that predominate the colonial archive. For Taylor, the "repertoire" is the substance of "embodied memory: performances, gestures, orality, movement, dance, singing—in short, all those acts usually thought of as ephemeral, nonreproducible knowledge." Taylor, *The Archive and the Repertoire,* 20. I am also influenced by Joseph Roach's conceptualization of "circum-Atlantic performance," and his insistence that the histories of such performances maybe be "forgotten" but they are "not gone." Roach, *Cities of the Dead,* 2.

30. Katrina Thompson theorizes the politics of Black music under slavery by developing a concept of "backstage." Thompson, *Ring Shout,* 99–128.

31. Stoever, *Sonic Color Line,* is indispensable on the subject of white listeners and the racialization of Black sonic expression.

32. Again, see Radano, *Lying up a Nation;* and Thompson, *Ring Shout.*

33. This project shares an impulse with Brooks's *Liner Notes for the Revolution.* Brooks focuses on how Black women musicians of the long-twentieth century enacted a cultural revolution, how they "made the modern world," and here I turn to their forebearers to illuminate the vastly underappreciated legacy of enslaved musicians. *Liner Notes,* 2–3.

34. For instance, Olaudah Equiano, also known as Gustavas Vassa, had his identity and origins questioned both in his own day and in modern scholarship by Vincent Carretta. Mary Prince, who was the first woman to publish a slave narrative and the first Caribbean, as well, also faced legal disputes concerning her personal history. Still today some historians discount her narrative because it was copied by amanuensis. There is voluminous scholarship on both authors engaging these subjects. For helpful bibliographic survey of the historical and contemporary debates about authors' truth-claims, see relevant chapters in Hanley, *Beyond Slavery and Abolition.*

1. Musical Encounters in Early Modern Atlantic Africa

1. Gronniosaw, *Narrative*. Gronniosaw's narrative was written via amanuensis. On Gronniosaw's narrative and connections to Calvinist Protestant discourse and pro-slavery argument, see Hanley, "Calvinism, Proslavery and James Albert Ukawsaw Gronniosaw." On Islam in Borno and Gronniosaw's clever narrative manipulation, see Harris, "Seeing the Light."

2. A similar story about Ottobah Cuogano's captivity as a teenager opens the first chapter of Mustakeem, *Slavery at Sea,* 19–20. See both Muskateem and Smallwood, *Saltwater Slavery,* for information about captives' experiences leading up to and during the Middle Passage.

3. Gronniosaw, *Narrative,* 6.

4. Olaudah Equiano, another young captive taken from what is now Nigeria and trafficked toward the Gold Coast, describes similar confusion in *The Interesting Narrative of the Life of Olaudah Equiano,* 61.

5. Gronniosaw, *Narrative,* 7.

6. Africans, Europeans, and Middle Easterners were influencing each other musically long before the dawn of chattel slavery. These encounters are also central to the story of how African music impacted the world. The spread of Islam spurred African musicians' influence on geographies northward in the medieval period. On the subject, see Sublette, *Cuba and Its Music,* chapter 1.

7. My ideas have been influenced by a swell of work in Atlantic and African history aiming to center African thought and action to the emergence of Atlantic and global trade. John Thornton addresses the topic throughout *Africa and Africans in the Making of the Atlantic World.* See also Bennett, *African Kings and Black Slaves,* on the importance of African statecraft and on the erasure of precolonial African history and influence on global trade and politics. See Wheat, *Atlantic Africa and the Spanish Caribbean* on Africa's centrality to Caribbean settlement; and Green, *A Fistful of Shells,* on West and West Central African kingdoms in the development of global trade in the early modern era.

8. Many early modern travel writers from Catholic empires were priests and missionaries. On Afro-Catholic musical production in Angola, Congo, and the Americas, see Fromont, ed. *Afro-Catholic Festivals;* Voigt, *Spectacular Wealth* (especially chapter 4); and Thornton, *Cultural History of the Atlantic World,*

387–96. Herman Bennett has examined the "pervasiveness with which European chroniclers and travel writers used Iberian royal tropes to describe the earliest encounters with Africans," arguing that scholars must consider European conceptualization of African sovereignty and statecraft as key to the emergence of colonialism and slavery; see Bennett, *African Kings and Black Slaves*, 2–3.

9. On visual representation in colonial travel literature, see especially Gaudio, *Engraving the Savage;* and Voigt and Brancaforte, "Traveling Illustrations." On the geographic imagination in colonial-era travel writing in the Americas, see Brückner, ed., *Early American Cartographies*, and Bauer, *The Cultural Geography.*

10. On De Bry, see Gaudio, *Engraving* (especially the introduction and chapters 1 and 2); and special issue of *Journal of Medieval and Early Modern Studies* edited by Maureen Quilligan, "Theodor De Bry's Voyages to the New and Old Worlds."

11. Bry et al., *Americae nona & postrema pars* . . . Plate XVIII, "QVOMODO HOLLANDI REGVLVM QVENDAM LITTORALIS tractus Guinaea inuiserint." The image is in book 9 under a section titled *Idaea vera et genvina praecipvarvm historiarvm omnivm, vt et varorvm ritvvm.*

12. On African fabrics from early modern central African kingdoms, see Fromont, "Common Threads," 842.

13. Woodfield discusses many of the issues addressed here. See Woodfield, *English Musicians,* on "musical diplomacy," 95–96, and on Mahu's voyage, 168–75.

14. While trumpeters were common on English and Dutch ships, Spanish and Portuguese sometimes used other instruments, including whistles and pipes, for similar purposes. On trumpeters' role at sea, see Woodfield, *English Musicians,* 51–74.

15. Behn, *Oroonoko,* 88.

16. On African musicians, Islam, and musical circulation to Moorish Iberia, see Sublette, *Cuba and Its Music,* chapter 1; and regarding the audible resonances of these histories in modern music, see Mackey, "Cante Moro." On the origins and spread of African lutes during the same time period, see Dubois, *The Banjo,* 25–31.

17. See Spohr, "'Mohr und Trompeter.'" On John Blanke, see Kaufmann, *Black Tudors,* 7–31; and Michael Ohajuru, *The John Blanke Project* (https://www .johnblanke.com/).

18. This detail about the King of Fatema is discussed in Thornton, *Cultural History of the Atlantic World,* 387. Thornton focuses specifically on the similarities between the patronage traditions in Europe and parts of West and Central Africa.

19. Lopes and Pigafetta, *Relatione del reame di Congo.* My direct citations are from the English version translated by Abraham Hartwell and printed by Iohn Wolfe in London in 1597, *Report of the Kingdome of Congo.* There is another

translation, from 1881, by Margarite Hutchinson. Both translations have their strengths and weaknesses. Ultimately, I chose to rely primarily on the earlier source.

20. Fromont, *Art of Conversion,* 26. Fromont's book is crucial reading on the subject of music in the Kingdom of Kongo and Atlantic trade and cultural exchange during the era.

21. The image comes from the original Italian edition of the narrative. The English translation includes a poor copy of the original, far less rich in style and detail. References to Mediterranean antiquity were common in European discussions of African politics and culture at the time, and they had to do with the way Europeans periodized African history. Whereas later generations of Europeans would resort to primitivizing narratives of Africa as pre-civilization, in the early modern period, references to civilizations in antiquity were more common. On early modern notions of antiquity in relation to global music, see Irving, "Ancient Greeks."

22. Lopes and Pigafetta, *Report of the Kingdome of Congo,* 49–50.

23. Fromont, *Art of Conversion,* 39–47.

24. Lopes and Pigafetta, *Report of the Kingdome of Congo,* 50–51.

25. Merolla da Sorrento, "Voyage to Congo," 561–62. The original Italian edition is Merolla, *Breue, e succinta relatione del viaggio nel regno di Congo nell' Africa meridionale.* The Italian edition contains an engraving that displays a lunga and other instruments (see p. 55). Describing the lunga and ivory horn the English translation of Merolla reads, "There are a sort of trumpets made of the finest ivory, being hollowed throughout in divers pieces, and are in all about as long as a man's arm; the lower mouth is sufficient to receive one hand, which by contracting and dilating of the fingers forms the sound; there being no other holes in the body as in our flutes or hautboys. A concert of these is generally six or four to one pipe. The *longa* (which is made of two iron bells joined by a piece of wire archwise) is founded by striking it with a little stick: Both these are carried also before princes, and that especially when they publish their pleasure to the people, being used as the trumpet is with us" (561–62).

26. Lopes and Pigafetta, *Report of the Kingdome of Congo,* 48–51.

27. On trumpeters' communication at sea, see Woodfield, *English Musicians,* chapter 4, "Signalling and Ceremonial Duties," 51–71.

28. Fromont, *The Art of Conversion,* 21–26. On the circulation to Brazil and transformation of *sangamentos* in the New World, see Dewulf, "From the Calendas," 21; and also Dewulf, "*Sangamentos* on Congo Square?: Kongolese Wrriors, Brotherhood Kings, and Mardi Gras Indians in New Orleans" in Fromont, ed., *Afro-Catholic Festivals.*

29. On knotlike Kongo designs, see Fromont, *Art of Conversion,* 76, and figure 21 in her book.

30. I have seen similar horns and carved ivory tusks in other museum collections, including the Museum Volkenkunde in Leiden, the Netherlands, where several carved tusks from the nineteenth century depict European colonial violence.

The art form appears to be linked to the history of European trade along the Atlantic coasts of Africa.

31. Corbin, *Village Bells;* and Rath, *How Early America Sounded,* chapter 2, "From the Sound of Things."

32. The quotations are respectively from Michael Angelo of Gattini, "Curious and Exact Account," 622; and Jobson, *Golden Trade,* 136.

33. Sarah Eyerly makes a similar point about the control of soundscapes in early North America, relating to the geographic boundaries enforced by settler and Native communities. Eyerly, *Moravian Soundscapes,* 13.

34. Petal Samuel addresses the long arc of sonic racism in Caribbean slave societies and how it persists into the postcolonial era. See forthcoming work and Samuel, "Timing to Descant." See also Gordon, "What Mr. Jefferson Didn't Hear," on sonic oppression under colonialism and slavery and particularly how white authorities misheard African diasporic performance in the Americas.

35. Charry, *Mande Music,* 109–10. Charry posits "griot" may be a derivation of an Arabic word "qawal." More accurate modern terminology includes "jali" (Fulbe), "gewel" (Wolof), and "jeli" (Maninka). Charry sites Alexis de Saint-Lô's *Relation du voyage du Cap-Verd* for early use of the term "guiriot."

36. See map 4, "Distribution of Griots in West Africa," in Charry, *Mande Music,* 108.

37. John Thornton also explains the overlaps between systems of musical patronage as key to musical encounter and change in the era. See Thornton, *Cultural History,* 365–96.

38. Jobson, *Golden Trade,* 105.

39. Jobson, *Golden Trade,* 105–8.

40. See the multi-media oeuvre of Tunde Jegede, composer, cellist, and Kora player in the Griot tradition whose discussions of African classical music influenced me to consider the similarities between European and African court musicianship in the period (www.tundejegede.org). We met at two conferences hosted in conjunction with the Yale Center for British Art, Historic Royal Palaces, and Hendrix and Handel House on the theme of Black Music in Eighteenth Century London.

41. Richard Jobson interprets the unique burial rites of griot to signify rejection by the larger community: "yet so basely do they esteem of the player, that when any of them die, they do not vouchsafe them burial, as other people have; but set his dead corpse upright in a hollow tree." He decried their spiritual beliefs, as well. Jobson, *Golden Trade,* 107–8.

42. Barbot, "Description of the Coasts," 55. This quote is from the English translation published in Churchill's *Voyages.*

43. Lopes and Pigafetta, *Report of the Kingdome of Congo,* 111–12.

44. The shift from early modern European investment in African sovereignty to racialized perceptions of Africa and Africans is the subject of Herman Bennett's *African Kings and Black Slaves.*

45. Southern, *Music of Black Americans,* 4–5; Epstein, *Sinful Tunes,* 4.

46. Jobson, *Golden Trade,* 136. Another example of English publications about the region include what is arguably the first slave narrative. Ayuba Diallo was the son of a powerful imam in Bundu, Senegal, who was sold into slavery and eventually made his way back home. His story was written in a narrative by Thomas Bluett, *Some Memoirs of the Life of Job* (1734).

47. See Charry, *Mande Music,* 9–11, on Mande music history and the bala; and 40–43, and on King Sunjata and the instrument's role in the foundation of the Malian empire.

48. On buzzy timbres in African music, see Driver, "Buzz Aesthetic and Mande Music."

49. Jobson, *Golden Trade,* 105–8.

50. Lopes and Pigafetta, *Report of the Kingdome of Congo,* 182.

51. Lopes and Pigafetta, *Report of the Kingdome of Congo.* The sonic descriptors in Italian are "le quali mádano fuori tintinno di varie maniere" and "un strepito intermisto." I am grateful to Susanna Ferlito for translating the passage for me and for helping me to discern the most useful translation to rely on here. Lopes and Pigafetta, *Relatione del reame di Congo,* 68.

52. Matthews, *Voyage to the River Sierra-Leone,* vii.

53. Matthews, *Voyage to the River Sierra-Leone,* vii, 105–6. An accompanying illustration portrays numerous instruments. Matthews' narrative was written in a different era, but his observations are still helpful because detailed portrayals of African music are relatively rare for much of the eighteenth century.

54. On African, Iberian, and Arab exchange connecting to tambourine-like instruments, see Fryer, *Rhythms of Resistance,* 2.

55. The origins of the bala are closely linked to blacksmithing, and as Eric Charry argues, the instruments construction and playing technique are connected to the craft. Charry, *Mande Music,* 10.

56. Green, *Fistful of Shells,* 115.

57. On theories of sound and vibration see especially Eidsheim, *Sensing Sound;* and Goodman, *Sonic Warfare.*

58. The idea of the "music of the spheres" or *musica universalis* hearkened to classical philosophers, and especially Pythagoras, who developed a mathematical theorization of music that still today influences European tuning.

59. Steven Feld's concept of "acoustemology" addresses the capacities of human hearing to attune to sonic specificities according to cultural and environmental surroundings, especially his work on the soundworlds of the Bosavi people of Papau, New Guinea. See Feld, "Acoustemology."

Studies of neuroplasticity within the field of audiology and specifically cochlear technology extensively explore the adaptivity of human hearing to evolving stimuli. For an explanation and critique of the discourse of auditory neuroplasticity in relation to cochlear therapies, see Mauldin, "Precarious Plasticity."

60. Mack Hagood makes transparent the production of race, class, and otherness through audio technology and the role of Western classical music for prominent tech corporations like Bose; see Hagood, "Quiet Comfort." See also Sterne, *MP3,* on the role of Western listening preferences in the laboratory development of audio technologies. To be sure, many musicians deploy modern technology in continuance of Black musical aesthetics. African diasporic artists have been innovators in the realm of music technology more generally. Examples include Dub Reggae artists, DJs, and electric guitarists like Jimi Hendrix. For further analysis of cultural politics of race, sound technology, and Black music, see Chude-Sokei, *Sound of Culture;* Jaji, *Africa in Stereo;* and Weheliye, *Phonographies.*

61. Driver, "Buzz Aesthetic and Mande Music," 103.

62. I wish to thank Louise Meintjes for bringing the significance of buzzing to my attention. Her work on musical production and recording in South Africa broadly influences my understanding of music, sound, collaboration, and technology. See Meintjes, *Sound of Africa!.*

63. See Pablo F. Gómez, *Experiential Caribbean,* for a study of experientiality and African knowledge systems in the Americas. Martin Munro's *Different Drummers* is relevant to much of my discussion here. Munro focuses on Western perceptions of rhythm and blackness in a deep history of rhythm in the circum-Caribbean, beginning in the late-eighteenth century. See especially the introduction on sensation, sound, and "rhythm."

64. On early modern early modern notions of antiquity in relation to global music, see Irving, "Ancient Greeks."

65. Jobson, *Golden Trade,* 105.

66. Stoever, *Sonic Color Line,* 7. On racialized sonic perception, see also Eidsheim, *Race of Sound.*

67. For a gloss of the term "fetish" and its use by Europeans, see Monique Allewaert, "Super Fly," 463. As an example of derogatory language describing indigenous African ritual, Girolamo Merolla described a performance as an "untunable discord of a great number of odd musical instruments" that composed a "hellish harmony." Merolla da Sorrento, "Voyage to Congo, and Several Other Countries Chiefly in Southern Africk," 561–62.

68. Mark, "Fetishers, 'Marybuckes' and the Christian Norm," 91.

69. Jobson, *Golden Trade,* 105–8. On Jobson's use of the term "Marybucke," see again, Mark, "Fetishers," 95. My interpretation of the word "changeling" is based on the various *Oxford English Dictionary Online* definitions of the word connected to the usage of the term in the early modern period. The term was at often used to refer to a child stolen by fairies, but it was also used to refer to people with intellectual disabilities.

70. "Changeling, n. and adj." OED Online. September 2021. Oxford University Press. https://www-oed-com.proxy.library.vcu.edu/view/Entry/30479?redirectedFrom=changeling.

71. Fromont, ed., *Afro-Catholic Festivals;* Fromont, *Art of Conversion.* On influence of Afro-Catholocism across the Atlantic, see also Dewulf, *Afro-Atlantic Catholics;* Valerio, *Sovereign Joy;* and Voigt, *Spectacular Wealth.*

72. On church music and African Catholicism see also Thornton, *Cultural History of the Atlantic World,* 388–99.

73. Merolla da Sorrento, "Voyage to Congo and Several Other Countries," 590. In the same collection, another Capuchin describes a Catholic mass that is directly followed by music and dancing rooted in Kongo tradition. See Michael Angelo of Gattina, "A Curious and Exact Account."

74. I am very grateful to Cécile Fromont for alerting me to the existence of this illustration, which is available online in the following collection: "Missione in prattica. Padri cappucini ne Regni di Congo, Angola et adiacenti," Central Public Library, Turin, ms. 457, https://bct.comune.torino.it/gallerie/missione-prattica.

75. Uring, *History,* 43–44.

76. Uring generally wrote favorably of music he witnessed, with the exception of religious and ritual performance. Uring, *History,* 46.

77. Uring, *History,* 45–46. I am grateful to Sarah Balakrishnan for raising the possibility that the practice may have been about spiritual deflection of unwelcome spirits rather than, or perhaps in addition to, grief over the child's death.

78. Again, see Stoever, *Sonic Color Line,* especially the introduction, and on the deadly consequences of white sonic racism, 2–3; also forthcoming work by Andy McGraw on sound and policing, "AudibleRVA: Mapping Sonic and Affective Geographies in Richmond, Virginia"; and forthcoming work by Petal Samuel on sonic oppression in the Caribbean.

79. Equiano, *Interesting Narrative,* 28–29.

80. Gronniosaw writes of his experiences crossing West African wilderness: "At night we secured ourselves from the wild beasts by making fires all around us; we and our camels kept within the circle, or we must have been torn to pieces by the Lyons . . ."; see Gronniosaw, *Narrative of the Most Remarkable Particulars,* 5.

81. Jobson, *Golden Trade,* 58.

82. Jobson, *Golden Trade,* 138.

83. Jobson, *Golden Trade,* 140–41.

84. Jobson, *Golden Trade,* 142.

85. Jobson, *Golden Trade,* 140.

86. Jobson, *Golden Trade,* 145.

87. Stoever, *Sonic Color Line,* 1. Stoever builds on W. E. B. Du Bois's theory of the color line, developed in Du Bois, *Souls of Black Folk.*

2. Circulating African Musical Knowledge to the Americas

1. I am not alone in turning to the histories of instruments in the examination of early African Atlantic music. Studies of the banjo in particular, have created significant inroads in the telling histories of early Black music. See especially

Dubois, *The Banjo;* Gaddy, *Well of Souls;* DjeDje, "The (Mis)Representation"; and Munro, *Different Drummers.*

2. I take inspiration here from Laurent Dubois' *The Banjo* and Kristina Gaddy's *Well of Souls,* both of which follow the story of the banjo to tell an expansive story about the origins of Black American music.

3. On Barbados history at the time of Ligon's arrival, see Kupperman, ed., *A True and Exact,* 1–35. On the status of Barbados and the rise of sugar slavery when Macow and Ligon lived there, see also Menard, *Sweet Negotiations,* 31.

4. Kupperman, ed., *A True and Exact,* 4–6.

5. Ligon, *A True and Exact,* 48–49.

6. Kupperman, Epstein, and Nunn all note Ligon's misinterpretation of Macow's instrument design. Nunn, "A Great Addition," 34–35; D. Epstein, *Sinful Tunes,* 57; Kupperman, ed., *A True and Exact,* 100n119.

7. Ligon, *A True and Exact,* 48–49.

8. This is, of course, what Michel Rolph-Trouillot made abundantly clear in *Silencing the Past,* by explaining the way powerful authors and narrators make historical truths invisible.

9. On various types of West African xylophones, see Maxwell, "West Africa: When the Xylophone Speaks," 51; and Agawu, *The African Imagination,* 98–99.

10. On xylophones and the Sundiata/Sunjata, see especially Charry, *Mande Music,* 133–45; and Maxwell, "West Africa," 58.

11. Charry writes, "Frame xylophones in West Africa are very similar to each other, and it is not too difficult to imagine a more unified West African xylophone culture sometime in the distant past." Charry, *Mande Music,* 135.

12. On the origins of the term balafon, again see Charry, *Mande Music,* 139. See also Bae, "The Distribution," 23.

13. On the influence of Kongo Christians on African diasporic culture across Latin America and the Atlantic World more broadly, again see Fromont, ed., *Afro-Catholic Festivals.* I discuss the subject further in chapter 4.

14. Jobson, *Golden Trade,* 107.

15. Froger, *Relation of a Voyage,* 561–62. Froger's narrative was translated into English and published before being published in French as François Froger, *Relation d'un voyage* (1700). Eric Charry describes the image as the earliest known pictorial representation of a Mande bala. Charry, *Mande Music,* 135.

16. Michael Angelo of Gattina, "A Curious and Exact Account," 622–23. Apparently, Portuguese friar João dos Santos also described African xylophones by comparing them to organs in 1586. See Agawu, *The African Imagination,* 68–70. Agawu cites secondary sources translating and transcribing the original, which appears to be João dos Santos, *Ethiopia Oriental, e Varia historia de cousas, notaueis do Oriente* (1609).

17. Traditionally, spider egg sacs were used as vibrational membranes on the gourds resonators of balas. Today, paper is more commonly used. See Charry, *Mande Music,* 139, and Maxwell, "West Africa," 62.

18. Ligon, *A True and Exact*, 46. David Eltis affirms the accuracy of Ligon's perception of the enslaved populations ethnicities through a study of relevant shipping records, see Eltis, *The Rise of African Slavery*, 246–47. "Guinny" (Guinea), "Buinny" (Benin), and the "River of Gambia" refer to the slave trading regions of West Africa, whereas Angola referred at the time broadly to the Kingdoms of Loango, Angola, and Kongo. "Cutchew" is a less familiar term that one scholar believes to be Cacheu in what is now Guinnea-Bissau. See Roper, *The English Empire*, 134.

19. Ligon, *A True and Exact*, 47.

20. On twin taboos and the history of missionizing and colonialism in Igbo territories, see Bastian, "The Demon Superstition," especially p. 18 on the ritual killing of mothers. On Yamba twin taboos and rituals in Cameroon see Gufler, "Yamba Twin Ritual."

21. Bae, "The Distribution," 16. These details are worth noting, but also very tenuous. I am very grateful to Otosirieze Obi-Young for consulting with me on the subject of Igbo xylophones.

22. See Morgan, *Laboring Women*.

23. Ligon, *A True and Exact*, 47.

24. Ligon, *A True and Exact*, 43–44.

25. Ligon, *A True and Exact*, 48.

26. See especially Nunn, "'A Great Addition.'" Erich Nunn reads Macow's and Ligon's musical encounter as exemplary of the exchanges between Black and white musicians that became foundational to American music and race in the wake of Atlantic slavery. We interpret the scene itself very similarly, although whereas Nunn views their encounter as an early indicator of a long-standing discourse, I examine the exchange for what it can teach us about Macow and Ligon's own historical moment. On Macow and Ligon see also Epstein, *Spiritual Tunes*, 26–27; 57.

27. Ethnomusicologists of Africa seem to be some of the only Western music scholars writing about music history of the region before the twentieth century. For example, Eric Charry explores early modern records extensively in *Mande Music*. I hope that future scholars, especially those from Africa and the Caribbean, will be able to find some use in my book because I have no doubt that they can and will offer a much richer understanding of the histories I touch on here.

28. Maxwell, "West Africa," 62. On "bigness" and "littleness" and other conceptualizations of instrument tuning and construction, see also Agawu, *The African Imagination*, 82–83.

29. Ligon, *A True and Exact*, 49.

30. Maxwell, "West Africa," 61–62; Ligon, *A True and Exact*, 99–100.

31. Ligon, *A True and Exact*, 49.

32. Maxwell goes on to explain, "Computer-generated analysis of this phenomenon shows that this 'hidden' pitch is intentionally created through skillful tuning techniques to produce an acoustic behavior known as beating. It allows

the players more melodic flexibility within the constraints of their fixed-keyed instrument so that if a C-sharp is desired it can be played although it does not physically exist on the actual keyboard." Maxwell, "West Africa," 63.

33. Dena Epstein cites the two 1770s Virginia sources mentioning balafons, noting the spellings "barrafou" "barrafoo." Epstein, *Sinful Tunes*, 57. William Young's narrative is printed at the end of Bryan Edwards, *An Historical Survey*, 276.

34. Dubois, *The Banjo*. See especially, chapter two, "The First African Instrument," 49–91 on the emergence of the instrument's identity in the Americas and for details about its construction and adaptivity to American materials.

35. On wood-curing for xylophone construction, see Charry, *Mande Music*, 138.

36. David Evans, in a study of "survivals of African instruments" notes the way that enslaved musicians repurposed found objects and reimagined traditional African instruments with new American materials. For instance, bamboo panpipes played within African American communities in the United States are known as "quills," likely because similar instruments are constructed using the quills of a very large species of porcupine in Africa. Evans, "The Reinterpretation," 383.

37. I am thinking, here, of West African "talking drums" that mimic speech sounds.

38. Rich Rath suggests that a fiddle technique from parts of the Southern U.S. known as "beating straws" or "fiddlesticks" also was born out of restrictions on drumming. In the second half of the eighteenth century and throughout the nineteenth, Black fiddlers became prominent musicians across the plantation Caribbean and North America. The "fiddlesticks" technique involves a second performer who stands to the side of the fiddler and taps out rhythms on the headstock using knitting needles or sticks. Rath, *How Early America Sounded*, 92–93. On Black fiddlers, see also, Jaqcueline Codgell DjeDje, "The (Mis)Representation," and forthcoming work by Maria Ryan, "White Ears Listening for Black Pedagogy."

39. Gilroy, *The Black Atlantic*, 78.

40. See Johnson, "Notes on Pans." Calypsonian Roger Gibbs told me in conversation that many of his musician peers believe steelpan emerged from Kongo drumming techniques.

41. See Minton, "West African Fiddles," 311, referring specifically to blues musician, Big Joe Williams.

42. For historically informed theoretical work on Black aesthetics and technological innovation, see especially Weheliye, *Phonographies;* and Chude-Sokei, *The Sound of Culture.*

43. Sounds travel across instruments in other traditions as well. For example, Irish and Scottish fiddling styles both replicate the sounds of the bagpipes.

44. In a similar vein, Lisa Gitelman argues that reading and writing practices were foundational to the way inventors like Edison conceived of possibilities

for inscribing sound into surfaces for the purpose of recording. See Sterne, *The Audible Past*; and Gitelman, *Scripts, Grooves*.

45. On African techniques and aesthetics influencing North American fiddling rhythm, see Jabbour, "In Search of the Source."

3. Plantation Gatherings and the Foundation of Black American Music

1. On death and dying in the eighteenth-century Caribbean, and Jamaica in particular, see Brown, *Reaper's Garden*.

2. In English at the time, a "kit" usually referred to a fiddle, but in describing African instruments the term probably referred to a small gourd fiddle or a strummed instrument like the banjo. I'm grateful to Pete Ross, luthier and specialist in the historical reconstruction of gourd banjos, for pointing this out to me.

3. Taylor, *Jamaica in 1687*, 269. For more on Taylor's life and writing, see the introduction to the published version of Taylor's manuscript, which was edited by David Buisseret in 2008. I cite the 2008 edition.

4. On firelight and evening musical customs in Africa, see Gronniosaw, *Narrative*, 5; and Jobson, *Golden Trade*, 58.

5. Discussing enslaved musical life in Barbados, Jerome Handler and Charlotte Frisbie also argue for the significance of Sundays and Christian feast days to the emergence of African diasporic tradition. They corroborate representations in travelogues with plantation records from the late eighteenth century to affirm that enslaved people were reprieved from work regularly in the fashion I describe. See Handler and Frisbie, "Aspects of Slave Life," 10, 27.

6. On African influences and Spanish Caribbean settlements and on Africans in musical trades, see Wheat, *Atlantic Africa and the Spanish Caribbean*, 12.

7. Cécile Fromont and Michael Iyanaga argue for the centrality of Afro-Catholic performance to the creation of Black Atlantic tradition, emphasizing in particular the role of the Central African Catholic Kingdom of Kongo in setting the stage for Black Atlantic celebration in the early modern era. Fromont and Iyanga, "Introduction." On Afro-Iberian Catholicism shaping Latin American and Caribbean tradition see also Voigt, *Spectacular Wealth*; and Dewulf, "From the *Calendas* to the *Calenda*"; and Dewulf, *From the Kingdom of Kongo*.

8. The origins of the 1619 African captives were discussed in a talk given by Michael Guasco, "1619: Rethinking the History of Africans and Slavery in Early America," held at Virginia Commonwealth University, January 31, 2019. Guasco further addresses the broad influence of Spanish colonial practice on early English slavery in *Slaves and Englishmen*, especially 80–120 and 195–226.

9. Christmas, for instance, was a time after harvest and before planting, and Pentecost occurred in some climates after first crop planting but before the extensive demands of the high growing season. Both of these holidays became an important time for African gatherings. I am grateful to Kristina Gaddy for bringing this to my attention.

10. For example, William Dickson described the differences between urban and rural gatherings in 1770s Barbados. Dickson, *Letters on Slavery*, 93.

11. Dena Epstein cites several descriptions of Sunday performances in *Sinful Tunes and Spirituals*, 38–42, noting that some observers in colonial North America decried the fact that the celebrations took place on the "Lord's Day." On the subject of Sunday gatherings in North America, see also Thompson, *Ring Shout, Wheel About*, 74–79. Regarding gatherings in colonial Philadelphia and Virginia, see also Southern, *Music of Black Americans*, 47–48. On Sunday gatherings in Mid-Atlantic cities, see Johnson, "Profane Language," 259. On urban Sunday gatherings in the eighteenth-century Anglo-Atlantic colonies, see Dickinson, *Almost Dead*, 86–114. And on Protestantism and slavery in the Caribbean, see Gerbner, *Christian Slavery*.

12. Ligon, *A True and Exact*, 48.

13. Sloane, *Voyage to the Islands*, lii.

14. Taylor, *Jamaica in 1687*, 269.

15. Charry, *Mande Music*, 93. This tradition is possibly changing. World-renowned contemporary musician Sona Jobarteh proudly claims to be "the first female within this tradition to become a professional virtuoso on the kora." https://Sonajobarteh.com.

16. See also Diana Paton, "Driveress and the Nurse," for information about enslaved women's domestic labor, especially childcare. She provides a model for how to interpret limited but significant evidence surrounding women's labor under slavery in the British Caribbean.

17. On gender roles in West Africa, see Morgan, *Laboring Women*, chapter 2, especially 62–63, and on women and African marketplaces and on transformation of these economic roles under slavery, 146.

18. Morgan, *Laboring Women*, 146.

19. On enslaved women, food production, and urban markets in the Atlantic world, see Young, "Nourishing Networks"; and Olwell, "Loose, Idle and Disorderly."

20. Dirk Valkenburg, *Slave Dance*, ca. 1707, housed at the Statens Museum for Kunst, Copenhagen; Zacharias Wagenaer, *Slaves Dancing*, housed at the Staatliche Kunstsammlungen, Dresden. On these paintings and the portrayals of African embodiment, see Brienen, "Embodying Race and Pleasure."

21. Sloane, *Voyage to the Islands*, xlviii.

22. Johnson, *Wicked Flesh*, 12.

23. Sloane. *Voyage to the Islands*, l–li.

24. Sloane, *Voyage to the Islands*, l.

25. There are earlier sources from the Americas that bear the mark of African musical influence. There are also records connected to African performers living in Iberia and elsewhere. The transcriptions inspired other documentarians of the Caribbean to address musical life in later works, but it was nearly one hundred years before another notated example of diasporic music from the British

Caribbean or North America enters the record (see chapter 6 of this book). I have done my best to gather all notated examples of plantation-era music from before 1800, but it is entirely possible that there are examples from the Spanish or Dutch Caribbean or other slave societies of which I am unaware.

26. In an earlier article, I discuss the musical notation extensively, as well as the mediating effects of representing enslaved performances in Western notation. See Lingold, "Peculiar Animations."

27. Rath, "African Music," 707. I cite Rath's 1993 article in discussing his interpretation of the pieces, but he also revisits much of this information in his monograph *How Early America Sounded*. A 2008 blog post, also titled "African Music in Seventeenth-Century Jamaica," briefly discusses the pieces and includes a recording in which Rath performs the pieces on mbira using midi technology. *Way Music* (blog), January 17, 2008, http://way.net/waymusic/?p=13.

28. Taylor, *Jamaica in 1687*, 270. Emphasis mine.

29. Sloane, *Voyage to the Islands*, xlviii–xlix.

30. Sloane, *Voyage to the Islands*, xlviii–xlix.

31. Dubois, *The Banjo*. On Baptiste's notation in Slone, and the image documenting the banjo, see especially pp. 59–71.

32. Rath, "African Music," 716; emphasis mine.

33. I am indebted to David Garner for noting the circularity of the melody in our ongoing conversations about the pieces while developing www.musical passage.org.

34. Vincent Brown discusses the complex significations of the term "Koromanti," often spelled "Coromantee." Vincent Brown, *Tacky's Revolt*, 90–91, 274–75n14.

35. In an online conversation about *Musical Passage: A Voyage to 1688 Jamaica* (musicalpassage.org), the journal *archipelagos* invited several scholars to discuss the website and the historical source that inspired it using the web-commenting platform *hypothes.is*. During the exchange, Kenneth Bilby, Jessica Krug, and Richard Rath had an interesting exchange regarding the complex possible meanings of the term Koromanti in 1688, and the legacies in Afro-Caribbean communities in the present. For more information and a link to the thread, see Dubois et al., "Caribbean Digital."

36. For more on African Muslims in the Americas, see Diouf, *Servants of Allah*, and on musical practices, see especially 270–75.

37. I am grateful to Matthew J. Smith for suggesting ululation as a possible meaning here.

38. Sloane, *Voyage to the Islands*, lvi.

39. Sloane, *Voyage to the Islands*, cxxiv.

40. On African medicine, its influence on planters, and connections with religion, see Wisecup, *Medical Encounters*, especially chapter 4, 127–60; and Parrish, *American Curiosity*, especially her discussion of the Surinam healer Graman

Kwasi or Quasi, in chapter 7, "African Magi, Slave Poisoners," 328–29. On Sloane and African and Indigenous American medicine, see Delbourgo, *Collecting the World,* especially chapters 2 and 3.

41. Early records of Myalism come from writing by Edward Long, an influential Jamaican enslaver who wrote a lengthy history of the island. He described Myalism in a tirade against Africanist efforts to resist white authority through spiritual means that he characterized as mere chicanery. He was virulently racist and pro-slavery in his writings, which also serve as the earliest written documentation of Myalism. Long, *History of Jamaica,* 2:416–17. On Myalism, see also Schuler, "Myalism and the African Religious Tradition in Jamaica." On modern Myal performance rituals, see Kenneth Bilby, "Surviving Secularization," 189–92. On Obeah, see Paton, *Cultural Politics of Obeah.* On the term "Obeah" and its meaning for enslaved people in contrast to the white observers who wrote about it, see Wisecup and Jaudon, "On Knowing and Not Knowing about Obeah."

42. Again, see Brown, *Reaper's Garden,* on the specter of death and dying in Jamaica. Brown writes extensively about burial rights of the enslaved, drawing from numerous sources (65–76). He also includes an excerpt of notation that attempted to portray a melody from a funereal song that was published in Alexander Barclay, *A Practical View of the Present State of Slavery in the West Indies* (London, 1826), 71. On funeral rites of the enslaved, see also Epstein, *Sinful Tunes,* 63–66.

43. Equiano, *Interesting Narrative,* 28–29; Uring, *History,* 46.

44. Planters, including Ligon, wrote about the perceived importance of blending African language groups and cultures in a given plantation population (Ligon, *A True and Exact,* 46). The idea was that doing so would make it difficult for the enslaved to communicate and coordinate revolt. That said, because of the logistical realities of the slave trade, there were still predominant groups of individual nations in many Caribbean settings, as Gwendolyn Midlo Hall documents extensively throughout *Slavery and African Ethnicities in the Americas.*

45. Taylor, *Jamaica in 1687,* 272.

46. On beliefs about returning to Africa after death, and especially suicide, see Handler and Lange, *Plantation Slavery in Barbados,* 211. The entire chapter "The Mortuary Patterns of Plantation Slaves" (171–215) is relevant here. Hans Sloane described similar practices in *Voyage to the Islands,* xlviii. See also Hughes, *The Natural History of Barbados,* 16n21.

47. For example, Toni Morrison writes about the mythology of the flying African in the novel *Song of Solomon,* citing the stories she heard as a child as inspiration for the narrative she created. The traditional gospel song "I'll Fly Away" about passage to heavenly realms is another North American referent to beliefs and stories rooted in this early era of enslavement. On the breadth and strength of the myth in Caribbean and African diasporic art and culture, see also McDaniel, "The Flying Africans."

48. On suicide and slavery, see Snyder, *Power to Die*. On suicides in the context of Middle Passage specifically, see Muskateem, *Slavery at Sea,* 106–30. Muskateem also discusses the role of music, particularly drumming, aboard slave ships, 119–21.

49. Taylor describes the dismembering practice in *Jamaica in 1687,* 273. Dismemberment was also a punishment for the living, commonly cited in portrayals of Caribbean slavery, including in Voltaire's fictional *Candide* (originally published in 1759), which depicts a dejected enslaved man from Suriname who is missing an arm and a leg. Voltaire, *Candide,* 48.

50. Uring, *History of the Voyages,* 46–47.

51. Sloane, *Voyage to the Islands,* lii.

52. Epstein, *Sinful Tunes,* 28.

53. See K. Gaddy, *Well of Souls,* 120–21.

54. See Smith, *Stono,* for multiple sources from the period about the Stono uprising as well as interpretations by historians.

55. On the significance of drumming in African tradition and the suppression of drums in the wake of uprisings, see Rath, "Drums and Power"; and Sullivan, "Talking Drums." On the prohibitions, see also Epstein, *Sinful Tunes,* 58–60, 62.

56. Also discussed in Thompson, *Ring Shout,* 99–103.

57. Brown, *Tacky's Revolt,* 172–73. On musical celebration during the uprising, 138; and on laws passed to curb future uprisings by repressing gatherings, 213–15.

58. Behn, *Oroonoko,* 260. In the narrative the title character, Oroonoko, also known as Caeser, an enslaved African prince, sends his musicians to entertain drunken planters while undertaking the revolt.

59. "An Account of a Remarkable Conspiracy formed by a Negro in the Island of St. Domingo," originally published in *Mercure de France* in 1787 and written by Monsieur de C. I used the English translation originally published in *Literary Magazine & British Review* (1789), later appearing in *New-York Magazine* (1796), and published by Duncan Faherty and Ed White on their web collection of early American literature *Just Teach One,* 4. A record of song incanted by Makandal's wife Brigitte and others survives in the memoir of his executioner, as discussed in Allewaert, "Super Fly," 465. Allewaert's essay also includes in depth discussion of numerous histories of Makandal, by Western professional historians and more regionalized oral and literary history as well. On African medicine and the Haitian Revolution, see Weaver, *Medical Revolutionaries.*

60. Dubois, *Avengers of the New World,* 100–102.

61. One short story from the post-revolutionary period emphasizes the lambi. Nau, "Le Lambi."

62. On "San Domingo," the Shand uprising, and music in Trinidad during the era, see Cowley, *Carnival, Canboulay and Calypso,* 13–16. I quote his version of the lyrics and his translation. There is some debate about whether or not the Trinidad plot was real, or if in fact it may even have been encouraged by Haitian leader Jean-Jacques Dessalines himself. For an extensive study of the surviving

records around the planned uprising in Trinidad as well as a thorough investigation of scholarship on the event, see Jenson, *Beyond the Slave Narrative,* 166–67. I am indebted to Roger Gibbs for discussing the song's history with me and for sharing his recorded rendition.

63. Ligon, *A True and Exact,* 48.

64. Blome, *A Description,* 90. In addition to drawing from earlier sources, Blome also apparently borrowed from the notes of Thomas Lynch, governor of Jamaica at the time.

65. Oldmixon, *The British Empire,* vol. 2., 123–24.

66. Leslie, *New History of Jamaica,* 310.

67. John Stedman's narrative is especially useful for understanding this process because his journals, manuscript, and published memoir all survive. The manuscripts are held at the James Ford Bell Library at the University of Minnesota. In their edited edition of Stedman's manuscript, Richard Price and Sally Price discuss the editorial changes that were made when Stedman's 1790 manuscript was transformed into a 1796 publication that sanitized much of the original content. The entire Stedman collection is available digitally, but for a readable version of Stedman's handwritten journals, see Stedman, *Journal of John Gabriel Stedman.*

68. Sloane's discussion is on the third-to-last page of the Preface, which is not numbered. He accused John de Laet of plagiarizing Francisco Hernández de Toledo, a court physician from Spain who traveled to Mexico in the sixteenth century and conducted natural historical observations, much in the same vein as Sloane.

69. Morgan, *Laboring Women,* 49. Morgan's study examines portrayals of enslaved women, citing many of the same sources key to my study, and Ligon in particular. Much of what she identifies about the impact of travel accounts on the emergence of racism rings true for portrayals of musical life.

70. John Taylor wrote that "on Saturday nights their masters allow 'em some rum and sugar, to make 'em a bowle of punch withal." Taylor, *Jamaica in 1687,* 266. John Stedman also wrote about a "Grand Ball" in Suriname that was held quarterly, "where the master often contributing to the happiness by his presence, or at least by sending them a present of a few jugs of *kill devil* or new rum." *Narrative,* 540–41.

4. Race and Professional Musicianship in the Early Carribean

1. Sloane, *Voyage to the Islands,* l.

2. Dubois et al., *Musical Passage.* See also the review of *Musical Passage* in *sx archipelagos: a journal of Caribbean digital praxis,* 1 (June 2016), http://archipelagosjournal.org/issue01/musical-passage.html; and Lingold, "Digital Performance and the Musical Archive of Slavery."

3. This point is elaborated in Lingold, "Peculiar Animations," 629–30; and in Dubois, *The Banjo,* 62.

4. This interpretation differs significantly from that of Richard Cullen Rath, who opens his article with an account of the scene that led to the notation's

production based on the idea that Mr. Baptiste was a French musician visiting Jamaica, and who was brought to the musical gathering along with Hans Sloane by a planter. See Rath, "African music," 700–701. In a later work, however, Rath describes this account as being an "imaginative reconstruction" based on Sloane's text; see Rath, *How Early America Sounded,* 201n44. While building on Rath's work, my conclusions here about Baptiste's background and the circumstances through which he came to produce the notations are different. Rath continues to explore the music, also using digital means, which he discusses in Rath, "Ethnodigital Sonics and the Historical Imagination."

5. On Vicente Lusitano see Floyd et al., *Transformation of Black Music,* 50–52. I'd like to thank participants at the Atlantic Crossings symposium for extending my knowledge of music in the Iberian Atlantic and for alerting me to Lusitano's work. On performers of African descent in Brazil and Portugal, see Budasz, "Black Guitar-Players." For a detailed study of the cultural representation of Africans in early modern Spain, see Jones, *Staging Habla de Negros.*

6. Minette's story was memorialized in a novel by Vieux-Chauvet, *Dance sur le volcan* (1957); for an English translation see Vieux-Chauvet, *Dance on the Volcano,* trans. K. Glover (Brooklyn, 2016). On Minette's life, music, and influence, see Dubois, "Heroines of the Haitian revolution"; Camier, "A 'Free Artist of Color' in Late-Eighteenth-Century Saint-Domingue"; and Prest, "Parisian Palimpsests and Creole Creations." On the Chevalier de Saint-Georges, see Banat, *Chevalier de Saint-Georges.* I am grateful to Tunde Jegede for alerting me to the biography of Joseph Emidy (1775–1835). Emidy had been enslaved as a child, and lived in Brazil and later Portugal, where he was emancipated. Although there are records describing his performances and his remarkable life, none of his compositions survive. Jegede explores Emidy's life and work in a multimedia theatre piece, "Emidy: He Who Dared to Dream," http://www.tundejegede.org/emidy-he-who -dared-to-dream.

7. On Black fiddlers in North America see DjeDje, "The (Mis)Representation"; Epstein, *Sinful Tunes and Spirituals,* 112–20; Jabbour, "In Search of the Source of American Syncopation"; Rath, *How Early America Sounded,* 89–94; and Lingold, "Fiddling with Freedom."

8. On cultural exchange between Africa and Europe, see Kaufmann, *Black Tudors;* Bennett, *African Kings and Black Slaves;* Sublette, *Cuba and Its Music;* Smith et al., *Early Modern Black Diaspora Studies;* Smith, *Black Africans in the British Imagination;* Hall, *Things of Darkness.* On the subject of music specifically, see Spohr "Mohr und Trompeter"; and Thornton, *Cultural History of the Atlantic World,* 386–96.

9. On Enlightenment-era scientific racism, colonialism, and slavery, see Chaplin, *Subject Matter;* Curran, *Anatomy of Blackness;* and Pratt, *Imperial Eyes.*

10. My thinking here is influenced by Smith, *Black Africans in the British Imagination,* 11. Smith argues questions of race in the early modern era should always first and foremost consider the experiences of those who endured the

effects of being racialized, rather than the conscious perceptions of those who inflicted racism. For a bibliography and critical genealogy of early modern Black diaspora studies, much of which addresses contested theories of race in the early modern era, see Smith et al., *Early Modern Black Diaspora Studies*, 1–9. Spohr's discussion of race and Black musicians in early modern Europe in "Mohr und Trompeter" is also very relevant here (617–18), with Spohr citing another foundational study of the topic, Hall, *Things of Darkness*, 7.

11. Newman, *Dark Inheritance*.

12. See Livesay, *Children of Uncertain Fortune*. Hans Sloane later welcomed an elite West African, Ayuba Diallo, to his home in London. Diallo, who was the son of an imam and literate in Arabic, had fled enslavement in Maryland and fought for his freedom. Diallo's reception by Sloane and other Londoners exemplifies the ways in which education and class were scrutinized more than emergent conceptions of race. In Diallo's case, his elite status within Senegambian community made him an important ally in terms of trade, and his literacy in Arabic caused English colonists to advocate for his freedom. See Bluett, *Some Memoirs of the Life of Job*.

13. Sloane, *Voyage to the Islands*, xlvi. Sloane's parsing of phenotype reflects Spanish colonial practice. On the history of the Spanish "sistema de castas," a hierarchical system of racial categorization based on blood purity, see Martínez, *Genealogical Fictions*.

14. On the generation of enslaved Africans who were culturally and linguistically defined by global trade in the Atlantic world, see Berlin, "From Creole to African." On Portuguese-African relations, see Heywood and Thornton, *Central Africans, Atlantic Creoles*, especially chapter 2, 49–108.

15. Record of John Baptiste's naturalization on July 17, 1714, Jamaica Land Patents File 1 B1 (B/11/1/16), Jamaica Archives, Spanish Town.

16. I also consulted Sloane's papers in the British Library, which have been extensively indexed. None of these papers appear to involve correspondence with a Baptiste. I also surveyed materials held in Jamaica National Library in Kingston, including *Journals of the Jamaican Assembly*, and also relevant documents at the Registar General's Department where wills and some parish registers from the period are housed.

17. Both documents are housed at Jamaica Archive and Records Department in Spanish Town. Jamaica Land Patents File 1 B1 (B/11/1/16), and St. Andrew Parish Baptisms Marriages and Burials (1B/11/1/1a), Marriages Anno 1689, "John Baptisto and Rachel Geanego . . . Feb. 10."

18. Thanks to Linda Sturtz for this suggestion and to Sturtz, James Robertson, Brooke Newman, and Jane Harwell for their help interpreting the land patent.

19. I found just one other possible family member of Rachel and Hannah, a man naturalized in 1683. Morris Jennico naturalization, February 1683, Jamaica Land Patents 10B, 189, Jamaica Archives, Spanish Town.

20. Law XVIII as transcribed in the John Taylor manuscript, *Jamaica in 1687*, 289.

21. Record of John Baptiste's naturalization.

22. John Baptista's estate inventory on August 7, 1717, Jamaica Inventories of Probated Estates, vol. 11 (1716–21), 68, Jamaica Archives, Spanish Town.

23. Opera singers from the era like Marie Pélissier provided their own costumes. Pélissier purchased a wardrobe from an actress who died in 1730, as explained in Rivera, "Marie Pélissier."

24. Typically witnesses to an estate inventory are close to those who have died. Given Wolmer's wealth and social prominence in Kingston, it would make sense that he would have been friendly with notable local musicians. The other witness to the estate, Stephen Guinnet, does not leave any records that would seem to explain his connection to Baptiste.

25. It is worth noting that Wolmer enslaved several individuals in his household, as documented in what survives of his will. "An Inventory of the estate of John Wolmer late of Kingston," Jamaica Inventories of Probated Estates, vol. 15 (1729–31).

26. Wolmer's school website, "School History," https://www.wolmersouth fla.org/about-us/school-history.

27. For more on difficulties faced by free people in the Caribbean, see Livesay, *Children of Uncertain Fortune;* and Newman, *Dark Inheritance.*

28. See Heywood and Thornton, *Central Africans, Atlantic Creoles, and the Foundation of the Americas,* especially chapter 2, 49–108.

29. Ligon, *A True and Exact,* 52.

30. On circum-Atlantic festivals and African-descended performers again see Fromont, ed., *Afro-Catholic Festivals;* Voigt, *Spectacular Wealth;* Dewulf, *Afro-Atlantic Catholics;* and Valerio, *Sovereign Joy.*

31. On boy choristers in Spain see Jiménez, "From Mozos de Coro Towards Seises." On how these educational practices were adapted to cathedral life in New Spain, see Lopez, "La enseñanza musical en la catedral de México." On race, status, and musicianship in cathedrals of colonial Mexico, see Ramos-Kittrell, *Playing in the Cathedral.*

32. Examples of sources from the period that document liturgical music in Kongo and Angola include Merolla da Sorrento, "Voyage to Congo," 590. In the same collection of travelogues, see also Angelo, "Curious and Exact Account of a Voyage to Congo," 622–23. Another example can be found in a manuscript painting from the 1740s (mentioned in chapter 1), which portrays African clerics kneeling and singing from what is likely a hymnal, flanked by a band of musicians playing traditional African instruments. "Missione in prattica. Padri cappucini ne Regni di Congo, Angola et adiacenti," Central Public Library, Turin, MSS 457. On church music in the Kingdom of Kongo as well as the Kingdom of Angola, again see Fromont, ed., *Afro-Catholic Festivals;* and Thornton, *Cultural History,* 388–99.

33. See Delany, *History of the Catholic Church in Jamaica;* and Osborne, *History of the Catholic Church in Jamaica.* One prominent priest, Don Juan

Baptista Dempsy was an influential member of this group of clergy, though I have no reason to believe him to be the author of the notation. There is no mention of Dempsy's musicianship, and it would be odd for Sloane not to have identified him outright given his close association with the island's elite.

34. He urged the Jamaican assembly to pass an act that would "encourage the conversion of slaves to the Christian religion" and requested laws that would prevent "wanton or willful killing of negroes." Albemarle's attempt to persuade the assembly to pass acts on these matters can be found in *Journals of the Assembly of Jamaica*, Feb. 18, 1687, p. 102, National Library of Jamaica. On differences regarding Christianity and slavery across empires, see Gerbner, *Christian Slavery*.

35. See Delany, *History of the Catholic Church in Jamaica*, 22–23.

36. Again, see Wheat, *Atlantic Africa*.

37. For more on this, again see Bennet, *African Kings and Black Slaves*, 6–7.

38. Pawson and Buisseret, *Port Royal, Jamaica*.

39. John Taylor, *Jamaica in 1687*, 240.

40. Scott, "London's Earliest Public Concerts." I am grateful to Matteo Pangallo for offering insight from the perspective of a theater historian.

41. Another well-known author, Aphra Behn, was a royalist who describes leaving England for the West Indies for similar reasons in *Oroonoko* (1688). Royalist Captain Henry Norwood fled to Virginia for political reasons in 1649, penning a travelogue later published as *A Voyage to Virginia* (1732).

42. Ligon, *A True and Exact*, 107.

43. *Jamaica Courant*, Wednesday, June 28, 1721. Scant issues of the journal from this period are available at the National Library of Jamaica on microfilm and also via a locally hosted database at the British Library. See also Woodfield, *English Musicians in the Age of Exploration*, for extensive study of the role of musicians on colonial voyages; on the slim record of music in the West Indian colonies, see especially p. 153.

44. Leslie, *New History of Jamaica*, 27.

45. Leslie, *New History of Jamaica*, 37.

46. My speculative biography of Baptise is inspired by Saidiya Hartman's concept, "critical fabulation." See "Venus in Two Acts" and *Wayward Lives*.

47. See Lingold, "Peculiar Animations." On the limitations of Western musical notation in terms of portraying non-Western traditions see Seeger, "Prescriptive and Descriptive Music-Writing"; Nettl, *Study of Ethnomusicology*, especially chapter 7; and Winkler, "Writing Ghost Notes." On musical transcriptions in the context of colonialism, slavery, and empire, see Wood, *Sounding Otherness in Early Modern Drama and Travel*; Goodman, "Sounds Heard, Meaning Deferred"; Bloechl, *Native American Song at the Frontiers of Early Modern Music*; Woodfield, *English Musicians in the Age of Exploration*; and Tomlinson, *The Singing of the New World*.

48. For more about contemporary performances of Baptiste's transcriptions see Lingold, "Digital Performance."

49. Blum puts pressure on conflating composition with Western conceptions of written notated works that are presumed to be "original." All music is derivative and collaborative. Blum, "Composition."

50. This is why projects like *Music by Black Composers* and *Music Theory Examples by Women* remain important for diversifying the canon and creating greater visibility around the history and influence of understudied composers. *Music by Black Composers* (founded by violinist Rachel Barton Pine) aims to "spread awareness of and access to music by Black composers" with the larger goal of encouraging more young Black musicians to pursue classical performance and thereby rectifying the historical erasure of legions of Black performers, past and present. "Our Mission & Story," *Music by Black Composers,* https://www.musicbyblackcomposers.org/about-us/our-mission-story/; *Music Theory Examples by Women* was created by Molly Murdock and Ben Parsell to bring women composers to the study of music theory. *Music Theory Examples by Women,* https://musictheoryexamplesbywomen.com/.

5. African Traditions and the Evolution of Caribbean Festival Culture in the Eighteenth Century

1. I am referring to the long-standing discussions and debates regarding cultural retentions and innovation in enslaved communities. On the subject of creolization, scholars of the African diaspora generally look to an unfolding debate that began with Melville Herskovits and E. Franklin Frazier in the first half of the twentieth century. Frazier believed that the stark traumas of slavery essentially erased African knowledge in slave societies, but Herskovitz disagreed and worked to document practices tied to African forms. Later, Sidney Mintz and Richard Price authored an influential corrective to Herskovitz, showing the importance of African American ingenuity. For Mintz and Price, African practices were influential, but these scholars sought to ascribe greater agency to Caribbean people for their active role in shaping the process they theorize as "creolization." Mintz and Price, *Birth of African-American Culture.* Foundational work by Kamau Brathwaite defining creolization also directed scholarly conversation during this period. See Brathwaite, *Development of Creole Society in Jamaica.* Kenneth Bilby addresses these unfolding debates at length in a review of one of Richard Price's more recent books, and I find his discussion of continuity and creativity informative. See Bilby, "African American Memory at the Crossroads." I also find the introduction to Fromont, ed., *Afro-Catholic Festivals,* 5–7, which was written by Fromont and Michael Iyanaga, to have an especially useful and succinct description of these long-standing debates and how they relate to the study of diasporic performance. Richard Rath also examines creolization debates extensively in terms of Caribbean music in "African Music in Seventeenth-Century Jamaica."

2. On issues of childbirth, population growth, and the degree to which it varied across slave societies in the era, see Morgan, *Laboring Women,* 107–9.

3. Gwendolyn Midlo Hall argues forcefully for the distinctive and lasting influence of African national traditions in the Americas in *Slavery and African Ethnicities in the Americas;* see especially 168–69. I also share the views of Jerome Handler and Charlotte Frisbie, who find considerable evidence that among enslaved communities in Barbados, traditions remained reflective of specific African genres for at least two centuries. Handler and Frisbie, "Aspects of Slave Life in Barbados," 36–37. Michael Dickinson also documents persistence of West African traditions and identities at urban musical gatherings in Anglo-Atlantic cities in the eighteenth century. See Dickinson, *Almost Dead,* 86–114.

4. John Thornton makes this point as well in Thornton, *Cultural History,* 390, citing Charles de Rochefort, *Historie naturelle et morale des illes Antilles de Amerique* (Rotterdam, 1658), 321–22, and also Du Tertre, *Histoire* (4 vols., Paris, 1667–71), 2:526–28.

5. See again Taylor, *Jamaica in 1687,* 269.

6. Sloane, *Voyage to the Islands,* l–li.

7. William Beckford, *Descriptive Account of the Island of Jamaica,* 2:215–18. Caramantee refers to the Akan people of modern Ghana, sometimes spelled Koromanti. Whydaw refered to the Kingdom of Whydaw (also spelled "Ouidah" in English at the time), which was a major slave-trading Atlantic port at the Bight of Benin.

8. Stedman, *Narrative,* 538–40.

9. Gaddy, *Well of Souls.* In addition to identifying musical connections between Suriname and South Carolina, Gaddy discusses Stedman's life and writings extensively throughout the book.

10. See Wood, *Black Majority,* 13–34.

11. The surviving written materials and paintings are housed in the James Ford Bell Library at the University of Minnesota. The instruments Stedman collected are part of the collection of the Museum Volkenkunde in Leiden, the Netherlands (a drum, RV-360–5685; a banjo, RV-360–5696; and a flute, RV-360–5699). On the instruments, see Richard Price and Sally Price, "John Gabriel Stedman's Collection."

12. Stedman, *Narrative.* See Price and Price's introduction, xiii–xcviii, for detailed information and analysis of the history of the publication, its author, and reception.

13. See Lingold, "Peculiar Animations," 642–44. This essay addresses the changes to the musical notation in Stedman's narrative.

14. On the history of Suriname Maroons, see Price, *Maroon Societies.*

15. See Polcha, "Voyeur in the Torrid Zone," which discusses Stedman's sexual violence against Joanna and other enslaved and free Black women of Suriname. On Joanna's biography, see also Aljoe, *Creole Testimonies,* 32–39; and K. Gaddy, *Well of Souls,* 56–62.

16. Journal, diaries, and other papers; 1772–1796, University of Minnesota Libraries, James Ford Bell Library. See also the published transcription of the

192 Notes to Pages 112–117

papers, *The Journal of John Gabriel Stedman,* ed. Stanbury Thompson (1962), and online digitized images of the manuscript at https://umedia.lib.umn.edu/item /p16022coll187:73. Page numbers cited here are from the 1962 transcription. On "mulatto" and "free negro" balls, see May 10, 1773 (p. 124) and January 18, 1776 (p. 161). Johnny's birthday noted Nov. 27, 1775 (p. 157). Playing banjar, and dancing baniard noted Nov. 27, 1775 (p. 157), Dec. 9, 1775 (p. 159), and June 12, 1776 (p. 175).

17. Gaddy, *Well of Souls,* especially xiii–xvii and 111–16.

18. Stedman, *Journal of John Gabriel Stedman,* June 8. "The 2 men, Vale and culner, play for my fiddle. It falls to Culner's share. The men dance." November 9 of that year, he noted that a Mrs. Rynsdorph gave him "musick," presumably sheet music, although it is not clear.

19. Stedman, *Narrative,* 292–93.

20. Stedman, *Narrative,* 292–93.

21. Jeroen Dewulf argues that many of these festival traditions have deep roots in Afro-Iberian and Afro-Catholic practices that took place long before the eighteenth century. See Dewulf, "From the Calendas" and "Rethinking."

22. On masking traditions, again see Kasfir, "Elephant Women, Furious and Majestic."

23. On women's fashion in late-eighteenth-century Jamaica, see Buckridge, *Language of Dress.* On African fabric trade and colonial travel, see Everill, "On Wednesdays We Wear Prints." On African-descended women's influential roles in the Atlantic economy, including aspects of material culture and taste, see also Johnson, *Wicked Flesh.* On textiles and the slave trade in the Kingdoms of Kongo, Loango, and Angola, and influence on Atlantic commerce, see Fromont, "Common Threads."

24. Stedman, *Narrative,* 540–41.

25. Stedman, *Narrative,* 540–41. Much of the scholarship on Koto is in Dutch. I am grateful to scholar of contemporary Koto dress, Ella Broek, for suggesting some titles to me, including van Russel-Henar et al., *Angisa tori;* and Henar-Hewitt, *Surinaamse koto's en angisa's.*

26. Young's narrative was published at the end of Edwards, *An Historical Survey.* Material on Christmas festivities is found on pp. 273, 275–76. On the influence of Catholicism on Caribbean festival tradition, again see Dewulf, "From the Calendas" and "Rethinking"; and Fromont, ed., *Afro-Catholic Festivals.*

27. The publication history of Bryan Edwards' writings about the West Indies, William Young's narrative, and the Brunias engraving is rather complicated, involving several editions and multiple titles, and a great deal of variation. The Brunias image is not present in all of the editions of Edwards and Young, but it can be found as "A Negro Festival Drawn from Nature in the Island of St. Vincent" opposite p. 184 in the second volume of Bryan Edwards, *The History, Civil and Commercial, of the British Colonies in the West Indies* (London, 1801).

28. Sarah Thomas, "Envisaging a Future for Slavery." See also Bagneris, *Colouring the Caribbean,* chapter 4, "Merry and Contented Slaves and Other Island Myths." The entire book, on Brunias, is relevant here. See also Kriz, *Slavery, Sugar, and the Culture of Refinement* on Brunias (especially chapter 2) and visual portrayals of the West Indies, more generally, and on portrayals of "happy slaves," Young, and these images, 43–44. For another example of a romanticized portrayal of enslaved peoples' performance from the time, see Beckford, *Descriptive Account of the Island of Jamaica,* 2:216–18.

29. Stedman, *Narrative,* 540.

30. Douglass, *Narrative of the Life of Frederick Douglass,* 14–15. The memorable passage has been discussed extensively by scholars. See Stoever, *Sonic Color Line,* 48–51; Moten, *In the Break,* 20–21. Douglass's sentiments are also echoed throughout W. E. B. Du Bois's influential "Sorrow Songs," the last chapter of *Souls of Black Folk* (1903).

31. On the African Atlantic history of the banjo, again see Dubois, *The Banjo.* Interestingly, Stedman also uses the term "Loango-bania" to refer to at type of kalimba or mbira that used a gourd resonator for amplification and sound design (there are many African names for such instruments).

32. See Price and Price, "John Gabriel Stedman's."

33. Price and Price, "John Gabriel Stedman's," 127.

34. See Lingold, "Peculiar Animations," for further discussion of enlightenment science, race, and music.

6. Songs from the 1770s

1. I am not aware of other notated examples from the eighteenth century specifically documenting vernacular music of the enslaved, except for the following, which gesture to enslaved performances: a transcription from a 1780s Peruvian manuscript commissioned by Baltasar Jaime Martínez Compañon, known as *Trujillo del Perú,* and housed in the Biblioteca del Palacio Real, MSS II/344, fol. 160, ca. 1789. The text is a multi-volume work that includes twenty pieces of music, of which the "Tonada el Congo," portrays and adapts music by enslaved people. "Tonada el Congo" features frequently in early music ensembles portraying colonial subjects. On representations of Afro-Peruvian music and dance in *Truijillo* see Valerio, *Sovereign Joy.* I am certain that other examples exist, probably in Spanish and Portuguese, and likely in manuscript form. I am grateful to Loren Ludwig for introducing me to another manuscript transcription entitled "Congo" from 1790 that likely references early Black performances in Virginia. See, Linnaeus Bolling, "Congo," in the Hubard Family Papers #360, Southern Historical Collection, UNC University Libraries, University of North Carolina at Chapel Hill. Kristina Gaddy has brought to light manuscript notation by Swedish doctor Christopher Carlander who documented music from the Swedish colony of St. Barthelemy, now held at Rijksarkivet in Stockholm. See

Gaddy, "Music in Well of Souls," which includes a useful representation of known sources from the period.

2. On women and French West Indies Theatre, see especially Powers, *From Plantation;* Camier, "A Free Artist"; and Prest, "Parisian Palimpsests."

3. Devin Leigh, "The Jamaican Airs," 12.

4. On theatre in Eighteenth-century Saint-Domingue, see Prest, "Parisian Palimpsests"; Powers, "From Plantation to Paradise?"; Dubois, "Minette's Worlds"; Camier, "Musique Coloniale et Sociéte à Saint-Domingue à La Fin Du XVIIIème Siècle" and "A Free Artist of Color"; and Jean Fouchard, *Le Théâtre à Saint-Domingue.*

5. "An African Song or Chant from Barbados," Gloucestershire Archives, Gloucestershire, England.

6. Dickson, *Letters on Slavery,* 93–94.

7. Dickson, *Letters on Slavery,* 93–94.

8. See Handler and Frisbie, "Aspects of Slave Life," 23n9, for a discussion of the Barbados song. I draw from their groundbreaking work on the Sharp/Dickson interaction here.

9. Equiano, *Interesting Narrative.*

10. On the music of British abolitionists, see Hamilton, "'African' Songs and Women's Abolitionism."

11. "An African Song or Chant from Barbados," *Unesco.org,* https://en.unesco.org/memoryoftheworld/registry/223. To hear Gibbs' version of the song, see Roger Gibbs, "Slave Chant c 1775 Roger Gibbs," *Youtube.* https://www.youtube.com/watch?v=mdFrNPy1wIw.

12. See Rickford and Handler, "Textual Evidence," 230–32 and 245n10; and Handler and Frisbie, "Aspects of Slave Life," 23–24 and 23n9.

13. In additions to conversations with Roger Gibbs, I also spoke to Jerry Handler, who has researched the song and is a specialist in Barbados history and culture, and his coauthor, historical linguist of the Caribbean John Rickford. I thank them both for their time and generosity. Unfortunately, neither of them have a clear sense of the term "regulaw." Lisa Voigt suggests that the word may derive from the Spanish "regalo," or gift, which is something I also considered and believe to be plausible given the presence of Spanish words and phrases in many Caribbean Creole languages.

14. See also Rickford and Handler, "Textual Evidence," 245n10, who note that the suggestion of suicide was raised by an anonymous reviewer of their article.

15. Hartman, *Scenes of Subjection,* 55.

16. Northup, *Twelve Years a Slave,* 226–27.

17. Le Page Du Pratz, *History of Louisiana,* book 4, chapter 4, section 2, 384.

18. On this point, see also Epstein, *Sinful Tunes,* 162.

19. On the subject of work songs in the Caribbean before 1800, see Epstein, *Sinful Tunes and Spirituals,* 68–74.

20. According to Karwan Fatah-Black enslaved laborers rowed barges to transport sugar and other commodities and trade goods, whereas tent boats ferried people. For more on Riverine travel in eighteenth-century Suriname, see Fatah-Black, *White Lies and Black Markets*, 126–35. Of tent boat rowers, Stedman compared them to "the *Lord Mayors Show* on the River Thames," noting that they could be quite resplendent. See Stedman, *Narrative*, 92.

21. Jerry Handler suggested to me in private conversation that the song was probably sung by both women and men, perhaps while hoeing and digging fields to prepare for planting.

22. Park, *Travels in the Interior Districts*.

23. Park, *Travels in the Interior Districts*, 197–98.

24. As Dena Epstein also notes, the work of childcare was commonly shaped by song. See Epstein, *Sinful Tunes*, 161–63.

25. On work song in modern African contexts see Agawu, *The African Imagination*, 36–37. Agawu also highlights women's domestic work song in terms of lullabies and weaving.

26. Beckford, *Descriptive Account*, 2:120–21.

27. On women's roles in Africa and on American plantations, again see Morgan, *Laboring Women*, 50–68.

28. *Marly; or, A Planter's Life in Jamaica*, 39.

29. Handler and Lange, *Plantation Slavery in Barbados*, 72–74. Children and women enslaved laborers on Newton plantation and elsewhere are also discussed extensively in Paton, "Driveress and the Nurse." Handler and Lange discuss the history of the term "gang" by plantation managers in Barbados on p. 72.

30. Smith, *Natural History of Nevis*, 230–31.

31. Again see Gibbs, "Slave Chant."

32. Colonial Williamsburg Foundation, *From Ear to Ear*.

33. On biological racism, enlightenment science, and Stedman's notation, see Lingold, "Peculiar Animations," 627.

34. See introduction to Stedman, *Narrative*, li–lxvi.

35. "Directions for the Plates" in Stedman's 1790 manuscript for the *Narrative*. Journal, diaries, and other papers, 1772–1796, University of Minnesota Libraries, James Ford Bell Library.

36. Stedman, *Narrative*, 516.

37. Stedman, *Narrative, of a Five Years' Expedition against the Revolted Negroes of Surinam, in Guiana, on the Wild Coast of South America: From the Year 1772, to 1777* [. . .] (London: Printed by J. Johnson, St. Pauls Church Yard, & J. Edwards, Pall Mall, 1796), 2:258. In "Peculiar Animations," I analyze this passage at length.

38. On tentboats and barges in Suriname, see Fatah-Black, "The Use of Wills," 126–35.

39. For more on the rangers, see introduction to Stedman, *Narrative*, xxiv.

40. Stedman, *Narrative*, 695n516.

41. See Leigh, "Jamaican Airs" and "The Jamaican Airs Exhibit." The manuscript pages are from "The Jamaican Airs" in "Revisions to Edward Long's *The History of Jamaica,* Volume II," C. E. Long Papers, Manuscripts Reading Room, British Library, London, Add. MS 12405, ff. 354–46. I consulted the materials as found on the *Early Caribbean Digital Archive.*

42. Long, *History of Jamaica.*

43. Leigh, "Jamaican Airs," 462–63.

44. A version of "Guinea corn" can also be found in Young, *West-India Melodies.*

45. On Long's record of Myalism, see Schuler, "Myalism and the African Religious Tradition." Long wrote about Myalism in the original published version of his book *History of Jamaica,* 2:416–17.

46. Forthcoming work by Maria Ryan and Wayne Weaver will expand understanding of the "Jamaican Airs." Indeed, I am grateful to both for sharing insights with me.

47. On Myalism, again see Schuler, "Myalism and the African Religious Tradition"; and Warner-Lewis, *Central Africa in the Caribbean,* 190–98. On Myalism, music and Jonkannu, see Bilby, "Surviving Secularization," 188–93.

48. Scholarship on the Caribbean in the era of the Haitian Revolution has emphasized the circulation of people, politics, and performance. See especially Johnson, *Fear of French Negroes;* and Scott, *Common Wind.* Sources examined in this chapter predate that era but suggest that Caribbean circulations were well-underway in the mid-eighteenth century.

49. "Characteristic Traits of the Creolian and African Negroes in this Island," *Columbian Magazine,* May 1797, 767, reproduced in Leigh, "Jamaican Airs Exhibit." The two pieces in the "Jamaican Airs," "Calemba" and "The Colymba," may refer to a related practice. "Kalimba" also is the name of a Central and Southern African instrument. The words are similar to "Calenda," one of the most prominently circulated Caribbean genres of the eighteenth century, as discussed extensively by Dewulf, "From the Calendas."

50. For a comparative study of Jonkanu traditions in the Caribbean, again see Bilby, "Surviving Secularization." For circulations of the practice in North America, including North Carolina, see Reed, "There Was No Resisting"; and Epstein, *Sinful Tunes,* 131, 138.

51. Leigh, "Jamaican Airs," 464, 475.

52. "Characteristic Traits," reproduced in Leigh, "The Jamaican Airs Exhibit."

53. Laws in England at the time were interpreted to mean that enslaved people who stepped foot in the nation could claim freedom, but their freedom was not guaranteed in the slave society from which they came. Prince, *The History of Mary Prince.*

54. "The Jamaican Airs," description of "Ranger" from the C. E. Long Papers, reproduced in Leigh, "Jamaican Airs Exhibit."

55. Saidiya Hartman has argued that enslaved people enacted subtle acts of resistance through everyday performance but also cautioned against romanticizing them. Hartman, *Scenes of Subjection*, 55. My understanding of the political message of the "Ranger Song" is influenced here by Vincent Brown, who also engages Hartman on the question of the limits and possibilities for enslaved political organizing. See Brown, "Social Death and Political Life."

56. Description of "Ranger," reproduced in Leigh, "Jamaican Airs Exhibit." The descriptions of the tunes in the handwritten manuscript are largely the same as what was printed in the Colombian Magazine in 1797, however in this instance, the magazine refers to the plant as "Poinciana" and the manuscript writes "Barbadoes Pride." These are similar flowering trees. I am grateful to Eric Martinel for sharing insights with me about this plant.

57. The author wrote of the song that "the first two bars of which one would almost suppose were taken from the Gavotte in Mr. Garth's 4th Sonata, Opera Quarto." He is probably referring to Garth, *A Second Sett*. I wish to thank Rebecca Geoffroy-Schwinden for consulting with me about Garth's piece and gavottes.

58. Again, see especially Fromont, ed., *Afro-Catholic Festivals;* and Dewulf, "Rethinking" and "From the Calendas."

59. Sturtz, "Sett Girls"; on differences between rural and urban sets, see especially p. 209.

60. Art historian Sidney Littlefield Kasfir argues for the strong connections between women's masquerades in the Caribbean and African masking traditions. See Kasfir, "Furious and Majestic."

61. On Jonkanu, see Smalligan, "Effigy for the Enslaved"; Warner-Lewis, *Central Africa in the Caribbean;* Bilby, "Secularization"; Dewulf, "Rethinking the Historical Development." Dewulf tracks the historical development of Jankunu to emphasize the Afro-Catholic influences on the tradition, working against notions that "creolization" between African and European tradition occurred most influentially in the Caribbean. Smalligan offers a useful bibliography of existing work on the tradition, of which there are numerous fragmentary studies across several fields. Warner-Lewis offers an interpretation of the etymology of the word Junkanoo, and Bilby analyzes the religious components of a practice long-interpreted as secular. The elaborately constructed replica of a building worn as a headpiece was documented memorably in Isaac Belisario's paintings, who also portrayed Set Girls. For information on Belisario and the Christmas festivities he documented, see Barringer et al., *Art and Emancipation in Jamaica.*

62. The anonymous author's characterization of the Set Girls foretells what Koritha Mitchell has termed, "know-your-place aggression." See Mitchell, "Identifying White Mediocrity."

63. Dillon, *New World Drama*, 199.

64. Sturtz, "Sett Girls," 207.

65. Johnson, *Fear of French Negroes*. On Set Girls, see chapter 4, "French Set Girls and Transcolonial Performance," 156–57.

66. Scott, *Common Wind*.

67. These remarks come from the general description of music that opens the "Jamaican Airs" manuscript, C. E. Long Papers. The page is numbered 3 in pencil. They are also repeated in the *Columbian Magazine* excerpt.

68. Set Girls notation is on page 338r of C. E. Long Papers, MS 12405. For an anonymous author's descriptions, see "Chap. Music." in Anon. and Edward Long, "Jamaican Airs," reproduced in Leigh, "The Jamaican Airs Exhibit."

69. M. G. Lewis (Matthew "Monk" Gregory), *Journal of a West India Proprietor, Kept during a Residence in the Island of Jamaica*, London: John Murray, 1834, 53.

70. On Caribbean military bands, see Cooper, "Playing against Empire," and also forthcoming work by Maria Ryan.

71. On Haitian Rara, see McAlister, *Rara!*; on baton twirling specifically, see especially p. 54.

Epilogue

1. Sandburg, *American Songbag*, 455. The pieces are primarily arranged for voice and piano, though many of the tunes could be played on a variety of instruments. On *The American Songbag*, see Niven, *Carl Sandburg*, especially part 3, "American Singer." John Lomax contributed to the volume and Ruth Crawford Seeger did much of the arranging. Benjamin Filene discusses the *Songbag* in relation to the emergent folklorist movement of the era and particularly his decision to publish a collection of sheet music rather than phonograph recordings. See Filene, *Romancing the Folk*, chapter 1.

2. Wallace-Sanders, *Mammy*. I examine the Mammy stereotype in relationship to Tena's story more extensively in Lingold, "Sonic Records," 174–76.

3. Lingold, "Tena, Too, Sings America."

4. Lingold, "Listening."

5. Phone call with Maggie MacRae, December 19, 2013.

6. Maggie MacRae shared details from the family's oral history with me during our phone conversation. Some of the information can also be found in Tracey, "Tina's Lullaby." However, the family incorrectly recalled that Alexander Spencer purchased Tena in 1854. Records show that he died in 1831 and that Tena was enslaved by him at that time. "Inventory and appraisement of the Personal Estate of Alexander Spencer deceased—made the 12th December, 1831," *Richmond County Years's Support Inventory & Appraisement Account Sales* D 1829–40, 98, held at the Augusta Genealogical Society in Augusta, Georgia.

7. On the illegal slave trade see Head, "Slave Smuggling." On slave smuggling across the Gulf of Mexico into Texas, see Maria Esther Hammack, "Illegal Slave Trade."

8. I believe Tena was probably purchased in 1830, because that is when Isabella Spencer (neé Bones) Coskery (1810–1883) was widowed by her first husband, William Bones (~1801–1830). The event may have been what prompted her father to purchase Tena to help her care for her children.

9. "Inventory and appraisement of the Personal Estate of Alexander Spencer." The names of Maria's children are listed but are more difficult to decipher. One was clearly named Harriet, and another may have shared the name Celia.

10. Claims to African nobility were common, especially as a selling point for traders or as a matter of claims to status and respectability for enslaved and free people. This is a thorny subject, one I hope to revisit in future scholarship, because even though tropes around African princes and princesses abounded, so did African princes and princesses. Here, the cultural discourse obscures historical realities. In this instance, I interpret the referent to Tena's nobility to be something that came from the white trader rather than her self-expression.

11. Regarding Tena's story, I examined relevant records connected to the Spencer heirs and descendants at the August Genealogical Society, Augusta, Georgia, and Probate Records at the Richmond County Courthouse in Augusta, Georgia. I also consulted online resources, such as U.S. Census data and other marriage and death records available on Ancestry.com. I inspected records of local cemeteries in Augusta, GA, as well, including Cedar Grove, where enslaved and free Black people were buried in the nineteenth century. Unfortunately, I have found no record of Tena's final resting place. I am deeply indebted to the volunteer staff at the Augusta Genealogical Society for their counsel during the research, and especially Gracie Joyce. I am also grateful to Cynthia Greenlee for suggesting that I consult with a local genealogical society in my research.

12. Berry, *Price for Their Pound of Flesh.*

13. Just a few years later, when part of the elder Spencer's estate was liquidated, several slaves were sold, including a woman, whose name appears to be spelled "Tenior," sold for $300.12. I initially thought this woman may have been Tena, but looking at earlier records, I believe it was the woman whose name is spelled Tamiar, or possibly Tamar, in the original estate inventory, where the price of $300.00 was ascribed to her. This prompted me to search other local planters' records for mentions of enslaved women named Tena. I found several in the Augusta area, but none seemed likely matches (given age and timing). The Spencer descendants maintain that Tena cared for a second generation of their ancestors, and I believe it likely, though I have not been able to confirm it. Census records and slave schedules from a crucial year, 1840, are missing for the family. "Sales at Auction for a/c of the Estate of A. Spencer died for order of J. Coskery Adm" in *Year's Support Inventory & Appraisment.*

14. The institutions and collections that Lomax and Tracey both built have done incredible work in recent decades to address inequities of the past with a focus, in particular, on repatriation and digital access. See, "ACE's Commitment," *culturalequity.org,* http://www.culturalequity.org/ace/commitment; Elijah

Madiba, "A Collaborative Approach." On Alan and John Lomax and the racialization of Black music, see Filene, *Romancing the Folk,* chapter 2. Filene discusses this in terms of what he calls the "cult of authenticity" that the Lomaxes helped to construct.

15. This radio program, also titled "Tina's Lullaby," was broadcast on September 10, 1957, as part of the *Sound of Africa Broadcast Series 3 Eastern Cape* (Transkei) in programme 2, part 1, and programme 2, part 2. These details are from my correspondence with the archivists at the International Library of African Music at Rhodes University, South Africa, where Tracey's papers and broadcast recordings are held. I am very grateful to the staff there for their generous assistance with my research. The radio show combines Tracey's narration with the story as told by the Johnson family on the tape they sent to him in South Africa. Much of the content is transcribed in the article version.

16. The family member speaking on the tape may be "Mrs. Clifford Stephens" or Mrs. Johnson. It is not clear from the records housed at ILAM, but Mrs. Johnson is the singer.

17. Sandburg recorded Tena's song on an album, *Carl Sandburg Sings His American Songbag* (1967). His performance indicates that he learned the song from notation, rather than the family. Several of the pieces in the *Songbag* are gathered from other collectors and musicologists.

18. Tracey's interpretive methods reinforced the perception that African sound and language is uninterpretable and irreproducible by non-Africans. He does so in a way that subtly essentializes and racializes Africanness, awhile also offering a largely ahistorical representation of Bantu language traditions.

19. "Sale of Negroes and Wines," *Charleston Courier,* July 20, 1804. Similar advertisements were made again in 1808.

20. According to my queries in the *Trans-Atlantic Slave Trade Database* (slavevoyages.org), there were many ships carrying captives to the Americas from the Eastern coasts during the era of Tena's enslavement, but primarily to Brazil. A handful of voyages landed in Cuba and one in Puerto Rico in 1824 and 1825, respectively. My query included ships containing slaves from "southeast Africa and Indian Ocean islands" between 1820–31. For example, one ship, #368, named *Bella Dolores* and captained by Antonio Guerrero, in 1824 went to Cuba. The *Orphee,* #2769, captained by "Jacques," also landed in Cuba in 1825. In 1824, #2754, *Chasseur,* captained by Françoise Thébaud, landed in Puerto Rico. *Trans-Atlantic Slave Trade Database.*

I am very grateful to Tsitsi Jaji for noting the commonality of the name Tinashe. I am also thankful to the librarian Tina at the Augusta Public library, and her assistant, (also named Tina), for directing me to the Augusta Genealogical Society and for reminding me of Tina's insistence.

21. Tracey, "Tina's Lullaby," 100.

22. *The Language You Cry In.* The Dawley family song also had been recorded in the 1930s by Lorenzo Turner, a pioneering researcher who explored

the African aspects of Gullah language and culture along the islands of coastal Georgia and South Carolina.

23. Du Bois, *Souls,* 254–55. Throughout *Souls,* each chapter begins with an excerpt of musical notation drawn from an African American spiritual. The final chapter, from which this excerpt comes, "On Sorrow Songs," is devoted entirely to the discussion of music and its central importance to black American history and culture.

24. Nabi Jah's remarks begin at about 50:00 in the film.

25. Richard Hall, "After 100 Years they Still Sing Tina's Song," *African Mail* (Lusaka), December 6, 1963; and W. Kasawira, "Tina Was a Nyasa," *African Mail,* January 24, 1964. A "press cutting" with the same content was published in Tracey's journal, *African Music.* See Kasawira, "Notes and News."

Bibliography

Abrahams, Roger D. *Singing the Master: The Emergence of African American Culture in the Plantation South.* New York: Pantheon Books, 1992.

Agawu, V. Kofi. *The African Imagination in Music.* New York, NY: Oxford University Press, 2016.

Aljoe, Nicole N. *Creole Testimonies: Slave Narratives from the British West Indies, 1709–1838.* New York: Palgrave Macmillan, 2012.

Allende-Goitía, Noel. "The Mulatta, the Bishop, and Dances in the Cathedral: Race, Music, and Power Relations in Seventeenth-Century Puerto Rico." *Black Music Research Journal* 26, no. 2 (2006): 137–64.

———. *Las músicas otras: Puerto Rico, el atlántico afrodiaspórico y otros ensayos de estudios culturales de la música,* 2014.

Allewaert, Monique. *Ariel's Ecology: Plantations, Personhood, and Colonialism in the American Tropics.* Minneapolis: University of Minnesota Press, 2013.

———. "Super Fly: François Makandal's Colonial Semiotics." *American Literature* 91, no. 3 (September 1, 2019): 459–90.

Bae, Yoo. "The Distribution, Construction, Tuning, and Performance Technique of the African Log Xylophone." ProQuest Dissertations Publishing, 2001.

Bagneris, Mia L. *Colouring the Caribbean: Race and the Art of Agostino Brunias.* Manchester: Manchester University Press, 2018.

Banat, Gabriel. *The Chevalier de Saint-Georges: Virtuoso of the Sword and the Bow.* Lives in Music Series; No. 7. Hillsdale, N.Y.: Pendragon Press, 2006.

Baraka, Amiri (neé Leroi Jones). *Blues People: Negro Music in White America.* New York: W Morrow, 1963.

Barbot, John. "A Description of the Coasts of North and South-Guinea; and of Ethiopia Inferior, Vulgarly Angola: A New and Accurate Account of the Western Maritime Countries of Africa In Six Books." In *A Collection of Voyages and Travels: Some Now First Printed from Original Manuscripts, Others Translated out of Foreign Languages, and Now First Published in English [. . .] In Six Volumes,* edited by Awnsham Churchill and John Churchill. Vol. V. London: Printed, by Assignment from Messs Churchill, 1732.

Barringer, Tim, Gillian Forrester, and Barbaro Martinez-Ruiz. *Art and Emancipation in Jamaica: Isaac Mendes Belisario and His Worlds*. New Haven: Yale Center for British Art in association with Yale University Press, 2007.

Bastian, Misty L. "'The Demon Superstition': Abominable Twins and Mission Culture in Onitsha History." *Ethnology* 40, no. 1 (2001): 13–27.

Bauer, Ralph. *The Cultural Geography of Colonial American Literatures: Empire, Travel, Modernity*. New York: Cambridge University Press, 2003.

Beckford, William. *A Descriptive Account of the Island of Jamaica: With Remarks upon the Cultivation of the Sugar-Cane [. . .] throughout the Different Seasons of the Year, and Chiefly Considered in a Picturesque Point of View, Also Observations and Reflections upon What Would Probably Be the Consequences of an Abolition of the Slave-Trade, and of the Emancipation of the Slaves*. London: Printed for T. and J. Egerton, Whitehall, 1790.

Behn, Aphra. *Oroonoko; or, the Royal Slave: A True History*. London: Printed for Will Canning, 1688.

Belisario, Isaac Mendes. *Sketches of Character, in Illustration of the Habits, Occupation, and Costume of the Negro Population, in the Island of Jamaica: Drawn after Nature, and in Lithography*. Published by the author: Kingston, 1837.

Bennett, Herman L. *African Kings and Black Slaves: Sovereignty and Dispossession in the Early Modern Atlantic*. Philadelphia: University of Pennsylvania Press, 2019.

Berlin, Ira. "From Creole to African: Atlantic Creoles and the Origins of African-American Society in Mainland North America." *William and Mary Quarterly* 53, no. 2 (1996): 251–88.

Berry, Daina Ramey. *The Price for Their Pound of Flesh: The Value of the Enslaved from Womb to Grave in the Building of a Nation*. Boston: Beacon Press, 2017.

Bilby, Kenneth M. "African American Memory at the Crossroads: Grounding the Miraculous with Tooy." *Small Axe: A Caribbean Journal of Criticism* 13, no. 2 (2009): 185.

———. "Surviving Secularization: Masking the Spirit in the Jankunu (John Canoe) Festivals of the Caribbean." *Nieuwe West-Indische Gids* 84, no. 3–4 (2010): 179–223.

Bilby, Kenneth M., and Fu-Kiau Kia Bunseki. "Kumina: A Kongo-Based Tradition in the New World." In *A Reader in African-Jamaican Music, Dance and Religion*, edited by Markus Coester and Wolfgang Bender. Kingston: Ian Randle Publishers, 2015.

Birenbaum Quintero, Michael. *Rites, Rights and Rhythms: A Genealogy of Musical Meaning in Colombia's Black Pacific*. New York: Oxford University Press, 2019.

Bloechl, Olivia A. *Native American Song at the Frontiers of Early Modern Music*. New York: Cambridge University Press, 2008.

Blome, Richard. *A Description of the Island of Jamaica; with the Other Isles and Territories in America, to Which the English Are Related, Viz. Barbadoes, St. Christophers, Nievis or Mevis, Antego, St. Vincent, Dominica, Montserrat, Anguilla, Barbada, Bermudes, Carolina, Virginia, Maryland, New-York, New England, New-Foundland. Taken from the Notes of Sr. Thomas Linch.* London: Printed by T. Milbourn and sold by J. Williams, 1672.

———. *The present state of His Majesties isles and territories in America* [. . .] *with new maps of every place: together with astronomical tables, which will serve as a constant diary or calendar, for the use of the English inhabitants in those islands, from the year 1686 to 1700* [. . .]. London: Printed by H. Clark, for D. Newman, 1687.

Bluett, Thomas. *Some Memoirs of the Life of Job, the Son of Solomon the High Priest of Boonda in Africa: Who Was a Slave about Two Years in Maryland, and Afterwards Being Brought to England, Was Set Free, and Sent to His Native Land in the Year 1734.* London: Printed for Richard Ford, 1734.

Blum, Stephen. "Composition." In *Grove Music Online.* Oxford Music Online. http://www.oxfordmusiconline.com/view/10.1093/gmo/9781561592630.001 .0001/omo-9781561592630-e-0000006216.

Brathwaite, Kamau. *The Development of Creole Society in Jamaica, 1770–1820.* Oxford: Clarendon Press, 1971.

Brienen, Rebecca Parker. "Embodying Race and Pleasure: Dirk Valkenburg's 'Slave Dance.'" *Nederlands Kunsthistorisch Jaarboek (NKJ) / Netherlands Yearbook for History of Art* 58 (2007): 242–64.

Brooks, Daphne. *Bodies in Dissent: Spectacular Performances of Race and Freedom, 1850–1910.* Durham: Duke Univ. Press, 2007.

———. *Liner Notes for the Revolution: The Intellectual Life of Black Feminist Sound.* Cambridge, MA: Belknap Press of Harvard University Press, 2021.

Brown, Vincent. *The Reaper's Garden: Death and Power in the World of Atlantic Slavery.* Harvard University Press, 2008.

———. "Social Death and Political Life in the Study of Slavery." *American Historical Review* 114, no. 5 (2009): 1231–49.

———. *Tacky's Revolt: The Story of an Atlantic Slave War.* Cambridge, MA: Harvard Belknap Press, 2020.

Browne, Randy M. *Surviving Slavery in the British Caribbean.* Philadelphia: University of Pennsylvania Press, 2017.

Brückner, Martin. *Early American Cartographies.* Chapel Hill: University of North Carolina Press, 2011.

Bry, Johann Theodor de, Gotthard Arthus, Zacharias Heyns, José de Acosta, Barent Jansz Potgieter, and Olivier van Noort. *Americae nona & postrema pars* [. . .] *Addita est tertio nauigatio recens, quam 4. nauium praefectus Olevier à Noort proximè suscepit: qui Freto Magellanico classe transmisso, triennij spatio vniuersum terrae orbem seu globum mira navigationis forte obiuit:*

annexis illis, quae in itinere isto singularia ac memorabiliora notata sunt. Francof[urt]: Apud Matth. Beckerum, 1602.

Buckridge, Steeve O. *The Language of Dress: Resistance and Accommodation in Jamaica, 1760–1890.* Mona, Kingston: University of the West Indies Press, 2004.

Budasz, Rogério. "Black Guitar-Players and Early African-Iberian Music in Portugal and Brazil." *Early Music* 35, no. 1 (February 2007): 3–21.

C., Monseiur de. "Account of a Remarkable Conspiracy Formed by a Negro in the Island of St. Domingo (1787)." Text prepared by Ed White and Duncan Faherty. Worcester, MA: Just Teach One, 2016. http://jto.common-place.org /just-teach-one-homepage/account-of-a-remarkable-conspiracy-makandal/.

Camier, Bernard. "A 'Free Artist of Color' in Late-Eighteenth-Century Saint-Domingue: The Life and Times of Minette." *International Journal for the Study of Music and Musical Performance* 1, no. 1 (2019): 1–26, 90.

———. "Musique Coloniale et Société à Saint-Domingue à La Fin Du XVIIIème Siècle." Université des Antilles-Guyane, 2004.

Cañizares-Esguerra, Jorge C, ed. *Entangled Empires: The Anglo-Iberian Atlantic, 1500–1830.* Philadelphia: University of Pennsylvania Press, 2018.

Chaplin, Joyce. *Subject Matter: Technology, Science, and the Body on the Anglo-American Frontier, 1500–1676.* Cambridge, MA: Harvard University Press, 2011.

Charry, Eric S. *Mande Music: Traditional and Modern Music of the Maninka and Mandinka of Western Africa.* Chicago: University of Chicago Press, 2000.

Chude-Sokei, Louis Onuorah. *The Sound of Culture: Diaspora and Black Technopoetics.* Middletown, CT: Wesleyan University Press, 2016.

Coester, Markus, and Wolfgang Bender. *A Reader in African-Jamaican Music, Dance and Religion.* Kingston: Ian Randle Publishers, 2015.

Cohen, Lara Langer, and Jordan Alexander Stein. *Early African American Print Culture.* Philadelphia: University of Pennsylvania Press, 2012.

Cohen, Matt. *The Networked Wilderness: Communicating in Early New England.* Minneapolis: University of Minnesota Press, 2010.

Conway, Cecelia. *African Banjo Echoes in Appalachia: A Study of Folk Traditions.* Knoxville: University of Tennessee Press, 1995.

Cooper, Elizabeth. "Playing against Empire." *Slavery & Abolition* 39, no. 3 (2018): 540–57.

Corbin, Alain. *Village Bells: The Culture of the Senses in the Nineteenth-Century French Countryside.* Translated by Martin Thom. Columbia University Press, 1998.

Cowley, John. *Carnival, Canboulay, and Calypso: Traditions in the Making.* New York: Cambridge University Press, 1996.

Cummings, Sherri V. "'They Are Delighted to Dance for Themselves': Deconstructing Intimacies—Moreau de Saint-Méry's 'Danse' and the Spectre of Black

Female Sexuality in Colonial Saint Domingue." *Journal of Caribbean History* 51, no. 2 (2017): 143–70.

Curran, Andrew S. *The Anatomy of Blackness: Science & Slavery in an Age of Enlightenment*. Baltimore: Johns Hopkins University Press, 2011.

Davies, Drew Edward. "Finding 'Local Content' in the Music of New Spain." *Early Music America* 19, no. 2 (Summer 2013): 64, 60–62.

Delany, Francis X. *A History of the Catholic Church in Jamaica, B.W.I. 1494–1929*. New York: Jesuit Mission Press, 1930.

Delbourgo, James. *Collecting the World: Hans Sloane and the Origins of the British Museum*. New York: Harvard University Press, 2017.

Dewulf, Jeroen. *Afro-Atlantic Catholics: America's First Black Christians*. South Bend: University of Notre Dame Press, 2022.

———. "From the Calendas to the Calenda: On the Afro-Iberian Substratum in Black Performance Culture in the Americas." *Journal of American Folklore* 131, no. 519 (2018): 3–29.

———. *From the Kingdom of Kongo to Congo Square: Kongo Dances and the Origins of the Mardi Gras Indians*. Lafayette, LA: University of Louisiana at Lafayette Press, 2017.

———. "Rethinking the Historical Development of Caribbean Performance Culture from an Afro-Iberian Perspective: The Case of Jankunu." *New West Indian Guide / Nieuwe West-Indische Gids* 95, no. 3/4 (July 28, 2021): 223–53.

Dickinson, Michael. *Almost Dead: Slavery and Social Rebirth in the Black Urban Atlantic, 1680–1807*. Athens, GA: University of Georgia Press, 2022.

Dickson, William. *Letters on Slavery, by William Dickson, Formerly Private Secretary to the Late Hon. Edward Hay, Governor of Barbadoes. To Which Are Added, Addresses to the Whites, and to the Free Negroes of Barbadoes; and Accounts of Some Negroes Eminent for Their Virtues and Abilities*. London: printed and sold by JPhillips, George-Yard, Lombard-Street [. . .], 1789.

Dickson, William, and Joshua Steele. *Mitigation of Slavery, in Two Parts*. London: Printed by R. and A. Taylor, 1814.

Dillon, Elizabeth Maddock. *New World Drama: The Performative Commons in the Atlantic World, 1649–1849*. Durham: Duke University Press, 2014.

Diouf, Sylviane A. *Servants of Allah: African Muslims Enslaved in the Americas*. New York: New York University Press, 1998.

DjeDje, Jacqueline Cogdell. "The (Mis)Representation of African American Music: The Role of the Fiddle." *Journal of the Society for American Music* 10, no. 1 (2016): 1–32.

———. *Turn up the Volume!: A Celebration of African Music*. Los Angeles: UCLA Fowler Museum of Cultural History, 1999.

Douglass, Frederick. *Narrative of the Life of Frederick Douglass: An American Slave*. Boston: Anti-Slavery Office, 1845.

Driver, Merlyn. "The Buzz Aesthetic and Mande Music: Acoustic Masks and the Technology of Enchantment." *African Music* 10 (2017): 95–118.

Du Bois, W. E. B. *The Souls of Black Folk: Essays and Sketches*. Chicago: A. C. McClurg, 1903.

Du Tertre, Jean Baptiste. *Histoire Generale Des Antilles Habitées Par Les Fran-çois: Tome II, Contenant l'histoire Naturelle [. . .]*. Paris: Chez Thomas Iolly, au Palais, en la Salle des Merciers, à la Palme, & aux Armes d'Hollande, 1667.

Dubois, Laurent. *Avengers of the New World: The Story of the Haitian Revolution*. Cambridge, MA: Harvard Belknap Press, 2004.

———. *The Banjo: America's African Instrument*. Cambridge, MA: Harvard Belknap Press, 2016.

———. "Heroines of the Haitian Revolution." *Public Books* (blog), April 28, 2017. https://www.publicbooks.org/heroines-of-the-haitian-revolution/.

———. "Minette's Worlds: Theater and Revolution in Saint-Domingue." *Studies in Eighteenth-Century Culture* 50, no. 1 (2021): 101–18.

Dubois, Laurent, David K. Garner, and Mary Caton Lingold. "The Caribbean Digital & Peer Review: A Musical Passage Hypothesis." *Archipelagos* 3 (2019).

———. *Musical Passage: A Voyage to 1688 Jamaica*. 2016. http://www.musicalpassage.org.

Dunbar, Erica Armstrong. *Never Caught: The Washingtons' Relentless Pursuit of Their Runaway Slave, Ona Judge*. New York: 37 Ink/Atria, 2017.

Edwards, Bryan. *An Historical Survey of the Island of Saint Domingo, together with an Account of the Maroon Negroes in the Island of Jamaica [. . .] also, A tour through the Several Islands of Barbadoes, St. Vincent, Antigua, Tobago, and Grenada, In the Years 1791 and 1792 by Sir William Young, Bart*. London: Printed for John Stockdale, Piccadilly, 1801.

———. *The History, Civil and Commercial, of the British Colonies in the West Indies*. London: Printed for John Stockdale, Piccadilly, 1801.

Eidsheim, Nina Sun. *The Race of Sound: Listening, Timbre, and Vocality in African American Music*. Refiguring American Music. Durham: Duke University Press, 2018.

———. *Sensing Sound: Singing and Listening as Vibrational Practice*. Durham: Duke University Press, 2015.

Eltis, David. *The Rise of African Slavery in the Americas*. New York: Cambridge University Press, 2012.

Epstein, Dena J. *Sinful Tunes and Spirituals: Black Folk Music to the Civil War*. Urbana: University of Illinois Press, 1977.

Equiano, Olaudah. *The Interesting Narrative of the Life of Olaudah Equiano, or Gustavus Vassa, the African. Written by Himself*. London, 1789.

Evans, David. "The Reinterpretation of African Musical Instruments in the United States." In *The African Diaspora: African Origins and New World Identities*, edited by Isidore Okpewho, Carole Boyce Davies, and Ali A. Mazrui, 379–90. Bloomington, IN: Indiana University Press, 1999.

Everill, Bronwen. "On Wednesdays We Wear Prints: Fashion Rules in the African Atlantic." *Junto* (blog), September 18, 2018. https://earlyamericanists.com/2018/09/18/22388/.

Eyerly, Sarah. *Moravian Soundscapes: A Sonic History of the Moravian Missions in Early Pennsylvania*. Bloomington: Indiana University Press, 2020.

———. "Mozart and the Moravians." *Early Music* 47, no. 2 (May 2019): 161–82.

Fatah-Black, Karwan. "The Use of Wills in Community Formation by Former Slaves in Suriname, 1750–1775." *Slavery & Abolition* 41, no. 3 (2020): 623–42.

———. *White Lies and Black Markets: Evading Metropolitan Authority in Colonial Suriname, 1650–1800*. Leiden: Brill, 2015.

Feld, Steven. "Acoustemology." In *Keywords in Sound*, edited by David Novak and Matt Sakakeeny, 12–21. Durham; London: Duke University Press, 2015.

Finley, Sarah. *Hearing Voices: Aurality and New Spanish Sound Culture in Sor Juana Inés de La Cruz*. Lincoln: University of Nebraska Press, 2019.

Floyd, Samuel A. *The Power of Black Music: Interpreting Its History from Africa to the United States*. New York; Oxford: Oxford University Press, 1997.

Floyd, Samuel L., Melanie Zeck, and Guthrie Ramsey. *The Transformation of Black Music: The Rhythms, the Songs, and the Ships of the African Diaspora*. Oxford, New York: Oxford University Press, 2017.

Fouchard, Jean. *Le Théâtre à Saint-Domingue*. Port-au-Prince: Imprimerie Henri Deschamps, 1988.

Froger, François. *Relation d'un voyage fait en 1695, 1696, & 1697, aux côtes d'Afrique, détroit de Magellan, Brezil, Cayenne, & isles Antilles, par une escadre des vaisseaux du roy, commandée par Monsieur de Gennes*. A Paris: chez Nicolas le Gras, 1700.

———. *A Relation of a Voyage Made in the Years 1695, 1696, 1697, on the Coasts of Africa, Streights of Magellan, Brasil, Cayenna, and the Antilles, by a Squadron of French Men of War, under the Command of M. de Gennes*. London: Printed for M. Gillyflower W. Freeman, M. Wotton J. Walthoe and R. Parker, 1698.

From Ear to Ear. Williamsburg, Va.: Colonial Williamsburg Foundation, 2006.

Fromont, Cécile, ed. *Afro-Catholic Festivals in the Americas: Performance, Representation, and the Making of Black Atlantic Tradition*. University Park, PA: Pennsylvania State University Press, 2019.

———. *The Art of Conversion: Christian Visual Culture in the Kingdom of Kongo*. Chapel Hill: University of North Carolina Press, 2017.

———. "Common Threads: Cloth, Colour, and the Slave Trade in Early Modern Kongo and Angola." *Art History* 41, no. 5 (2018): 838–67.

Fryer, Peter. *Rhythms of Resistance: African Musical Heritage in Brazil*. London: Pluto Press, 2000.

Fuentes, Marisa J. *Dispossessed Lives: Enslaved Women, Violence, and the Archive.* Philadelphia: University of Pennsylvania Press, 2016.

Fuller, Harcourt. "Maroon History, Music, and Sacred Sounds in the Americas: A Jamaican Case." *Journal of Africana Religions* 5, no. 2 (2017): 275–82.

Gaddy, Kristina. *Well of Souls: Uncovering the Banjo's Hidden History.* New York: W.W. Norton & Company, 2022.

———. "Music in Well of Souls: Uncovering the Banjo's Hidden History." *Kristinagaddy.com* (blog) September 26, 2022. https://www.kristinagaddy.com/blog/music-in-well-of-souls-uncovering-the-banjos-hidden-history

Garth, John. *A Second Sett of Six Sonata's for the Harpsichord Piano Forte and Organ; with Accompaniments for Two Violins and a Violoncello.* London, n.d.

Gaudio, Michael. *Engraving the Savage the New World and Techniques of Civilization.* Minneapolis: University of Minnesota Press, 2008.

Geoffroy-Schwinden, Rebecca Dowd. "Digital Approaches to Historical Acoustemologies: Replication and Reenactment." In *Digital Sound Studies,* edited by Whitney Trettien, Mary Caton Lingold, and Darren Mueller, 231–249. Durham, NC: Duke University Press, 2018. https://www.doabooks.org/doab?func=search&query=rid:32429.

Gerbner, Katharine. *Christian Slavery: Conversion and Race in the Protestant Atlantic World.* Philadelphia: University of Pennsylvania Press, 2018.

Gilroy, Paul. *The Black Atlantic: Modernity and Double Consciousness.* Cambridge, MA: Harvard University Press, 1993.

Gitelman, Lisa. *Scripts, Grooves, and Writing Machines: Representing Technology in the Edison Era.* Stanford: Stanford University Press, 1999.

Gómez, Pablo F. *The Experiential Caribbean: Creating Knowledge and Healing in the Early Modern Atlantic.* Chapel Hill: University of North Carolina Press, 2017.

Goodman, Glenda. "Sounds Heard, Meaning Deferred: Music Transcription as Imperial Technology." *Eighteenth-Century Studies* 52, no. 1 (2018): 39–45.

Goodman, Steve. *Sonic Warfare: Sound, Affect, and the Ecology of Fear.* Cambridge, MA: MIT Press, 2010.

Gordon, Bonnie. "What Mr. Jefferson Didn't Hear." In *Rethinking Difference in Music Scholarship,* edited by Olivia Bloechl, Melanie Lowe, and Jeffrey Kallberg, 108–32. New York: Cambridge University Press, 2015.

Gordon-Reed, Annette. *The Hemingses of Monticello: An American Family.* New York: Norton, 2008.

Green, Toby. *A Fistful of Shells: West Africa from the Rise of the Slave Trade to the Age of Revolution.* Chicago: University of Chicago Press, 2019.

Gronniosaw, James Albert Ukawsaw. *A Narrative of the Most Remarkable Particulars in the Life of James Albert Ukawsaw Gronniosaw, an African Prince, as Related by Himself.* 1772. Documenting the American South, https://docsouth.unc.edu/neh/gronniosaw/gronnios.html.

Guasco, Michael. "1619: Rethinking the History of Africans and Slavery in Early America." Virginia Commonwealth University, January 31, 2019.

———. *Slaves and Englishmen: Human Bondage in the Early Modern Atlantic World*. Philadelphia: University of Pennsylvania Press, 2014.

Gufler, Hermann. "Yamba Twin Ritual." *Anthropos* (1996): 33–51.

Gura, Philip F., and James F Bollman. *America's Instrument: The Banjo in the Nineteenth Century*. Chapel Hill: University of North Carolina Press, 1999.

Hagood, Mack. "Quiet Comfort: Noise, Otherness, and the Mobile Production of Personal Space." *American Quarterly* 63, no. 3 (2011): 573–89.

Hall, Gwendolyn Midlo. *Slavery and African Ethnicities in the Americas: Restoring the Links*. Chapel Hill: University of North Carolina Press, 2005.

Hall, Kim F. *Things of Darkness: Economies of Race and Gender in Early Modern England*. Ithaca: Cornell University Press, 1995.

Hamilton, Julia. "'African' Songs and Women's Abolitionism in the Home, 1787–1807." *Studies in Eighteenth-Century Culture* 50, no. 1 (2021): 153–68.

Hammack, Maria Esther. "The Illegal Slave Trade in Texas, 1808–1865." *Not Even Past*, September 27, 2016. https://notevenpast.org/the-illegal-slave-trade-in-texas-1808-1865/.

Handler, Jerome S., and Charlotte J. Frisbie. "Aspects of Slave Life in Barbados: Music and Its Cultural Context." *Caribbean Studies* 11, no. 4 (1972): 5–46.

Handler, Jerome S., and Frederick W. Lange. *Plantation Slavery in Barbados: An Archaeological and Historical Investigation*. Cambridge, MA: Harvard University Press, 1978.

Hanley, Ryan. *Beyond Slavery and Abolition: Black British Writing, c. 1770–1830*. New York: Cambridge University Press, 2019.

———. "Calvinism, Proslavery and James Albert Ukawsaw Gronniosaw." *Slavery & Abolition* 36, no. 2 (2015): 260–381.

Harris, Jennifer. "Seeing the Light: Re-Reading James Albert Ukawsaw Gronniosaw." *English Language Notes* 42, no. 4 (June 1, 2005): 43–57.

Hartman, Saidiya V. *Scenes of Subjection: Terror, Slavery, and Self-Making in Nineteenth-Century America*. Race and American Culture. New York: Oxford University Press, 1997.

———. "Venus in Two Acts." *Small Axe* 12, no. 2 (July 17, 2008): 1–14.

———. *Wayward Lives, Beautiful Experiments: Intimate Histories of Social Upheaval*. New York: W.W. Norton & Company, 2019.

Head, David. "Slave Smuggling by Foreign Privateers: The Illegal Slave Trade and the Geopolitics of the Early Republic." *Journal of the Early Republic* 33, no. 3 (2013): 433–62.

Henar-Hewitt, Ilse. *Surinaamse koto's en angisa's*. Paramaribo, Suriname: Offsetdrukkerij Westfort, 1997.

Heywood, Linda M., and John K. Thornton. *Central Africans, Atlantic Creoles, and the Foundation of the Americas, 1585–1660*. New York: Cambridge University Press, 2007.

Hill, Errol. *The Jamaican Stage, 1655–1900: Profile of a Colonial Theatre.* Amherst: University of Massachusetts Press, 1992.

Hughes, Griffith. *The Natural History of Barbados. In Ten Books. By the Reverend Mr. Griffith Hughes, A. M. Rector of St. Lucy's Parish, in the Said Island, and F. R. S.* London: Printed for the author, 1750.

Hulme, Peter. *Colonial Encounters: Europe and the Native Caribbean, 1492–1797.* London; New York: Methuen, 1986.

Hunter, David. "The Beckfords in England and Italy: A Case Study in the Musical Uses of the Profits of Slavery." *Early Music* 46, no. 2 (2018): 285–98.

Hurston, Zora Neale. "How It Feels to Be Colored Me." *World Tomorrow,* May 1928.

Iannini, Christopher P. *Fatal Revolutions: Natural History, West Indian Slavery, and the Routes of American Literature.* Chapel Hill: University of North Carolina Press, 2012.

Irving, David R. M. "Ancient Greeks, World Music, and Early Modern Constructions of Western European Identity." In *Studies on a Global History of Music: A Balzan Musicology Project, 2013–2015,* edited by Reinhard Strohm, 24–41. New York: Routledge, 2018.

Jabbour, Alan. "In Search of the Source of American Syncopation." *Strings* 16, no. 8 (June 2002): 46–56.

Jaji, Tsitsi. *Africa in Stereo: Modernism, Music, and Pan-African Solidarity.* New York: Oxford University Press, 2014.

Jegede, Tunde. "African Classical Music: The Griot Tradition." Paper presented at Black Music: Its Circulation and Impact in Eighteenth-Century London, Yale Center for British Art, Yale University, April 2019.

Jenson, Deborah. *Beyond the Slave Narrative Politics, Sex, and Manuscripts in the Haitian Revolution.* Liverpool: University Press, 2011.

Jobson, Richard. *The Golden Trade: Or, A Discovery of the River Gambra, and the Golden Trade of the Aethiopians [. . .].* London: Printed by Nicholas Okes, 1623.

Johnson, Daniel. "'Profane Language, Horrid Oaths and Imprecations': Order and the Colonial Soundscape in the American Mid-Atlantic, 1650–1750." *Social History* 46, no. 3 (July 3, 2021): 255–77.

Johnson, Jessica Marie. *Wicked Flesh: Black Women, Intimacy, and Freedom in the Atlantic World.* Philadelphia: University of Pennsylvania Press, 2020.

Johnson, Sara E. *The Fear of French Negroes: Transcolonial Collaboration in the Revolutionary Americas.* Berkeley: University of California Press, 2012.

Johnson, Walter. "On Agency." *Journal of Social History* 37, no. 1 (2003): 113–24.

Jones, Nicholas R. *Staging Habla de Negros: Radical Performances of the African Diaspora in Early Modern Spain.* University Park: The Pennsylvania State University Press, 2019.

Kasawira, W. "Notes and News." *African Music* 3, no. 2 (1963): 50–54.

Kasfir, Sidney Littlefield. "Elephant Women, Furious and Majestic: Women's Masquerades in Africa and the Diaspora." *African Arts* 31, no. 2 (1998): 18.

Kaufmann, Miranda. *Black Tudors: The Untold Story*. London: Oneworld Publications, 2017.

Kriz, Kay Dian. *Slavery, Sugar, and the Culture of Refinement: Picturing the British West Indies, 1700–1840*. New Haven: Yale University Press, 2008.

Kupperman, Ordahl, ed. *A True and Exact History of the Island of Barbados*, by Richard Lignon. Indianapolis: Hackett Pub. Co., 2011.

The Language You Cry In. Dir. Angel Serrano and Alvaro Toepka. San Francisco: California Newsreel, 1998.

Le Guin, Elisabeth. "'One Fine Night in Veracruz.'" *American Music* 39, no. 3 (October 1, 2021): 265–300.

Le Page du Pratz, M. *The History of Louisiana, or the Western Parts of Viginia and Carolina* [. . .] *Translated from the French of M. Le Page Du Pratz; With some Notes and Observations relating to our Colonies*. London: Printed for T. Becket, 1774.

Leigh, Devin. "The Jamaican Airs: An Introduction to Unpublished Pieces of Musical Notation from Enslaved People in the Eighteenth-Century Caribbean." *Atlantic Studies* 17, no. 4 (October 21, 2019): 462–84.

———. "The Jamaican Airs Exhibit." *Early Caribbean Digital Archive*. Northeastern University. ecda.northeastern.edu/Jamaican-music-exhibit-leigh/.

Léry, Jean de. *Histoire d'un voyage faict en la terre du Bresil, autrement dite Amerique*. Geneve: A. Chuppin, 1580.

Leslie, Charles. *A New History of Jamaica, from the Earliest Accounts, to the Taking of Porto Bello by Vice-Admiral Vernon*. London: Printed for J. Hodges, 1740.

Lewin, Olive. *Rock It Come Over: The Folk Music of Jamaica*. Kingston: University of the West Indies Press, 2001.

———. "Traditional Music in Jamaica." *Caribbean Quarterly* 29, no. 1 (March 1983): 32–43.

Lhamon, W. T. *Raising Cain: Blackface Performance from Jim Crow to Hip Hop*. Cambridge, MA: Harvard University Press, 1998.

Ligon, Richard. *A True and Exact History of the Island of Barbados*. London: Printed for Humphrey Moseley, 1657.

Lindsay, Lisa A., and John Wood Sweet. *Biography and the Black Atlantic*. Philadelphia: University of Pennsylvania Press, 2014.

Lingold, Mary Caton. "Digital Performance and the Musical Archive of Slavery: 'Like Running Home.'" *Studies in Eighteenth-Century Culture* 49, no. 1 (2020): 109–25.

———. "Fiddling with Freedom: Solomon Northup's Musical Trade in 12 Years a Slave." *Sounding Out!* (blog), December 16, 2013.

———. "In Search of Mr. Baptiste: On Early Caribbean Music, Race, and Colonial Composition." *Early Music*, 49, no. 1 (2021): 49–66.

———. "Listening to the Past: An African-American Lullaby." *Appendix* 1, no. 3 (July 2013). http://theappendix.net/issues/2013/7/listening-to-the-past-an -african-american-lullaby.

———. "Peculiar Animations: Listening to Afro-Atlantic Music in Caribbean Travel Narratives." *Early American Literature* 52, no. 3 (2017): 623–50.

———. "Sonic Records: Listening to Early Afro-Atlantic Literature and Music, 1650–1850," 2017. https://dukespace.lib.duke.edu/dspace/handle/10161 /14352.

———. "Tena, Too, Sings America: Listening to an Enslaved Woman's Musical Memories of Africa." *C19* podcast. https://soundcloud.com/c19podcast /tena-too-sings-america-listening-to-an-enslaved-womans-musical-memories -of-africa.

Lingold, Mary Caton, Darren Mueller, and Whitney Trettien, eds. *Digital Sound Studies*. Durham: Duke University Press, 2018.

Linhart Wood, Jennifer. *Sounding Otherness in Early Modern Drama and Travel: Uncanny Vibrations in the English Archive*. New York: Palgrave Macmillan, 2019.

Livesay, Daniel. *Children of Uncertain Fortune: Mixed-Race Jamaicans in Britain and the Atlantic Family, 1733–1833*. Chapel Hill: University of North Carolina Press, 2018.

Long, Edward. *The History of Jamaica. Or, General Survey of the Antient and Modern State of That Island: With Reflections on Its Situation, Settlements, Inhabitants, [. . .] In Three Volumes. Illustrated with Copper Plates*. Vol. 2. London: Printed for T. Lowndes, 1774.

Lopes, Duarte, and Filippo Pigafetta. *Relatione del reame di Congo et delle circonvicine contrade Tratta dalli Scritti & ragionamenti di Odoardo Lopez Portogheses Per Filippo Pigafetta [. . .]*. Roma: Appresso Bartolomeo Grassi, 1591.

———. *A Report of the Kingdome of Congo, a Region of Africa: And of the Countries That Border Rounde about the Same [. . .]*. London: Printed by Iohn Wolfe, 1597.

———. *A Report of the Kingdom of Congo, and of the Surrounding Countries; Drawn out of the Writtings and Discourses of the Portuguese, Duarte Lopez, by Filippo Pigafetta, in Rome, 159, translated by Margarite Hutchinson. London*. London: Printed by John Murray, 1881.

Lott, Eric. *Love and Theft: Blackface Minstrelsy and the American Working Class*. New York: Oxford University Press, 1993.

Mackey, Nathaniel. "Cante Moro." In *Sound States: Innovative Poetics and Acoustical Technologies*, edited by Adalaide Kirby Morris, 194–212. Chapel Hill: University of North Carolina Press, 1997.

Madiba, Elijah. "A Collaborative Approach to Revitalisation and the Repatriation of IsiXhosa Music Recordings Archived at the International Library of African Music (ILAM) in South Africa." *Ethnomusicology Forum* 30, no. 1 (January 2, 2021): 52–62.

Marín Lopez, Javier. "La Enseñanza Musical En La Catedral de México Durante El Periodo Virreinal." *Música y Educación* 76 (2008): 8–19.

Mark, Peter. "Fetishers, 'Marybuckes' and the Christian Norm: European Images of Senegambians and Their Religions, 1550–1760." *African Studies Review* 23, no. 2 (September 1980): 91–99.

Marke, Peter. "The Evolution of 'Portuguese' Identity: Luso-Africans on the Upper Guinea Coast from the Sixteenth to the Early Nineteenth Century." *Journal of African History* 40, no. 2 (1999): 173–91.

Marly; or, A Planter's Life in Jamaica. Glasgow, 1828. Matthews, John. *A Voyage to the River Sierra-Leone on the Coast of Africa: Containing an Account of the Trade and Productions of the Country* [. . .] *with an Additional Letter on the Subject of the African Slave Trade*. London: B. White and Son, 1791.

Mauldin, Laura. "Precarious Plasticity: Neuropolitics, Cochlear Implants, and the Redefinition of Deafness." *Science, Technology, & Human Values* 39, no. 1 (2014): 130–53.

Maxwell, Heather. "When the Xylophone Speaks." In *Turn up the Volume!: A Celebration of African Music*, edited by Jacqueline Cogdell DjeDje, 58–67. Los Angeles: UCLA Fowler Museum of Cultural History, 1999.

May, Robert E. *Yuletide in Dixie: Slavery, Christmas, and Southern Memory*. Charlottesville: University of Virginia Press, 2019.

McAlister, Elizabeth A. *Rara!: Vodou, Power, and Performance in Haiti and Its Diaspora*. Berkeley: University of California Press, 2002.

McDaniel, Lorna. *The Big Drum Ritual of Carriacou: Praisesongs in Rememory of Flight*. Gainesville: University Press of Florida, 1998.

———. "The Flying Africans: Extent and Strength of the Myth in the Americas." *New West Indian Guide / Nieuwe West-Indische Gids* 64, no. 1/2 (1990): 28–40.

Meintjes, Louise. *Sound of Africa!: Making Music Zulu in a South African Studio*. Durham: Duke University Press, 2003.

Menard, Russell R. *Sweet Negotiations: Sugar, Slavery, and Plantation Agriculture in Early Barbados*. Charlottesville: University of Virginia Press, 2006.

Merolla da Sorrento, Jerom. "A Voyage to Congo, and Several Other Countries Chiefly in Southern Africk." In *A Collection of Voyages and Travels: Some Now First Printed from Original Manuscripts, Others Now First Published in English in Six Volumes*, edited by Awnsham Churchill and John Churchill, Vol. 1, 3rd Edition. London, 1744.

Merolla, Girolamo. *Breue, e succinta relatione del viaggio nel regno di Congo nell' Africa meridionale, fatto dal P. Girolamo Merolla da Sorrento, sacerdote cappuccino, missionario apostolico: continente variati clima, arie, animali, fiumi, frutti, vestimenti con proprie figure, diuersità di costumi, e di viueri per l'vso humano*. Napoli: Francesco Mollo, 1692.

Michael Angelo of Gattina. "A Curious and Exact Account of a Voyage to Congo, in the Years 1666 and 1667." In *A Collection of voyages and travels: some now first printed from original manuscripts, others translated out of Foreign Languages, and now first published in English* [. . .] *the whole illustrated with a great number of useful maps, and cuts, all engraven on copper,* edited by Awnsham Churchill and John Churchill, vol. 1. London: Printed for Henry Lintot and John Osborn, 1728.

Millward, Jessica. *Finding Charity's Folk: Enslaved and Free Black Women in Maryland.* Athens: University of Georgia Press, 2015.

Minton, David. "West African Fiddles in Deep East Texas." In *Juneteenth Texas: Essays in African-American Folklore,* edited by Francis E. Abernethy, Patrick B. Mullen, and Alan B. Govenar, 291–314. Denton: University of North Texas Press, 1996.

Mintz, Sidney W., and Richard Price. *The Birth of African-American Culture: An Anthropological Perspective.* Boston: Beacon Press, 1992.

Mitchell, Koritha. "Identifying White Mediocrity and Know-Your-Place Aggression: A Form of Self-Care." *African American Review* 51, no. 4 (2018): 253–62.

Morgan, Jennifer L. *Laboring Women: Reproduction and Gender in New World Slavery.* Philadelphia: University of Pennsylvania Press, 2004.

Morrison, Matthew D. "Blacksound." In *The Oxford Handbook of Western Music and Philosophy,* edited by Tomás McAuley, Nanette Nielsen, Jerrold Levinson, and Ariana Phillips-Hutton, 555–78. New York: Oxford University Press, 2021.

Moten, Fred. *In the Break: The Aesthetics of the Black Radical Tradition.* Minneapolis: University of Minnesota Press, 2003.

Munro, Martin. *Different Drummers: Rhythm and Race in the Americas.* Berkeley: University of California Press, 2010.

Mustakeem, Sowande' M. *Slavery at Sea: Terror, Sex, and Sickness in the Middle Passage.* Urbana: University of Illinois Press, 2016.

Nau, Ignace. "Le Lambi." *L'Union,* April 20, 1837.

Nettl, Bruno. *The Study of Ethnomusicology: Twenty-Nine Issues and Concepts.* Urbana: University of Illinois Press, 1983.

Newman, Brooke N. *A Dark Inheritance: Blood, Race, and Sex in Colonial Jamaica.* New Haven: Yale University Press, 2018.

Niven, Penelope. *Carl Sandburg: A Biography.* New York: Scribner's, 1991.

Northup, Solomon. *Twelve Years a Slave: Narrative of S. Northup, a Citizen of New York, Kidnapped in Washington City in 1841, and Rescued in 1853.* London, 1853.

Norwood, Henry. "A Voyage to Virginia. By Colonel Norwood." In *A Collection of Voyages and Travels: Some Now First Printed from Original Manuscripts, Others Now First Published in English,* edited by Awnsham Churchill and John Churchill, vol. 6. London, 1732.

Novak, David, and Matt Sakakeeny. *Keywords in Sound.* Durham: Duke University Press, 2015.

Ochoa Gautier, Ana María. *Aurality: Listening and Knowledge in Nineteenth-Century Colombia.* Durham: Duke University Press, 2014.

Oldmixon, John. *The British Empire in America, Containing the History of the Discovery, Settlement, Progress and present State of all the British Colonies on the Continent and Islands of America.* London: Printed for John Nicholson, 1708.

Olwell, Robert. "'Loose, Idle and Disorderly': Slave Women in the Eighteenth-Century Charleston Marketplace." In *More than Chattel: Black Women and Slavery in the Americas,* edited by Darlene Clark Hine and Barry David Gaspar, 97–110. Bloomington: Indiana University Press, 1996.

O'Malley, Gregory E. *Final Passages: The Intercolonial Slave Trade of British America, 1619–1807.* Chapel Hill: University of North Carolina Press, 2014.

Osborne, Francis. *A History of the Catholic Church in Jamaica.* New Orleans: Loyola University Press, 1977.

Park, Mungo. *Travels in the Interior Districts of Africa: Performed under the Direction and Patronage of the African Association, in the Years 1795, 1796, and 1797.* London: Printed by W. Bulmer and Co., 1799.

Parrish, Susan Scott. *American Curiosity: Cultures of Natural History in the Colonial British Atlantic World.* Chapel Hill: University of North Carolina Press, 2006.

Paton, Diana. "Enslaved Women and Slavery before and after 1807." *History in Focus,* no. 12. https://archives.history.ac.uk/history-in-focus/Slavery/articles/paton.html.

———. *The Cultural Politics of Obeah: Religion, Colonialism and Modernity in the Caribbean World.* Critical Perspectives on Empire. New York: Cambridge University Press, 2015.

———. "The Driveress and the Nurse: Childcare, Working Children and Other Work Under Caribbean Slavery." *Past & Present* 246, supplement 15 (December 5, 2020): 27–53.

———. "Mary Williamson's Letter, or Seeing Women and Sisters in the Archives of Atlantic Slavery." *Transactions of the Royal Historical Society* 29 (December 2019): 153–79.

Pawson, Michael, and David Buisseret. *Port Royal, Jamaica.* Oxford: Clarendon Press, 1975.

Pestana, Carla Gardina. "The Jamaica Maroons and the Dangers of Categorical Thinking." *Common-Place* 17, no. 4 (2017). http://common-place.org/book/vol-17-no-4-pestana/.

Philip, Marlene Nourbese, and Setaey Adamu Boateng. *Zong!,* Middelton, CT: University of Wesleyan Press, 2011.

Polcha, Elizabeth. "Voyeur in the Torrid Zone: John Gabriel Stedman's *Narrative of a Five Years Expedition against the Revolted Negroes of Surinam, 1773–1838.*" *Early American Literature* 54, no. 3 (2019): 673–710.

Powers, David M. *From Plantation to Paradise?: Cultural Politics and Musical Theatre in French Slave Colonies, 1764–1789.* East Lansing: Michigan State University Press, 2014.

Pratt, Mary Louise. *Imperial Eyes: Travel Writing and Transculturation.* London: Routledge, 1992.

Prest, Julia. "Pale Imitations: White Performances of Slave Dance in the Public Theatres of Pre-Revolutionary Saint-Domingue." *Atlantic Studies* 16, no. 4 (October 2, 2019): 502–20.

———. "Parisian Palimpsests and Creole Creations: Mme Marsan and Dlle Minette Play Nina on the Caribbean Stage." *Early Modern French Studies* 41, no. 2 (July 3, 2019): 170–88.

Price, Richard. *Maroon Societies: Rebel Slave Communities in the Americas.* Baltimore: Johns Hopkins University Press, 1996.

Price, Richard, and Sally Price. "John Gabriel Stedman's Collection of 18th-Century Artifacts from Suriname." *New West Indian Guide / Nieuwe West-Indische Gids* 53, no. 3/4 (1979): 121–40.

Prince, Mary. *The History of Mary Prince, a West Indian Slave.* London: F. Westley and A. H. Davis, 1831.

Quilligan, Maureen, ed. "Theodor De Bry's Voyages to the New and Old Worlds." *Journal of Medieval and Early Modern Studies* 41, no. 1 (January 1, 2011): 1–12.

Radano, Ronald Michael. *Lying up a Nation: Race and Black Music.* Chicago: University of Chicago Press, 2003.

Ramos-Kittrell, Jesús A. *Playing in the Cathedral: Music, Race, and Status in New Spain.* New York: Oxford University Press, 2016.

Rath, Richard. "Drums and Power: Ways of Creolizing Music in Coastal South Carolina and Georgia, 1730–1790." In *Creolization in the Americas,* edited by Steven Reinhardt and David Buisseret, 99–130. College Station: Texas A&M Press, 2000.

Rath, Richard Cullen. "African Music in Seventeenth-Century Jamaica: Cultural Transit and Transition." *William and Mary Quarterly* 50, no. 4 (1993): 700–726.

———. "Ethnodigital Sonics and the Historical Imagination." In *Digital Sound Studies,* edited by Mary Caton Lingold, Darren Meuller, and Whitney Trettien, 29–46. Durham: Duke University Press, 2018.

———. *How Early America Sounded.* Ithaca: Cornell University Press, 2003.

Reed, Peter. "There Was No Resisting John Canoe: Circum-Atlantic Transracial Performance." *Theatre History Studies* 27 (2007): 65–85.

Rickford, John R., and Jerome S. Handler. "Textual Evidence on the Nature of Early Barbadian Speech, 1676–1835." *Journal of Pidgin and Creole Languages* 9, no. 2 (1994): 221–55.

Rivera, Gina. "Marie Pélissier (1707–49), the Diva of the Dulis Affair." *Early Music* 43, no. 2 (May 1, 2015): 309–17.

Roach, Joseph R. *Cities of the Dead: Circum-Atlantic Performance.* New York: Columbia University Press, 1996.

Roberts, John Storm. *Black Music of Two Worlds: African, Caribbean, Latin, and African-American Traditions.* New York: Schirmer Books, 1998.

Roberts, Peter A. *A Response to Enslavement: Playing Their Way to Virtue.* Kingston: University of the West Indies Press, 2018.

Robertson, James. "Late Seventeenth-Century Spanish Town, Jamaica: Building an English City on Spanish Foundations." *Early American Studies* 6, no. 2 (2008): 346–90.

Roper, L. H. *The English Empire in America, 1602–1658: Beyond Jamestown.* London: Pickering & Chatto, 2009.

Ruiz Jiménez, Juan. "From Mozos de Coro Towards Seises: Boys in the Musical Life of Seville Cathedral in the Fifteenth and Sixteenth Century." In *Young Choristers: 650–1700,* edited by Susan Boynton and Eric Rice, 86–103. Woodbridge, UK: Boydell Press, 2008.

Russel-Henar, Christine van, Chandra van Binnendijk, and Stichting Fu Memre Wi Afo. *Angisa tori: de geheimtaal van Suriname's hoofddoeken = Angisa tori: the secret code of Surinamese headkerchiefs.* Paramaribo: Stichting Fu Memre Wi Afo, 2008.

Ryan, Maria. "'The Influence of Melody upon Man in the Wild State of Nature': Enslaved Parishioners, Anglican Violence, and Racialized Listening in a Jamaica Parish." *Journal of the Society for American Music* 15, no. 3 (2021): 268–86.

Sandburg, Carl. *The American Songbag.* New York: Harcourt, Brace & World, 1927.

———. *Carl Sandburg Sings His American Songbag.* New York: Caedmon, 1967.

Samuel, Petal. "Timing to Descant: The Colonial Ear and Afro-Caribbean Women Writers' Decolonial Soundscapes." Dissertation. Vanderbilt University, 2016.

Santos, João dos. *Ethiopia Oriental, e Varia historia de cousas, notaueis do Oriente.* Impressa no Conuento de S. Domingos de Euora [. . .] por Manoel de Lira, 1609.

Schuler, Monica. "Myalism and the African Religious Tradition in Jamaica." In *Africa and the Caribbean: The Legacies of a Link,* edited by Margaret E Crahan and Franklin W Knight, 65–79. Baltimore: Johns Hopkins University Press, 1979.

Scott, Hugh Arthur. "London's Earliest Public Concerts." *Musical Quarterly* 22, no. 4 (1936): 446–57.

Scott, Julius Sherrard. *The Common Wind: Afro-American Currents in the Age of the Haitian Revolution.* London: Verso, 2018.

Seeger, Charles. "Prescriptive and Descriptive Music-Writing." *Musical Quarterly* 44, no. 2 (1958): 184–95.

Shibli, Fatima El. "Islam and the Blues." *Souls* 9, no. 2 (June 6, 2007): 162–70.

Skeehan, Danielle. "Black Atlantic Acoustemologies and the Maritime Archive." In *Acoustemologies in Contact: Sounding Subjects and Modes of Listening in Early Modernity,* edited by Emily Wilbourne and Suzanne G. Cusick, 107–33. Cambridge: Open Book Publishers, 2021.

———. "Deadly Notes: Atlantic Soundscapes and the Writing of the Middle Passage." *Appendix* 1, no. 3 (July 2013). http://theappendix.net/issues/2013/7/deadly-notes-atlantic-soundscapes-and-the-writing-of-the-middle-passage.

———. *The Fabric of Empire: Material and Literary Cultures of the Global Atlantic, 1650–1850.* Baltimore: Johns Hopkins University Press, 2020.

Sloane, Hans. *A Voyage to the Islands Madera, Barbados, Nieves, St. Christophers and Jamaica, with the Natural History* [. . .] *of the last of those Islands.* London: Printed by B.M. for the Author, 1707.

Small, Christopher. *Musicking: The Meanings of Performing and Listening.* Hanover: University Press of New England, 1998.

Smalligan, Laura M. "An Effigy for the Enslaved: Jonkonnu in Jamaica and Belisario's *Sketches of Character.*" *Slavery and Abolition* 32, no. 4 (December 2011): 561–81.

Smallwood, Stephanie E. *Saltwater Slavery: A Middle Passage from Africa to American Diaspora.* Cambridge, MA: Harvard University Press, 2007.

Smith, Cassander L. *Black Africans in the British Imagination: English Narratives of the Early Atlantic World.* Baton Rouge: Louisiana State University Press, 2016.

Smith, Cassander L., Nicholas R. Jones, and Miles P. Grier, eds. *Early Modern Black Diaspora Studies: A Critical Anthology.* New York: Palgrave Macmillan, 2018.

Smith, Mark M. *Listening to Nineteenth-Century America.* Chapel Hill: University of North Carolina Press, 2001.

———. *Stono: Documenting and Interpreting a Southern Slave Revolt.* Columbia: University of South Carolina Press, 2005.

Smith, William. *A Natural History of Nevis, and the Rest of the English Leeward Charibee Islands in America.* [. . .] *In Eleven Letters from the Revd Mr. Smith.* London: J. Bentham, 1745.

Snyder, Terri L. *The Power to Die: Slavery and Suicide in British North America.* Chicago: University of Chicago Press, 2015.

Southern, Eileen. *The Music of Black Americans: A History.* New York: Norton, 1971.

Southern, Eileen, and Josephine Wright. *African-American Traditions in Song, Sermon, Tale, and Dance, 1600s–1920: An Annotated Bibliography of Literature, Collections, and Artworks.* New York: Greenwood Press, 1990.

Spencer, Robert. "Chitarrone, Theorbo and Archlute." *Early Music* 4, no. 4 (1976): 407–23.

Spohr, Arne. "'Mohr Und Trompeter': Blackness and Social Status in Early Modern Germany." *Journal of the American Musicological Society* 72, no. 3 (2019): 613–63.

Stedman, John Gabriel. *Narrative of a Five Years Expedition against the Revolted Negroes of Surinam: Transcribed for the First Time from the Original 1790 Manuscript,* edited by Richard Price and Sally Price. Baltimore: Johns Hopkins University Press, 1988.

———. *The Journal of John Gabriel Stedman, 1744–1797: Soldier and Author, Including an Authentic Account of His Expedition to Surinam in 1772.* Mitre Press, 1962.

Sterne, Jonathan. *The Audible Past: Cultural Origins of Sound Reproduction.* Durham: Duke University Press, 2003.

———. *MP3: The Meaning of a Format.* Durham: Duke University Press, 2012.

Stevenson, Robert. "A Caribbean Music History: A Selective Annotated Bibliography." *Inter-American Music Review* 4, no. 1 (1981): 1–84.

———. *Music in Aztec & Inca Territory.* Berkeley: University of California Press, 1968.

———. "Vicente Lusitano New Light on His Career." *Journal of the American Musicological Society* 15, no. 1 (1962): 72–77.

Stoever, Jennifer Lynn. *The Sonic Color Line: Race and the Cultural Politics of Listening.* Postmillennial Pop. New York: New York University Press, 2016.

Sturtz, Linda. "The Sett Girls and the Pedagogy of the Streets: An Aural Black Counterpublic." In *Caribbean Reasonings: Rupert Lewis and the Black Intellectual Tradition,* edited by Clinton A. Hutton, Maziki Thame, Jermaine McCalpin, 207–38. Kingston: Ian Randle Publishers, 2018.

Sublette, Ned. *Cuba and Its Music: From the First Drums to the Mambo.* Chicago: Chicago Review Press, 2004.

Sullivan, John Jeremiah. "Death Rattle: Searching for the old jawbone." *Oxford American,* 99, Winter 2017. https://oxfordamerican.org/magazine/issue-99 -winter-2017/death-rattle

———. "Talking Drums," *Oxford American,* 107, Winter 2019. https://main .oxfordamerican.org/magazine/item/1855-talking-drums.

Sweet, James H. *Domingos Álvares, African Healing, and the Intellectual History of the Atlantic World.* Chapel Hill: University of North Carolina Press, 2011.

Taylor, Diana. *The Archive and the Repertoire: Performing Cultural Memory in the Americas.* Durham: Duke University Press, 2003.

Taylor, John. *Jamaica in 1687: The Taylor Manuscript at the National Library of Jamaica.* Kingston: University of the West Indies Press, 2008.

Thomas, Sarah. "Envisaging a Future for Slavery: Agostino Brunias and the Imperial Politics of Labor and Reproduction." *Eighteenth-Century Studies* 52, no. 1 (2018): 115–33.

Thompson, Katrina Dyonne. *Ring Shout, Wheel About: The Racial Politics of Music and Dance in North American Slavery.* Urbana: University of Illinois Press, 2014.

Thornton, John K. *Africa and Africans in the Making of the Atlantic World, 1400–1800.* New York: Cambridge University Press, 1998.

———. *A Cultural History of the Atlantic World, 1250–1820.* New York: Cambridge University Press, 2012.

Tomlinson, Gary. *Singing of the New World: Indigenous Voice in the Era of European Contact.* New York: Cambridge University Press, 2009.

Tracey, Hugh. "Tina's Lullaby." *African Music* 2, no. 4 (1961): 99–101.

Trouillot, Michel-Rolph. *Silencing the Past: Power and the Production of History.* Boston: Beacon Press, 1995.

Uring, Nathaniel. *A History of the Voyages and Travels of Captain Nathaniel Uring: with New Draughts of the Bay of Honduras and the Caribbee Islands* [. . .]. London: Printed by W. Wilkins, for J. Peele, 1726.

Valerio, Miguel. *Sovereign Joy: Afro-Mexican Kings and Queens, 1539–1640.* New York: Cambridge University Press, 2022.

Vazquez, Alexandra T. *Listening in Detail: Performances of Cuban Music.* Durham: Duke University Press, 2013.

Vieux-Chauvet, Marie. *Dance on the Volcano.* Translated by Kaiama Glover. New York: Archipelago Books, 2016.

Voigt, Lisa. *Spectacular Wealth: The Festivals of Colonial South American Mining Towns.* Austin: University of Texas Press, 2016.

Voigt, Lisa, and Elio Brancaforte. "The Traveling Illustrations of Sixteenth-Century Travel Narratives." *PMLA* 129, no. 3 (2014): 365–98.

Voltaire. *Candide and Other Stories.* Translated by Roger Pearson. New York: Oxford University Press, 2006.

Wallace-Sanders, Kimberly. *Mammy: A Century of Race, Gender and Southern Memory.* Michigan: University of Michigan Press, 2010.

Warner-Lewis, Maureen. *Central Africa in the Caribbean: Transcending Time, Transforming Cultures.* Kingston: University of the West Indies Press, 2003.

Weaver, Karol Kimberlee. *Medical Revolutionaries: The Enslaved Healers of Eighteenth-Century Saint Domingue.* Urbana: University of Illinois Press, 2006.

Weheliye, Alexander G. *Phonographies: Grooves in Sonic Afro-Modernity.* Durham: Duke University Press, 2005.

Wheat, David. *Atlantic Africa and the Spanish Caribbean, 1570–1640.* Chapel Hill: University of North Carolina Press, 2016.

Wheeler, Roxann. *The Complexion of Race: Categories of Difference in Eighteenth-Century British Culture.* Philadelphia: University of Pennsylvania Press, 2000.

White, Shane, and Graham J White. *The Sounds of Slavery: Discovering African American History through Songs, Sermons, and Speech.* Boston: Beacon Press, 2005.

Wilbourne, Emily, and Suzanne G. Cusick, eds. *Acoustemologies in Contact: Sounding Subjects and Modes of Listening in Early Modernity.* Cambridge: Open Book Publishers, 2021.

Winans, Robert B. *Banjo Roots and Branches*. Urbana: University of Illinois Press, 2018.

Winkler, Peter. "Writing Ghost Notes: The Poetics and Politics of Transcription." In *Keeping Score: Music, Disciplinarity, Culture,* edited by David Schwarz and Anahid Kassabian, 169–203. Charlottesville: University Press of Virginia, 1997.

Wisecup, Kelly. *Medical Encounters: Knowledge and Identity in Early American Literatures*. Boston: University of Massachusetts Press, 2013.

Wisecup, Kelly, and Toni Wall Jaudon. "On Knowing and Not Knowing about Obeah." *Atlantic Studies* 12, no. 2 (April 3, 2015): 129–43.

Woodfield, Ian. *English Musicians in the Age of Exploration*. Stuyvesant, NY: Pendragon Press, 1995.

Young, Ashley Rose. "Nourishing Networks: The Public Culture of Food in Nineteenth-Century America." ProQuest Dissertations Publishing, 2017. https://search.proquest.com/docview/1981985669?pq-origsite=summon.

Young, Philip, ed. *West-India Melodies; or Negro Tunes. Adapted for the Piano-Forte. As Performed by the Negroes in the West-Indies, with the Regular Negro Beat Imitated as Made by Various African Instruments They Use.* London: H. R. Young, 1830.

Index

abolition: Black, 87–88, 148; in Britain, 110, 125–28; of international slave trade, 150; and portrayals of music and slavery, 5–6, 117–18, 124; in the United States, 118

acoustemology, 174n59

aesthetics. *See* musical aesthetics

Africa: centering the region, 4–5, 16, 22, 33; circulation of musical practices within, 36, 54; diversity within, 22, 33, 34; early modern music in, 16–17, 19–49; scholarship on history of, 170n7; slave trafficking in, 19–21; and trade with the Middle East and Mediterranean, 36, 170n6, 171n16. *See also* kingdoms in early modern Africa; *and names of individual nations, ethnic groups, languages, and regions*

African Atlantic music: calendrical rhythms and, 46, 67–71; challenges of studying early periods, 7–12, 15, 41, 106–7; circularity and repetition in, 80–81, 149; composers of, 95, 105–7, 148; definition of, 3; in early modern Africa, 16–17, 19–49; embodiment and, 38–41, 42, 74, 113; emergence of diasporic genres of, 2, 62–64, 108–22; enslaved peoples' agency in creating, 7, 62–66, 67–68, 88–89, 91–93; humor and, 142–43; influence of on modern genres, 2, 62–64; innuendo and, 128, 143–44; literary accounts and the study of, 2, 9–12; manuscript sources and, 11, 110; maritime trade and, 3, 22–23; memorialization of, 162–63; origins and rise of, 1–5, 8–9, 42, 50–52, 56, 64–66, 67–71,

78, 88–93, 119, 122, 144–45; and perceptions of historical lostness, 7, 15–16, 64–66, 163; and performing in the present, 78–79, 105, 124, 128, 134, 155–57; playing technique and, 35–38, 52–53, 144; political critique and, 128–30, 142–43, 151; references to antiquity and, 27, 40, 172n21; scholarship related to history of, 7–9; sonic methods and the study of, 12–14, 152, 163; theatrical elements and, 112; white colonists participation in, 112, 126, 145; white critiques of, 147–48. *See also* circulation of music; dance; fashion and costuming; festivals; happy slave trope; instruments; musical gatherings; prohibitions against music in slave societies; racialization of sound and music; religion and spiritual practice; sex and sexuality; Sundays; survival of African identities and practices in the Americas; vocal arts

African history, silencing of, 53, 56, 102

African listeners, in Africa, 33, 45, 48–49, 59–60

African Mail, 162–63

Agawu, V. Kofi, 169n28, 196n25

age of exploration, 22, 54

agricultural labor, 67–69, 125–35; and timing of musical festivities, 70, 71

Akan people, 37, 81–82

Albemarle, Duke of, 95, 102, 104

Albert, James. *See* Gronniosaw, Ukawsaw

alcohol and alcoholism. *See* food and drink; rum

Aljoe, Nicole, 168n24

Allewaert, Monique, 184n59

amelioration of slavery, 117–18
American Songbag, 153–55
ancestral memory, 161–62
Angola, Kingdom of, 31, 42, 54, 57, 70, 80
"Angola" (song), 77–78; possible origins of, 80
ansokko-bania, 120–21
Antigua, 115
antiquity, 27, 40, 172n21
Appendix (journal), 156–57
Arawak people, 103
archival silence, 14, 152, 163; sound and performance as solution for, 14, 169n29
assiento, 102
Atlantic world: centering Africa in studies of, 4–5, 16, 22, 33; definitions of, 3
authenticity, questions of in Black music history, 15–16

Bagneris, Mia L., 117
Bahamas, 142, 145
balas. *See* xylophones
banjos, 51, 61–62, 69, 77, 79–80, 90, 112, 119–21; scholarship on, 8
Bantu languages, 160
baptism, 134
Baptiste, Mr., 11, 75–82, 92–93, 94–107, 109, 123
Barbados, 1–2, 17, 50–53, 56–59, 66, 71–72, 89–90, 97, 103–4, 112, 114, 120, 123–30, 133–35, 144
Barbados pride plant, 144
Barbados work song, 123–35, 144
Barbot, John, 33
barge rowers, 131–32, 137
Bartholemew, Ruth, 160
baton twirling, 149
Beckford, William, 109–10, 132–33, 193n28
Behn, Aphra, 25–26, 87
Belisario, Isaac, 150, 197n61
Belize, 142, 145
Benin, 56, 80–81
Bennett, Herman, 33–34, 170n8
benta. *See* mouth bows
Bermuda, 114, 143
Bilby, Kenneth, 190n1, 197n61
birdsong, 135
Blackface minstrelsy, 6, 61, 118, 151
Blackfriars Theatre, 103–4

Black music: caricatures of, 6; defining, 3, 165n3; historical scholarship on, 7–8; and innovative uses of sound technology, 62–64, 175n60. *See also* African Atlantic music
Black musicality, stereotypes of, 21, 35, 38–41
blacksmithing, 36–37, 174n55
Blake, William, 110
Blanke, John, 26
Blome, Richard, 90–91
Bluett, Thomas, 174n46, 187n12
bogas. *See* barge rowers
Brathwaite, Kamau, 190n1
Brazil, 70, 74
British Caribbean, 16, 124; development of plantations colonies in, 51, 71–72; prominence of musical gatherings in, 89–91; Sunday music and, 70–71. *See also* Caribbean; English travel accounts; *and individual place names*
British Library, 139
British Museum, 106
British North America, 70. *See also individual place names*
Brooks, Daphne, 169n33
Brown, Vincent, 83, 182n34, 183n42, 198n55
Brunias, Agostino, 115–17
buck-dancing, 63
buzzing sounds, 35–41, 56, 63, 79

calabash. *See* gourd resonators
Calemba, 142
Calenda, 196n49
call-and-response, 80, 127–28, 133, 135, 138, 148
Calypso, 128, 134
Cameroon, 57
Candomblé, 83
Cape Verde, 22–27
Caribbean: as central to slavery and African Atlantic music, 3–4; interconnections between British, French, and Spanish territories, 94, 100–101. *See also* British Caribbean; France: plantation colonies of; Spain: colonies of; *and individual place names*
Carlander, Christopher, 193n1
Carnivale, 149
Castillo, Juan de, 102

Catholicism, 23, 26, 41–42, 54; Catholic empires' influence on enslaved gatherings, 69–71; and free Black and enslaved musician, 95–96, 101–2, 104–5; in Jamaica, 101–2; in St. Vincent, 115
Celia, 158
Central Africa, 22, 36. *See also individual places*
chain gangs, 132
Charles, 158
Charleston, South Carolina, 158, 161
Charleston Courier, 161
Charry, Eric, 32
childbirth, 109
children and childcare, 19–21, 43–45, 45–48, 74, 109, 132–34, 155–56; African children's songs and their survival under slavery, 161–63; enslaved women caretakers of white children, 158–60
Chimanyika, 160–61
choristers, 101
Christianity and slavery, 69–71, 87, 102
Christmas, 71, 78, 104, 113, 115, 124, 141, 145–46
circulation of music: from Africa to America, 50–60, 62–66; from America to Africa, 152; around Atlantic Africa, 36, 54; around the Caribbean, 142, 145–49, 151
clapping, 75, 90, 112, 115
Clarissa, 158
class: in colonial Caribbean, 94, 96–98, 101, 116; and European perceptions of musicians in Atlantic Africa, 33–34
clothing. *See* fashion and costuming
C19 Podcast, 156
Code Noir, 86
Colombia, 131, 133
Colonial Williamsburg, 134
Columbian Magazine, 139, 141
Compañon, Baltasar Jaime Martínez, 193n1
composers, 95, 105–7, 148
conch shell, 120–21; and iconography of Caribbean liberty, 87–88. *See also* lambi
Coromantee. *See* Koromanti people
Coskery, Isabella Bones, 158
cotton plantations, 130
cotton-weaving, 132
country dances, 149
Cowley, John, 184–85n62

creole languages, 128–29, 138
Creole people (American born in colonial era), 97, 112, 119–21
creolization, 77–78, 108–10, 144, 190n1
Crop Over, 114
Cuba, 100
Cuogano, Ottobah, 170n2
Curaçao, 142

dance: in Africa, 28–29, 46–48, 85; and bala music in St. Vincent, 61; British planter practices of, 104; fashion and, 114–15, 145–50; gender roles and, 48, 72, 74, 114; as integral to African Atlantic music, 2, 5, 13; and Jamaican Set Girls, 145–51; military exercises and, 28; origins of patting juba, buck-dancing, and tap, 63; and plantation Caribbean, 61, 68–69, 72, 79, 90, 112–19, 129, 137, 139, 141–42; religious practices and, 82–83, 87; revolt and, 85–86; sexuality and, 74; and Trinidad regiments, 87
Danish colonies, 88
Dawley, Amelia, and family, 161
death, 43–45, 83–85, 152; beliefs about African homegoing in the afterlife, 84; and mortality rates among enslaved, 67, 72, 109; musical lyrics about, 127–29, 134, 148–49; suicide and, 84, 129
de Bry, Theodor, 24–26, 30
De Graav, Mr., 112–13
Dempsy, Don Juan Baptista, 188–89n33
Dewulf, Jeroen, 192n21, 197n61
Diabaté, Toumani, 39
Diallo, Ayuba, 174n46, 188n12
Diarra, Duga Koro, 59
Dickinson, Michael, 192n3
Dickson, William, 125–28
diddley bows, 63–64
Dillon, Elizabeth, 145–48
disability, 42, 159
divine implements, 41, 43–45
Dominica, 115
Douglass, Frederick, 118
Driver, Merlyn, 39–40
drivers, 130
drums and drumming: in Africa, 20, 34, 43, 47; in America, 58, 63, 73, 89–90, 112, 116, 120–22, 145, 149; restrictions on drumming in American plantation societies, 86–87

Dubois, Laurent, 61, 78–80, 95
Du Bois, W. E. B., 134, 161–62
Dutch: portrayals of enslaved gatherings
in visual art, 74; slave trading and, 20,
161; travelers and travel accounts of,
23–25, 109–15, 117–22. *See also* Brazil;
de Bry, Theodor; Mahu, Jacob; Stedman, John; Suriname; Valkenburg, Dirk;
Wagenaer, Zacharias

Edison, Thomas, 64
Edwards, Bryan, 116, 192–93n27
elders, 48, 158, 162–63
Emidy, Joseph, 96
England, 96, 103, 143, 146, 148, 149;
music houses in during the Interregnum,
103
English Civil War, 51, 103
English trade in Africa, 34–35, 43–45,
46–49, 55
English travel accounts: of the Caribbean
(*see* Beckford, William; Blome, Richard;
Edwards, Bryan; Leslie, Charles; Lewis,
Matthew "Monk" Gregory; Ligon,
Richard; Long, Edward; Oldmixon,
John; Sloane, Hans; Smith, William;
Stedman, John; Young, William, Jr.); of
Africa, 41–42 (*see also* Jobson, Richard;
Matthews, John; Park, Mungo; Uring,
Nathaniel)
Enlightenment, the, theories of race, sci-
ence, and knowledge of, 14, 96, 106,
122, 135
Epstein, Dena, 131, 166n12
Equiano, Olaudah, 11, 45, 83–84, 127,
170n34
estate records, 99–100, 159
ethnomusicology, and the study of early
African and African diasporic music, 8,
59, 178n27
European music: enslaved and free Black
musicians and, 8, 94–96; records of in
the plantation Caribbean, 103–4, 111;
and scientific theories of, 38, 58; and
systems of notation, 76–77, 96
Evans, David, 179n36
Eyerly, Sarah, 173n33

fashion and costuming: in Caribbean festivals, 74–75, 79, 114–16, 118, 145–51;
and cotton-weaving in Africa, 132; and

garments worn by the enslaved, 89; as
integral to African Atlantic music, 13;
worn by African musicians, 35; worn
by Jamaican Set Girls, 145–51; worn by
professional European and Caribbean
musicians, 100
Fatah-Black, Karwan, 195n20
Feld, Steven, 174n59
festivals, 17; Catholicism and, 69–70;
emergence of in plantation Americas,
67–71; and enslaved uprisings, 86–87,
92–93; evolution of in the eighteenth-
century Caribbean, 109–22, 145–51;
and policing of enslaved people, 85–86;
in 1688 Jamaica, 75–78; in 1620s Gambia, 46–49. *See also* Christmas; musical
gatherings; Sundays
fetishes. *See* divine implements
fiddles: enslaved performers of, 65, 180n2;
European violins in the Caribbean,
104–5, 111, 121; and Jamaican Set
Girls, 145–46, 148–49; and practice
known as fiddlesticks or beating straws,
179n38
Filene, Benjamin, 198n1
fires, 19, 46–47, 62, 69
Fisk Jubilee Singers, 134, 166n8
Florida, 86
flutes, 104, 109, 120–21
flying African mythology, 84
food and drink: and alcoholism, 141; and
enslaved people's dietary provisions,
58, 71, 131; at a festival in West Africa,
47–48; and festivals in the Caribbean,
92, 116, 118, 145–46; as oblations at
gravesites, 84
found objects: and African diasporic aesthetics, 51, 62–64, 144
France: plantation colonies of, 86, 87–88,
100–101, 115, 124, 148; professional
musicians in, 96, 100; and trade in early
modern Africa, 42. *See also* French
travel accounts; Guadeloupe; Haiti
Frazier, E. Franklin, 190n1
freedom, complexities of, 144
free people of African descent: in the
Caribbean, 111–12, 135, 138; in early
British Jamaica, 96–98; in Europe, 26; as
professional musicians, 95–96; in slave-
trading regions of Africa, 47. *See also*
Baptiste, Mr.

French travel accounts, 32–33, 37, 54, 55–56. *See also* Barbot, John; Froger, François
Frisbie, Charlotte, 180n5, 191n3
Froger, François, 37, 55–56
Fromont, Cécile, 26, 28–29, 42, 168n24, 181n7, 190n1
Fulbe people, 32, 34
funerals. *See* religion and spiritual practice: mourning and

Gaddy, Kristina, 110, 112, 191n9
Gambia and the Gambia river region, 32–33, 34–37, 40, 42, 46–49, 55–57
gangs of plantation laborers, 133
Garifuna, 142, 145
Garner, David, 78–79, 95
Garth, John, 144
gatherings. *See* festivals; musical gatherings; Sundays
Gattina, Michael Angelo of, 56, 188n32
Geanego, Rachel, 98–99
gender, impact of on musicianship, 57. *See also* women
genres, modern: development and origins of, 131; influence of enslaved musicians on, 2, 63–64
gentrification, 45
Georgia, U.S. state of, 11, 18, 152–65
Germany, African musicians in, 26
Gibbs, Roger, 128, 134, 179n40
Gilroy, Paul, 63
Gitelman, Lisa, 179–80n45
Goji fiddle, 30
Gold Coast, 22, 36–37
Gombey, 114
goombay, 145
Gordon, Bonnie, 173n34
gourd resonators, 35–36, 38, 53–54, 55–56, 63, 69, 79, 90, 120–21
grand balls, 111, 113–17. *See also* festivals
Green, Toby, 37
griot, 30–34, 35, 37, 54, 72
Gronniosaw, Ukawsaw, 11, 19–21
Guadeloupe, 96
Guinea, 56
"Guinea Corn" (song), 141
Guinnet, Stephen, 188n24
Gulf of Mexico, 158
Gullah people, 154, 161–62

habla de negros, 6
Hagood, Mack, 175n60
Haiti, 96, 100, 114, 149, 151; caricatures of Black music and, 6; and figure of Makandal, 87; Set Girls in Jamaica, 147–48; theater in, 125
Haitian Revolution, 87–88, 120, 148, 151
Hall, Gwendolyn Midlo, 183n44, 191n3
Handler, Jerome, 129, 180n5, 191n3, 195n21
Hanover Plot, 125
happy slave trope, 5–6, 117–19, 146–47
harps, 79
harpsichords, 38; comparisons with African xylophones, 55–56
Hartman, Saidiya, 129, 152, 189n46, 197n55
Hay, Edward, 125
hearing, science of, 39, 59; and theories and critiques of neuroplasticity, 174n59
Henry, 158
Herskovitz, Melville, 190n1
hip-hop, 63
history from below, 7
horns: and African influences on European trombone and tambourine, 36; in African kingdoms, 20, 24–26, 34, 172n30; in Americas, 120–21; in European courts, maritime trade, and military practice, 24–26, 28; and restrictions of use on plantations, 34, 86
horse teeth, 145

Iberian Atlantic: Africans in, 11, 69–70, 100–101; music scholarship and, 8. *See also* Portugal; Spain
Igbo people, 45, 57, 84
imperialism: cultural, 14, 53; European, 23–26
indentured servants, 99
Indigenous Americans, 82, 83, 103, 108, 122, 131, 142, 145. *See also individual names*
instruments: as artifacts of music history, 1–2, 50–52; artistic renderings of, 31, 37, 55, 75, 119–22; construction of in American slave societies, 61–64, 79–80, 121–22; as recording devices, 64–66; and sound design in early modern Africa, 35–41, 56, 59–60; survivals and innovations in Americas under slavery,

instruments (*continued*)
61–64, 79, 144; and use of found
objects, 51, 62–64, 144. *See also names
of individual instruments and instrument
types*
interdisciplinarity, 11–12, 14–16
International Library of African Music,
160
Ireland, 103
Islam: on American plantations, 82; and
memorization, 64; spread of in Africa,
170n6; in West Africa, 34, 41–42; and
xylophone performance, 55–56
Italy: theorbos from, 52; trade and missionizing in early modern Africa, 42;
travelers and travel accounts, 26, 36, 42,
69, 115–17. *See also* Brunias, Agostino;
Gattina, Michael Angelo of; Lopes,
Duarte; "Missione in prattica"; Sorrento, Girolamo Merolla da
Iyanaga, Michael, 180n7, 190n1

Jack, 158
Jah, Nabi, 162
Jamaica, 68, 71–72, 75–88, 89–93,
94–107, 109–10, 124–25, 139–51;
archives in, 95, 98–101. *See also indi-
vidual cities and parish names*
Jamaican Airs, 124–25, 139–51
James, 158
James Ford Bell Library, 111
jazz, 131
Jegede, Tunde, 173n40, 186n6
jeli. *See* griot
jenkoving, 90–91
Jennico, Hannah, 98–99
Jewish people, 26, 103
jingling and tinkling sounds, 35–41, 63, 79
Joanna, 111–12
Jobarteh, Sona, 181n15
Jobson, Richard, 32, 34–35, 39–40, 42,
46–49, 55
Johnson, Jessica Marie, 74
Johnson, Margaret, 154, 160
Johnson, Sara E., 147–48
Jonkanu, 142, 145–46
juba. *See* patting juba

kalimba, 79, 193n31, 196n49
Kasiwira, W., 162
Kikongo language, 54

kingdoms in early modern Africa, 16–17,
19–20; and court music, 30–34; military
music in, 26–31; and trade and diplo-
macy between Africans and Europeans,
21–26. *See also* Angola, Kingdom of;
Kongo, Kingdom of; Loango, Kingdom
of; Mali, Empire of
Kingston, Jamaica, 85, 99–100, 102–3, 139
Kongo, Kingdom of, 23–24, 26–31, 42,
54, 56, 70, 80, 101
kora, 39
"Koromanti" (song), 80–81
Koromanti people, 81, 109, 119
Koto, 114
Kouyate, Bala Faseke, 54
Kupperman, Karen, 51

lambi, 87–88
Language You Cry In, The (film), 161–62
Latin America, 8; boat rowers in, 131–32;
xylophones in, 54, 61
laws prohibiting enslaved music and
instruments. *See* prohibitions against
music in slave societies
Leigh, Devin, 125, 139
Leslie, Charles, 90–91, 104
Lewin, Olive, 166n12
Lewis, 158
Lewis, Matthew "Monk" Gregory, 149
liemba-toetoe, 120–21
Ligon, Richard, 1–2, 5, 50–53, 56–62,
65–66, 71–72, 89–91, 101
listening practices: cultural specificity of,
12–14, 39–40, 44–45, 55–56, 59–60,
76–77; as research method, 155–65. *See
also* African listeners
Loango, Kingdom of, 43–45, 54, 80, 84,
85–86, 112–13, 119
Lomax, Alan, 160
Long, Edward, 83, 139–42, 183n41
Lopes, Duarte, 26–30, 33–34, 36; transla-
tions of, 171n19, 171n21
Lost Cause, 157–58
Louisiana, 130–31, 158
lullabies, 132, 155
lunga, 28
Lusitano, Vicente, 96
lutes, 33, 52, 79, 90

Macow, 1–2, 5, 17, 50–54, 56–62, 65–66,
120

MacRae, Maggie, 198nn5–6
Mahu, Jacob, 23–26
Makandal, 97
Malawi, 162
Mali, 39–40, 59; work song in Segou, 132
Mali, Empire of, 34, 54
Malimba, Masucca, 44
Mallè, Brehman, 59
mammy iconography, 154
Mande people, 32, 34, 52, 115
Mardi Gras, 113–14
Maria, 158
marimba. *See* xylophones
Mark, Peter, 41–42
market women, 73, 116
Marly; or, A Planter's Life in Jamaica (1828), 133
Maroons, 81, 88, 111, 124, 142–43
Mary, 158
material culture: decorative sonic implements and, 35–38. *See also* fashion and costuming
Matthews, John, 36
Maxwell, Heather, 59–60
mbira, 38, 79, 120–21
medicine, 43, 82–83. *See also* religion and spiritual practice: healing and
Meintjes, Louise, 175n62
metalwork in Africa, 27–28, 35–38
Middle Passage, 19, 158; survivors of, 5, 8–9, 50, 61, 66, 108–10, 113, 118–19, 124, 152, 154, 162
military practice: in colonial Americas, 110, 112, 137, 145, 149; in early modern Africa, 22, 26–31
Minette, 96
minstrelsy. *See* Blackface minstrelsy
Mintz, Sidney, 190n1
misogyny and misogynoir, 57, 73–75. *See also* women
missionaries, 23, 42. *See also* "Missione in prattica"
"Missione in prattica," 176n74, 188n32
Mitchell, Koritha, 197n62
mixed-race people, 34, 97, 99, 111, 131
molasses, 92
Montego Bay, Jamaica, 145
Morgan, Jennifer, 73, 91, 185n68
Morrison, Toni, 63, 183n47
Mosquito people, 103
mouth bows, 109, 120–21

Mozambique, 161
multisensory properties of music, 36–41
Mumbo Jumbo, 115
Munro, Martin, 175n63
music, definitions of, 12–13. *See* African Atlantic music
musical aesthetics: African diasporic, 62–64, 144, 179n42; in early modern Africa, 34–41, 51
musical diplomacy, 21–26
musical gatherings: and the foundation of Black music, 67–93; in plantation Caribbean, 64–93; and policing of enslaved people, 85–86; prominence and acceptability of, 67–71, 89–93; in Protestant vs. Catholic colonies, 70–71; in urban vs. rural settings, 70, 126; visual portrayals of, 74, 115–16. *See also* Christmas; festivals; grand balls; Sundays
Musical Passage: A Voyage to 1688 Jamaica (website), 78–79, 95
Music by Black Composers, 190n50
music houses, 103
musicking, 169n27
musicology, and the study of early Black music, 7–9
Music Theory Examples by Women, 190n50
Muskateem, Sowande, 185n48
Myalism, 83, 141–42

natural history, 75, 122, 135
naturalization records, 99–100
Nevis, 133–34
Newton Plantation, 133
Nigeria, 19–21, 45, 57
North Carolina, 155
Northup, Solomon, 130–31
notation, musical: challenges of interpreting, 76–77, 79, 105–6, 156–57; examples of, 65, 75–82, 123–51, 152–63, 183n42, 193n1; limitations and politics of, 96, 105–6, 144–45; scholarship on transcriptions of non-Western music and, 168n22
Nunn, Erich, 178n26
Nyasaland, 163

Obeah, 83
Ochoa-Gautier, Ana Maria, 131
Oldmixon, John, 90–91

oral history, 31, 32, 157, 158
organs, comparisons of with xylophones,
    55–56, 60
Oroonoko; or, the Royal Slave. See Behn,
    Aphra
Ouidah, 109

Paine University, 160
Pan-Africanism, 147
"Papa" (song), 77–78, 80–82
Park, Mungo, 132
paternalism among planters and colonists,
    92
Paton, Diana, 181n16
patting juba, 63
Pélisser, Marie, 189n23
performance: concepts of, 12; as research
    method, 155–57
Peru, 193n1
Pigafetta, Filippo. *See* Lopes, Duarte
pipes, 33, 145, 149; on Spanish and Portu-
    guese ships, 171n14
plagiarism in travel writing, 88–93
plantation slavery. *See* slavery and enslaved
    people
poisoning, 85, 87
Polcha, Elizabeth, 191n15
Popo people, 80–82, 120–21
Port Royal, Jamaica, 99–103
Portugal: and Afro-Catholicism, 69–70,
    100–101; Afro-descendants in Portugal
    and Portuguese-Atlantic contexts, 34,
    96, 100–101; and trade and cultural
    exchange in Africa, 23–31, 37, 42. *See
    also* Lopes, Duarte; Lusitano, Vicente;
    musical diplomacy; Santos, João dos
Pratt, Mary Louise, 168n23
Pratz, Le Page du, 130–31
Price, Richard, 111, 138, 190n1
Price, Sally, 111, 138
Prince, Mary, 143, 170n34
professional musicians, 8, 32, 95–96, 98,
    100–107. *See also* Baptiste, Mr.
prohibitions against music in slave socie-
    ties, 68, 85–88; failures of, 88–89
Protestantism, 70–71, 85

qua-qua, 120–21

racial identity: in the Caribbean, 96–98,
    116–17; in comparison to modern

conceptions, 166n3; in Spanish colonies,
    187n13
racialization of sound and music, 33–34,
    39–41, 45, 49, 112, 120–21, 135, 160
Radano, Ronald, 165n7
railroads, 132
rangers, 111, 124, 137–39, 141–45, 151
"Ranger Song," 141–45, 148, 151
Rara, 149
Rath, Richard, 78, 80, 179n38, 185–86n4,
    190n1
rattles and rattling objects, 33, 36–38, 43,
    120–21, 144; women and, 73, 79
recording technology: and African classical
    musics, 39–40; musical instruments as,
    64–66
regiments, 87–88
regulation of enslaved musical practices.
    See prohibitions against music in slave
    societies
religion and spiritual practice, 13; Afro-
    catholic liturgical practice, 42, 54, 96–97,
    101; in Atlantic Africa, 21, 40, 41–45;
    under Catholic vs. Protestant colonial
    rule, 102; ecstatic praise and spiritual
    embodiment, 42; healing and, 42–43;
    82–83; herbal medicine, 83; mourn-
    ing and, 43–45, 83–85; in plantation
    Americas, 69–71, 82–85, 87–88, 141–42;
    and ritual circumcision, 46–49; and upris-
    ings, 87–88. *See also* Catholicism; divine
    implements; missionaries; Myalism;
    Obeah; Protestantism; sorcery; Vodou
resistance: to European intrusion in the
    context of communal ritual in Africa,
    47–48; to slavery through music, 20,
    29–30, 68, 85–88, 129–30, 152, 159
resonators. *See* gourd resonators
revolt. *See* uprisings
Rhodesia, 162–63
rhythm, 42, 58, 63, 65, 80, 138; European
    perceptions of, 40; and work song, 131,
    134. *See also* drums and drumming
Rickford, John, 128
rivers and water: and the circulation of
    African Atlantic music, 131–32; imagery
    of, 128–29, 134
Roach, Joseph, 169n29
royalists, 51, 103–4
rum, 84, 131. *See also* food and drink
Ryan, Maria, 196n46

Saint-Domingue. *See* Haiti
Saint-Georges, Chevalier de (Joseph
Bulogne), 96
Samgully, 46–49
Samuel, Petal, 173n34
Sancho, Ignatius, 135
Sandburg, Carl, 11, 153–55, 157, 160
Sangamentos, 28–29
sansa, 120–21
Santos, João dos, 177n16
science. *See* natural history
Scotland, 112, 149, 158
Scott, Julius, 148
self-emancipation. *See* freedom; Maroons
Senegambia, 22, 36, 41–42
sermons, 134
Set Girls, 115, 124–25, 141–42, 145–51
sex and sexuality: sexuality and, 74–75,
128; between white colonists and
enslaved women, 111–12
Sharp, Granville, 125–28
Shona people and language, 161
Sierra Leone, 26, 36
silence. *See* archival silence
singing. *See* vocal arts
sistema de castas, 187n13
slave narratives, 11, 130. *See also* Cuogano, Ottobah; Diallo, Ayuba; Douglass,
Frederick; Equiano, Olaudah; Gronniosaw, Ukawsaw; Northup, Solomon;
Prince, Mary
slavery and enslaved people: agency and,
7; difficult conditions of life under,
58, 64, 72, 83–84, 109–10, 112–13,
117–19, 126–35, 144; musical sources
and the study of, 123–24; paternalism
and, 92; personal histories and biographies of, 10–11; rise of, 8–9, 16, 23,
50–51, 67; urban slavery, 70, 126–27,
145, 158. *See also* amelioration of
slavery; Celia; Charles; children and
childcare; Clarissa; Cuogano, Ottobah;
Diallo, Ayuba; Douglass, Frederick;
drivers; Emidy, Joseph; Equiano, Olaudah; freedom; free people of African
descent; gangs of plantation laborers;
Gronniosaw, Ukawsaw; Henry; Jack;
James; Joanna; Lewis; Macow; Makandal; Maria; market women; Mary;
Prince, Mary; rangers; resistance; Set
Girls; Stedman, Johnny; Tamar; Tena;

uprisings; Washington; Wheatley Peters,
Phillis; women; Young Lewis
slavery and music: and debates about abolition, 5–6, 116–17; and the happy slave
trope, 5–6, 117–19, 146–47; in modern
public discourse, 3–5; romanticization
of, 6–7
slavery studies, research methods in, 9–12,
152, 163
slave trade: abolition of internationally,
150; in East Africa, 161; in West Africa,
19–21
Sloane, Hans, 11, 17, 71–72, 74–75,
75–82, 86, 89–93, 94, 97, 100, 101–2,
104, 106, 109, 123, 135, 139
Small, Christopher, 169n27
Smalligan, Laura M., 197n61
Smith, Cassander, 169n24, 186–87n10
Smith, William, 133–34
sonic prejudice, 14–15, 20–21, 29–30,
33–34, 39–41, 58–59; of enslaved music,
68–69; of religious music in Africa,
41–45, 49
sorcery, 83, 87
Sorrento, Girolamo Merolla da, 42, 54–55,
175n67, 188n32
sorrow songs, 134
Souls of Black Folk. See Du Bois, W. E. B.
sound: as artifact and archive, 13–14, 45,
152, 163, 169n29; and Black studies, 169n26; cross-cultural perceptions
of, 19–21, 29–30, 35, 38–41, 48–49,
122; as distinguished from music, 12;
embodied characteristics of, 34–41;
and histories of colonialism and global
contact, 169n26; and instrument design,
35–38, 122, 175n60; and methods for
music history, 12–14; multi-modality of,
35–41, 48, 145; and the production of
power, 29–30, 44–45, 49; and recording technology, 13, 39–40, 64–66; and
slavery, 2, 12–14, 153, 163; transferring
of across instruments and found objects,
62–64. *See also* archival silence; buzzing
sounds; jingling and tinkling sounds;
listening practices; racialization of sound
and music; sonic prejudice; twangy
sounds
South Africa, 11
South Carolina, 4, 86–87, 112
Southern, Eileen, 166n12

Southern history and culture (U.S.), 157–58

Spain: caricatures of Black music in, 6; and church musicians in colonial Americas, 101; colonies of, 86, 100, 101–3, 187n13; and influence on early Black music, 69–70; and Jamaica, 102–3; and racial identity, 187n13; and the slave trade, 70, 102; and trade and cultural exchange in Africa, 42

Spanish Jamaica, 102–3

Spanish language, 155–56

Spanish Town, Jamaica, 98

Spencer, Alexander, 158–59

spirituals, 134

Sranan Tongo, 138

St. Andrews Parish, Jamaica, 98

St. Bartolomey, 193n1

"St Domingo" (song), 87–88

St. Elizabeth Parish, Jamaica, 149

St. Thomas, 88

St. Vincent, 61, 115–17, 142

Stedman, John, 109–15, 117–22, 124, 131; notation and, 135–39

Stedman, Johnny, 111–12

steelpan, 63

Sterne, Jonathan, 64, 175n60

stilt-walking, 115

Stoever, Jennifer, 40, 49, 169n31

Stono Rebellion, 86–87

Sturtz, Linda, 145, 147

sugar plantations, 51, 71, 89, 97, 102, 130; and use of work songs on, 132–34

suicide, 84

Sundays: domestic labor and, 71–75, 89–90; enslaved music on, 17, 58, 69–71, 75, 78, 85–87, 89–92, 109

Sundiata, King, 52

Super Sunday, 114

Suriname, 4, 16, 73, 97, 109–15, 117–22, 124, 131, 133, 135–39, 143

survival of African identities and practices in the Americas, 77–78, 81–82, 91, 108–22, 125–27, 142, 184n44

tabors, 145

Tacky's Revolt, 87

Tamar, 158

tambourines, 36; women and, 73, 116

Taylor, Diana, 169n29

Taylor, John, 68–69, 71–72, 78, 84, 103

tempo, politics of, 130–31; utility of, 133–34. *See also* rhythm

Tena, 11, 18, 152–63

tent boats. *See* barge rowers

Texas, 158

theater, 6, 103–4, 112

theorbos, 1, 52, 65

Thomas, Sarah, 117

Thompson, Katrina, 169n30

Thornton, John, 171n18, 173n37

Tinashe, 161

Togo, 80

Tonada el Congo, 193n1

Tracey, Hugh, 160–62

Transatlantic Slave Trade Database, 200n20

travel writing: challenges in interpreting, 10, 48; copying and plagiarism in, 88–93; editorializing and, 110–11, 116, 138; genre conventions of and the portrayal of music, 9–10, 88–93; as historical sources for the study of slavery, 9–11, 110–11; and perceptions of musical gatherings, 88–93. *See also* *individual names of travel authors*

Trinidad and Tobago, 63, 87–88

Trouillot, Michel-Rolph, 177n8

True and Exact History of the Island of Barbados. *See* Ligon, Richard

Trujillo del Perú. *See* Compañon, Baltasar Jaime Martínez

trumpets. *See* horns

tuning: African systems of, 59–60; European systems of, 53, 174n58

Turner, Lorenzo, 200–201n22

twangy sounds, and modern genres of blues, zydeco, hip-hop, and rock, 63

twin taboo, 57

ululation, 75, 82. *See also* vocal arts

uprisings, 68, 85–88; and religious practice, 87–88. *See also* Haitian Revolution; Hanover Plot; Stono Rebellion; Tacky's Revolt

Uring, Nathaniel, 43–45, 83–84, 85–86

Valkenburg, Dirk, 74

Vassa, Gustavus, 11, 45, 83–84. *See also* Equiano, Olaudah

Vere, Parish of, 98–99

vibration: in aesthetics and theory of Atlantic African music, 38–40, 63; of the spheres, 38

violins. *See* fiddles
Virginia, 61, 70, 103
vocal arts, 48, 114–15; ritual lamentations, 43–45, 84; singing, 18, 43, 80, 84, 90, 118, 127–35, 135–39, 145, 152–63; ululation, 75, 82
vocal masks, 38
Vodou, 87
Voigt, Lisa, 194n13
Voyage to the Islands of Madera, Barbados, Nieves, St. Christophers and Jamaica. See Sloane, Hans

Wagenaer, Zacharias, 74
Walltown Children's Theatre, 155–56
war. *See* military practice
Warner-Lewis, Maureen, 197n61
Washington, 158
Weaver, Wayne, 196n46
West-India Melodies, 196n44
Wheatley Peters, Phillis, 135
whistles, on Spanish and Portuguese ships, 171n14
white fear, 20–21, 29–30, 85–88
whiteness, 44–45, 49, 106, 157–58; historical records and, 14; musical tastes and, 14; perceptions of Black music and, 14, 38–41, 52–53, 89–92, 113
Whydaw. *See* Ouidah
Wolmer, John, 100
Wolof people, 32
women: as composers of original music, 148; as dancers, 47–48, 61, 112–13; and fashion, 114–15, 145–47; growing musical prominence of during eighteenth-century, 124, 141; as healers, 43, 83; labor shaping musical lives of, 71–75, 116, 124; marital violence against, 57;

as mothers, 46–48, 155–59, 162–63; as mourners, 43; and origins of work songs in Africa and America, 132–33; portrayals as mammies, 154–55; and restriction of musical roles, 57, 72–73; and roles in Sunday gatherings, 71–75; sexualized portrayals of in visual art, 73–74; sexual violence and exploitation of, 111–12; as vocalists, 43, 48, 96, 148–51, 152–65; white critiques of sartorial style, 147–48. *See also* market women; Set Girls
Woodfield, Ian, 25–26, 171n13
work song, 125–35; in Africa, 132; barge rowers and, 132–33, 137; politics of tempo and, 130–31; women and children and, 132–33
wrestling, 90
Wright, Margarett Clarissa Bones, 160

xylophones, 1–2, 17, 50–56, 63, 65; in America, 61–62, 115, 120; balas, 1, 30, 35–36, 47, 53–56, 60–62, 79, 115; in Central Africa, 54; construction of, 52–53, 59–60, 62; history of in Africa, 53–56; history of the word *balafon*, 54–56, 60; marimbas, 1, 54; tuning of, 59–60

Yamba people, 57
Yoruba people, 57
Young, Philip, 196n44
Young, William, Jr., 115–17
Young, William, Sr., 115–17
Young Lewis, 158

Zambia, 11, 162
Zimbabwe, 160
zithers, 63–64

RECENT BOOKS IN THE SERIES
New World Studies

The Literatures of Spanish America and Brazil: From Their Origins through the Nineteenth Century
Earl E. Fitz

Break and Flow: Hip Hop Poetics in the Americas
Charlie D. Hankin

Looking for Other Worlds: Black Feminism and Haitian Fiction
Régine Michelle Jean-Charles

The Epic of Cuba Libre: The Mambí, *Mythopoetics, and Liberation*
Eric Morales-Franceschini

The Mambi-Land, or Adventures of a Herald *Correspondent in Cuba*
James J. O'Kelly, edited by Jennifer Brittan

Fictions of Whiteness: Imagining the Planter Caste in the French Caribbean Novel
Maeve McCusker

Haitian Revolutionary Fictions: An Anthology
Edited and with translations by Marlene L. Daut, Grégory Pierrot, and Marion C. Rohrleitner

Rum Histories: Drinking in Atlantic Literature and Culture
Jennifer Poulos Nesbitt

Imperial Educación: Race and Republican Motherhood in the Nineteenth-Century Americas
Thomas Genova

Fellow Travelers: How Road Stories Shaped the Idea of the Americas
John Ochoa

The Quebec Connection: A Poetics of Solidarity in Global Francophone Literatures
Julie-Françoise Tolliver

Comrade Sister: Caribbean Feminist Revisions of the Grenada Revolution
Laurie R. Lambert

Cultural Entanglements: Langston Hughes and the Rise of African and Caribbean Literature
Shane Graham

Water Graves: The Art of the Unritual in the Greater Caribbean
Valérie Loichot

The Sacred Act of Reading: Spirituality, Performance, and Power in Afro-Diasporic Literature
Anne Margaret Castro

Caribbean Jewish Crossings: Literary History and Creative Practice
Sarah Phillips Casteel and Heidi Kaufman, editors

Mapping Hispaniola: Third Space in Dominican and Haitian Literature
Megan Jeanette Myers

Mourning El Dorado: Literature and Extractivism in the Contemporary American Tropics
Charlotte Rogers

Edwidge Danticat: The Haitian Diasporic Imaginary
Nadège T. Clitandre

Idle Talk, Deadly Talk: The Uses of Gossip in Caribbean Literature
Ana Rodríguez Navas

Crossing the Line: Early Creole Novels and Anglophone Caribbean Culture in the Age of Emancipation
Candace Ward

Staging Creolization: Women's Theater and Performance from the French Caribbean
Emily Sahakian

American Imperialism's Undead: The Occupation of Haiti and the Rise of Caribbean Anticolonialism
Raphael Dalleo

A Cultural History of Underdevelopment: Latin America in the U.S. Imagination
John Patrick Leary

The Spectre of Races: Latin American Anthropology and Literature between the Wars
Anke Birkenmaier

Performance and Personhood in Caribbean Literature: From Alexis to the Digital Age
Jeannine Murray-Román

Tropical Apocalypse: Haiti and the Caribbean End Times
Martin Munro

Market Aesthetics: The Purchase of the Past in Caribbean Diasporic Fiction
Elena Machado Sáez

Printed in the USA
CPSIA information can be obtained
at www.ICGtesting.com
LVHW091918011123
762773LV00002B/6